win

www.hants.gov.uk/library

Hampshire
County Council

Love
YOUR LIBRARY

Tel: 0300 555 1387

WOUNDS

FERGAL KEANE

WOUNDS

a memoir of war & love

WILLIAM
COLLINS

William Collins
An imprint of HarperCollins*Publishers*
1 London Bridge Street
London SE1 9GF

WilliamCollinsBooks.com

First published in Great Britain in 2017 by William Collins

1

Copyright © Fergal Keane 2017

Fergal Keane asserts the moral right to be
identified as the author of this work

A catalogue record for this book is
available from the British Library

ISBN 978-0-00-818925-9 (hardback)
ISBN 978-0-00-822537-7 (trade paperback)

Maps by Martin Brown

Printed and bound in Great Britain by
CPI Group (UK) Ltd, Croydon

MIX
Paper from
responsible sources
FSC C007454

This book is produced from independently certified FSC paper
to ensure responsible forest management

For more information visit: www.harpercollins.co.uk/green

For Dan and Holly, children of peace

Contents

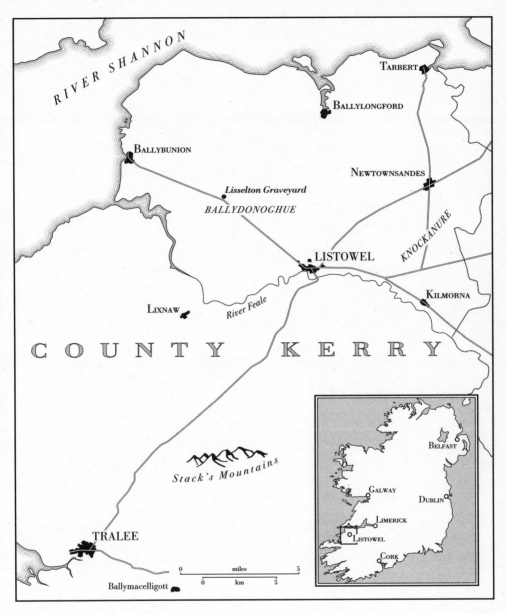

North Kerry, War of Independence, 1919–21

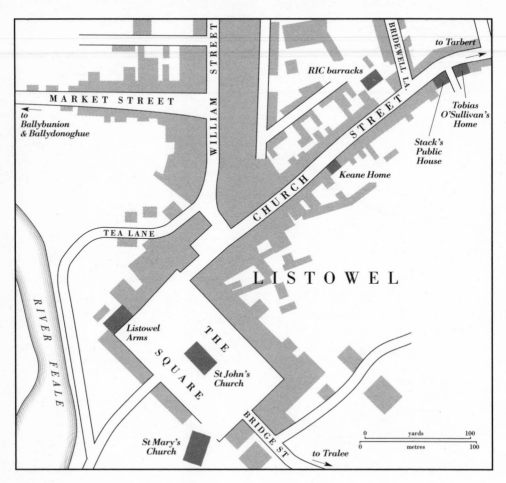

Listowel, 20 January 1921

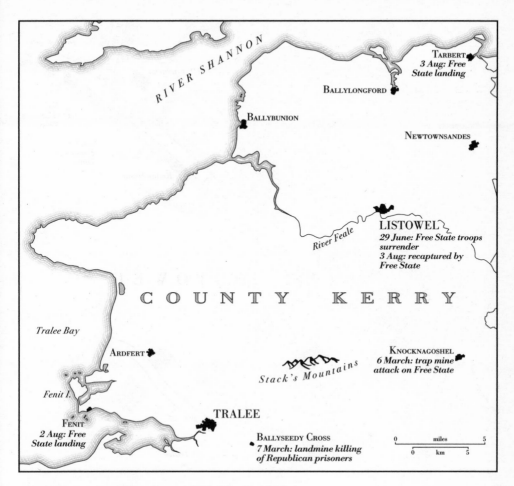

RIVER SHANNON

TARBERT
*3 Aug: Free
State landing*

BALLYLONGFORD

BALLYBUNION

NEWTOWNSANDES

River Feale

LISTOWEL
*29 June: Free State troops
surrender
3 Aug: recaptured by
Free State*

C O U N T Y   K E R R Y

Tralee Bay

ARDFERT

KNOCKNAGOSHEL
*6 March: trap mine
attack on Free State*

Stack's Mountains

Fenit I.

FENIT
*2 Aug: Free
State landing*

TRALEE

BALLYSEEDY CROSS
*7 March: landmine killing
of Republican prisoners*

0   miles   5
0   km   5

North Kerry, Civil War, June 1922–March 1923

Prologue

We Killed All Mankind

His manner was that the heads of all those (of what sort so ever they were) which were killed in the day, should be cut off from their bodies, and brought to the place where he encamped at night: and should there be laid on the ground, by each side of the way leading into his own tent: so that none could come into his tent for any cause, but commonly he must pass through a lane of heads ... and yet did it bring great terror to the people when they saw the heads of their dead fathers, brothers, children, kinsfolk, and friends lie on the ground before their faces, as they came to speak with the said Colonel.

Thomas Churchyard, *A Generall Rehearsall of Warres*, 1579

I

This is the story of my grandmother Hannah Purtill, who was a rebel, and her brother Mick and his friend Con Brosnan, and how they took up guns to fight the British Empire and create an independent Ireland. And it is the story of another Irishman, Tobias O'Sullivan, who fought against them because he believed it was his duty to uphold the law of his country. It is the story too of the breaking of bonds and of civil war and of how the wounds of the past shaped the island on which I grew up. Many thousands of people took part in the War of Independence and the Civil War that followed. The story of my own family is one that might differ in some details but is shared by numerous other Irish families. They may have taken different sides but all were changed in some way, and lived in a new state defined by the costs of violence. I have spent much of my life trying to understand why people will kill for a cause and how the act of killing reverberates through the generations. This book is, in part, an attempt to understand my own obsession with war.

It starts in my grandmother's house in the north Kerry town of Listowel, in the middle of the 1960s.

The house is asleep. My brother and sister are in beds at the other side of the room. My mother is in the room across the landing, next to the door leading up into the attic where cracked uncle Dan once lived among the cobwebs and the crows. The last drinkers have left Alla Sheehy's next door. His wife Nora Mai is sweeping the floor. She will be muttering, drawing hard on a cigarette, cursing the hour and the work, under the eternal gaze of the stuffed fox on the counter. A Garda will pass soon on his rounds, his ear alert for the murmur of secret drinkers. There are several dozen pubs in Listowel and he will stop to listen at each one. But the only noise is from the dogs barking in the lane between the houses and the sports field.

'They can sense it,' my father says. 'Stay quiet now. Stay quiet and you will hear them.' He sits at the end of my bed. I can only make out his shape. There is comfort in the tiny orange glow of his cigarette. 'Listen close,' he says again, 'the riders will come soon.'

I am ten years old. My imagination swells in the darkness. My father lives between the story and the reality. He has spent his life faltering between the two. It is his gift and his tragedy. He can make me believe anything.

'Now! Now! Sit up,' he says. 'Do you hear them? They are riding to hell!'

2

I hear everything that he wills into being: the hooves pounding the midnight earth, the hard music of armour, sword and spur and men's voices shouting in the late autumn of 1600. Captain Wilmot's cavalry – armed with the finest muskets Queen Elizabeth's treasury can procure – stop before the gates of Listowel Castle and by the banks of the River Feale, which flows out of the mountains in neighbouring County Limerick, meandering around Listowel on its way to the Atlantic coast nearby. The garrison refuse to surrender. Above the swift water heads fly. The blood seeps into the salmon pools. Nine Englishmen are killed, but the Irish cannot hold out. They beg for terms but are refused. They must accept the captain's discretion, which means death in a more or less dreadful form. Wilmot kills them by hanging, a comparative leniency by the bloody standards of the day, according to my father. After the surrender, the legs of eighteen suffocating men kick to the laughter of Wilmot's men. My father reaches to his throat to mimic the act of hanging.

The priest who is found with the garrison is spared, however. Not for him the breaking of joints with heavy irons, the agonising death that is the fate of another clergymen found near Dingle. The priest has a bargain to offer. He tells Wilmot that the rebel Lord Kerry's son, 'but 5 years old … almost naked and besmirched with dirt',[1] has been smuggled out of the castle by an old woman. Who better than the heir to lure the lord into surrender? The old woman and boy are found in a hollow cave and are sent to Dublin with the priest, but their fate is not recorded.

My father pulls ghosts out of history every night. I know that in reality there are no riders as the field behind my grandmother's house is unmarked when I check it the next morning. 'Sure that's your father for the stories,' Hannah jokes to me when I return. My grandmother has stories too. She is part of more recent wars. If only she would tell me. She fought the English and was threatened with execution. But her stories will remain untold in her own voice.

* * *

I am grown and my father is dead when I discover how faithfully he brought the Elizabethan past to life. In the late sixteenth century the conquering English had swept their enemies before them. After capturing Listowel they rode on into Limerick. The president of Munster, Sir George Carew, reported back to London that they had killed 'all man-kind that were found therein, for a terror to those that should give relief to renegade traitors; thence we came into Arlogh Woods [in County Limerick] where we did the like, not leaving behind us man or beast or corn or cattle'.[2] Livestock was slain by the thousand and corn trampled and burned. The Irish peasants were butchered or driven away so that rebels and plotting Spaniards 'might make no use of them'.[3] Ireland was a nest of potential traitors. The possibility of the invasion of England through the 'back door', to the west, loomed large in the imaginations of Tudor statesmen and soldiers. Rebellions supported by the pope and the Spanish king reinforced the English terror of the Protestant Reformation being reversed. Such endings, they knew well, only came in tides of blood. Elizabeth's spymaster Sir Francis Walsingham had been in Paris on 24 August 1572 and lucky to escape the St Bartholomew's Day massacre of Protestant Huguenots. A delighted Pope Gregory XIII offered a Te Deum and had a special medal struck rejoicing that the Catholic people had triumphed 'over such a perfidious race'.[4]

The European wars of religion brought an exterminatory savagery to Ireland. In the Munster of my ancestors unknown thousands were killed in battle, slaughtered out of hand, and starved or killed by disease. The severed heads that lined the path to the tent of Sir Humphrey Gilbert — celebrated soldier–explorer and half-brother of Sir Walter Ralegh — were deemed a necessary price for making Ireland a land ripe for the benefits of English civilisation, lining the pockets of English adventurers, and keeping England safe from the existential threat posed by the kings of Catholic Europe.

II

History began with my father's stories. It was *our* history. He had no interest in complex agency, only in the evidence of English perfidy of which there was abundant evidence on our long walks during holidays around the ruined castles of north Kerry. Eamonn was a professional actor, one of the most gifted of his generation, and his voice, the rich, beguiling voice of those stories, has followed me all my days. I walked beside him through the lands of the O'Connors – taken by the English Sandes family, who came with Cromwell in 1649 – to Carrigafoyle Castle with its gaping breach where the Spaniards and Italians, and their Irish allies, were massacred fleeing into the mud of the estuary – and to Teampallin Ban on the edge of Listowel where, under the thick summer grass, lay the bones of the Famine dead. That was the 'hungry grass' said my father. Walk on the graves and you would always be hungry.

In those days Eamonn was a romantic nationalist. My mother Maura was a supporter of the Irish Labour Party and a committed feminist. She disdained nationalist politics. For her the struggle to achieve equal pay and control over her own body were the greater causes. A memory: being sent to Gleeson's chemist on the corner in Terenure, five minutes' walk from home, to ask for a package. The brown paper envelope I carried home contained 'the pill', something so secret I could not tell a soul. Only later did I learn how the chemist and my mother, in their quiet way, defied the law of the land which forbade women the right to decide if and when they would have children. Maura was raised in a house where no politics was spoken. Her father, Paddy Hassett, had been an IRA man in Cork but he had left the movement when the Civil War started in 1922. Most of his colleagues took up arms against the new Irish state. The only other trace of the revolutionary past I can find in my mother's life was her friendship with our neighbour, Philippa McPhillips, niece of Kevin O'Higgins, the Free State Justice Minister assassinated by the IRA in 1927 in revenge for his part in the draconian

My father the actor

policy of executing Republican prisoners during the Civil War. It
was not a political friendship – they were good neighbours – but
my mother always spoke of O'Higgins as a man who had been doing
what he believed was his best for the country. He was a man we
should remember, she said. Still, when my father suggested I should
be named after a dead IRA man, my mother acquiesced: Eamonn
Keane was a force of nature and not easily refused. Twenty-year-old
Fergal O'Hanlon had been killed during a border campaign raid on
an RUC barracks on New Year's Day 1957. The raid was a disaster,
and the IRA campaign faded away for lack of support. But O'Hanlon
and his comrade Sean South were ritually immortalised by way of
ballad:

Oh hark to the tale of young Fergal Ó hAnluain
Who died in Brookboro' to make Ireland free
For his heart he had pledged to the cause of his country
And he took to the hills like a bold rapparee

And he feared not to walk to the walls of the barracks
A volley of death poured from window to door
Alas for young Fergal, his life blood for freedom
Oh Brookboro' pavements profused to pour.
(Maitiú Ó'Cinnéide, 1957)

I grew up in Dublin. The city of the mid- to late 1960s was a place of rapid social change. The crammed tenements of James Joyce's 'Nighttown' with its 'rows of flimsy houses with gaping doors',[5] were mostly gone, their residents dispatched to the suburban council estates and tower blocks as a new Ireland, impatient for prosperity, straining to be free of dullness and small horizons, came into being. Nationalism had a grip on us still. But it had to compete with other temptations. The city of elderly rebels and glowering bishops was also the home to the poet Seamus Heaney, the budding rock musician Phil Lynott, the young lawyer and future president Mary Robinson; the theatres and actors' green rooms of my father's professional life were filled with characters who seemed to live bohemian lives untroubled by the orthodoxies of church and state. The country's most famous gay couple – though it could never be stated openly – ran the Gate Theatre next to the Garden of Remembrance where the heroes of the 1916 rebellion were commemorated. My mother intimated that Micheál McLiammóir and Hilton Edwards were 'different' and left it at that. To me they were simply a slightly more mysterious element in the noisy, extravagant, colourful world through which my father moved in the late 1960s. They were part of my cultural milieu, along with English football teams and imported American television series. Still, my father's attachment to romantic nationalism defined how I saw history. Or I should say how I 'felt' history – because thinking played much the lesser part of all that I absorbed in those days.

Dominic Behan visited our home in Dublin. So did the Sinn Féin leader and IRA man Tomás Mac Giolla, and several other Republican luminaries, though by then the IRA was drifting far to the left. My father played the role of the martyred hero Robert Emmet in a benefit concert for Sinn Féin. By that stage the leadership of the organization had drifted to the left, towards doctrinaire Marxism and away from the militarist nationalism of earlier times, but it could still summon up the martyred dead to rally more traditional supporters. My father never hated the English as a people. In drink he would swear damnation on the ghost of Cromwell and weep over the loss of 'the north'. But he was too imbued with the magic of the English language to be capable of cultural or racial chauvinism. Shakespeare and Laurence Sterne and John Keats had lived in his head since childhood. In one of his many flights of fancy he would even claim kinship with the great Shakespearean English actor Edmund Kean.

Irish history for my father was a series of tragic episodes culminating in the sacred bliss of martyrdom and national redemption. In 1965, the year I was sent to school, Roger Casement's remains were finally brought home to Ireland. The British had hanged Casement as a traitor in 1916 after he attempted to bring German guns ashore to support the Easter Rising. For nearly fifty years the authorities had refused to allow Casement's body to be exhumed from his grave in London's Pentonville Prison, and repatriated. When in March his body was finally brought back to Dublin for burial, my father placed a portrait of Casement on our living-room mantelpiece and told me to be proud of a man who had given up all the honours England could offer in order to fight for Ireland.

On the day of his belated state funeral we were given a half day off from school. The ceremony was broadcast on national television. Our eighty-two-year-old President, Éamon de Valera, defied the advice of his doctors and went to Glasnevin cemetery to tell the nation that Casement's name 'would be honoured, not merely here, but by oppressed peoples everywhere'. The following year, Ireland commemorated the fiftieth anniversary of the Rising. I remember a ballad that was constantly on the radio. We sang it when we played games of the 'Rebels and the English' in the lanes of Terenure in the suburbs of Dublin. I can recall some of the words still:

> And we're all off to Dublin in the green, in the green
> Where the helmets glisten in the sun
> Where the bay'nets flash and the rifles crash
> To the rattle of a Thompson gun ...[6]

The song, by 'Dermot O'Brien and his Clubmen', stayed in the charts at number one for six weeks. There was also a slew of commemorative plays, concerts and films for the fiftieth anniversary. Nineteen sixty-six was a big year for my father. He played the hero William Farrell in the television drama *When Do You Die, Friend?*, which was set during the failed rebellion of 1798. The performance won him the country's premier acting award. I watched a video of the production for the first time a few years ago. There is a wildness in my father's eyes. It erupted suddenly in my present. I felt shaken as the old wildness in his nature flashed before me.

I was later sent to school at Terenure College, a private school run by the Carmelite order, where there was conspicuously little in the way of nationalism apart from some small echoes in the singing classes of Leo Maguire, a kind man we nicknamed 'The Crow', whose radio programme on RTE featured such staples as 'The Bold Fenian Men' and 'The Wearing of the Green', harmless stuff in those becalmed days. What I did not know was that during the Civil War the IRA blew up a Free State armoured car outside our school, badly wounding three soldiers and two civilians. None of that bloody past whispered in the trees that lined our rugby pitches.

On Easter Sunday 1966, my father took me into Dublin to watch the anniversary parade of soldiers passing Dublin's General Post Office. De Valera was there to take the salute, although he stood too far above the heads of the crowd for me to see. Elderly men with medals formed a guard of honour below the reviewing stand. They did not look like heroes; they were just old men in raincoats and hats. Only the dead could be heroes. Like Patrick Pearse, my personal idol in those days. He was handsome and proud and gloriously doomed. My father often recited his poems and speeches.

I read them now and shiver. After nearly three decades reporting conflict I recognise in the words of Pearse a man who spoke of the glory of war only because he had not yet known war: 'We must accustom ourselves to the thought of arms, to the use of arms. We may make mistakes in the beginning and shoot the wrong people,' he wrote, 'but bloodshed is a cleansing and a sanctifying thing, and a nation which regards it as the final horror has lost its manhood. There are many things more horrible than bloodshed; and slavery is one of them.'[7]

In Ireland they were still shooting the 'wrong' people a hundred years after Pearse's death. The dissident Republican gunmen who swore fealty to his dream, and the criminal gangs who killed with weapons bought from retired revolutionaries, were at it still.

The following year, at Dublin's Abbey Theatre, my father played the lead role in Dion Boucicault's *The Shaughraun*, a melodrama set during the Fenian struggles of the mid-nineteenth century. Early in the play one of the characters speaks of the dispossession of her people by the English and swears vengeance: 'When these lands were torn from Owen Roe O'Neal in the old times he laid his curse on the spoilers . . . the land seemed to swallow them up one by one.'[8] Eamonn played a roguish poacher who outwits the devilish oppressors. During the play he was shot and seemed to be dead. I had been warned that it would happen but the impact of the gunfire, the sight of him falling, apparently dead, was still traumatic. Afterwards I found him alive backstage. My first experience of the power of the gun ended in smiles and embraces.

I was sent to Scoil Bhríde, an Irish-speaking school in the city which had been founded by Louise Gavan Duffy, a suffragist and veteran of the 1916 Rising, and built on land where Patrick Pearse first established a school in 1908. Michael Collins reputedly hid there during the guerrilla war against British rule in Ireland. We children read aloud the 1916 Proclamation of the Republic and memorised the names of the fallen leaders. 'We stood twice as tall,' Bean Uí Cléirigh, my old teacher, told me years later. 'We felt we could stand with any nation on earth.'[9] All I had to do was breathe the air of the place to feel pride in the glorious dead.

I learned that heroism in battle came from a time before the wars with the English. My father read to me the legend of Cù Chulainn, our greatest hero, who loomed out of the mythic past dripping in the gore of his enemies. Pitiless and self-distorting violence runs through the narratives:

> The first warp-spasm seized Cú Chulainn, and made him into a monstrous thing, hideous and shapeless, unheard of. His shanks and his joints, every knuckle and angle and organ from head to foot, shook like a tree in the flood or a reed in the stream. His body made a furious twist inside his skin, so that his feet and shins switched to the rear and his heels and calves switched to the front . . . The hair of his head twisted like the tangle of a red thornbush stuck in a gap; if a royal apple tree with all its kingly fruit were shaken above him, scarce an apple would reach the ground but each would be spiked on a bristle of his hair as it stood up on his scalp with rage.[10]

Cù Chulainn met his end strapped to a stone, sword in hand, facing the corpses of his enemies piled in walls around him, a raven perched on his shoulder as he faced his last reckoning with the enemies of Ulster. He died gloriously, of course.

My father was of a generation schooled in classical literature. He could read in ancient Greek, in which he came first in Ireland in the Leaving Certificate exams, and as a boy heard his father read Homer's *Iliad* aloud, until he was old enough to read it for himself. In the previous century, Irish peasant children had listened to the stories of Achilles and Ulysses from roadside teachers. A German travel writer visiting north Kerry in 1842 discerned a more dutiful reason for the prevalence of Latin speakers among local shepherds, recording that it was 'generally acquired in reference to the church

... it has not been purely for the sake of the aesthetic enjoyment to derived from it or simply for the cultivation of their minds'.[11] But such rich cultural reference did influence minds, and it took no vast leap of the imagination to see in our own Cù Chulainn a hero to compete with Achilles.

For Sunday outings my parents would sometimes take us to Tara, seat of the ancient kings, or to nearby Newgrange, where each December the winter solstice illuminated the tombs of our ancient Irish ancestors. I did not need heroes from American films or English comic books. I was a suggestible child, borne along by my father's passion, my teachers' certainty and the vividness of our native legends. History and mythology, one blending seamlessly with the other. I was now acutely conscious of my father's alcoholism. And so I learned the consolation of stories. I escaped the painful present by entering into the heroic past.

In that same year, 1966, events were beginning to unravel in the north that would change all of our lives. The sight of marching nationalists in the Republic unsettled the working-class Protestants of the north, where a Unionist government maintained all power in the hands of the Protestant majority. In the north, the commemoration of the Easter Rising had been a muted affair, but it took little in the way of nationalist self-assertion to prompt a return to the old habit of sectarian murder in Belfast. The Ulster Volunteer Force, named after an earlier Protestant militia, shot and killed two Catholic men in May and June. A Protestant pensioner died when flames from a burning Catholic pub spread to her home. The UVF followed up with a general warning that foreshadowed the murderous years to come. 'From this day, we declare war against the Irish Republican Army and its splinter groups,' it announced. 'Known IRA men will be executed mercilessly and without hesitation. Less extreme measures will be taken against anyone sheltering or helping them, but if they persist in giving them aid, then more extreme methods will be adopted ... we solemnly warn the authorities to make no more speeches of appeasement. We are heavily armed Protestants dedicated to this cause.'[12]

Violence permeated the memory of the Republic. It pulsed through the everyday reality of the north. IRA membership was not an essential qualification for murder at the hands of loyalists. At times any Catholic would do. But the early Troubles did not impinge on my life. The north was far away. In 1968, as the first big civil rights marches were taking place, I went on a trip to Belfast with my mother's school. I remember the surprise of seeing red pillar boxes, a Union flag flying at the border, the model shop on Queen Street where I bought toy soldiers, the coach stopping on the coast at Newcastle on the way back so that we could hunt under the stones for eels and crabs. It was a brief moment of calm. The following year catastrophe enveloped the six counties. It lasted for decades, long enough for me to grow to adulthood and eventually move the hundred or so miles north to work as a journalist in Belfast.

The Troubles confounded my father. He and my mother had visited Belfast the year before I was born. They'd stayed in a theatrical boarding house on Duncairn Gardens in the north of the city. It was run by Mrs Burns, a kind-hearted Protestant woman who had welcomed generations of actors. But less than a decade later, the district had become a notorious sectarian flashpoint. Near where my parents had once walked freely, a 'peace' wall would be erected to keep Protestants and Catholics apart. My father's romantic nationalism could not survive the onset of the Troubles. He veered between outrage at the British and outrage at the Provisional IRA. When IRA bombs killed civilians he would insist that these new guerrillas had nothing in common with the 'Old IRA', in which his mother Hannah and her brother had served. My father believed in the story of the good clean fight. He denied any kinship between the IRA Flying Columns of north Kerry and the men in balaclavas from the Falls Road and Crossmaglen. By then, the rebel in him had vanished.

How could he rhapsodise about the glorious dead of long ago while we watched on the nightly news the burned remains of civilians being gathered up on Bloody Friday? Neither my father nor my mother, or any of my close relatives, understood the north. Until 1969 it had had no practical impact on their lives. They watched from Dublin as curfews were declared and the first British troops arrived. Then came refugee camps in the south for embattled Catholics: 10,000 crossed into the Republic in 1972 – the year of Bloody Sunday, and Bloody Friday;* the year my parents broke up; the year we escaped my father's headlong descent into alcoholism. The north was burning and blowing up but I was lost in the small room of my own sorrow. Nothing made sense.

The refugees were kept further north. But I remember a group came to the seaside in Ardmore, County Waterford, one weekend in August in the early seventies. They were hard kids from the streets of Belfast and they scared us. An Irish government file from the time gives a good indication of how many southerners felt about the new arrivals: 'Refugees are not always frightened people who are thankful for the assistance being given them. Some of them can be very demanding and ungrateful, even obstreperous and fractious – as well as, particularly in the case of teenage boys, destructive.'[13] Oh yes, we in the Republic had moved a long way from the destructive impulses of war. When crowds clashed with police outside the British embassy in Dublin, a Garda told the *Guardian* newspaper that 'We didn't know what was happening in the North until this lot attacked us.'[14]

The Provisional IRA became active in the Republic, training and hiding and, very occasionally, shooting at our own security forces. We had army patrols outside the banks, special courts to try IRA suspects and a 'Heavy Gang' of policemen who battered confessions out of prisoners. The word 'subversive' entered our daily vocabulary.

---

* On 30 January 1972, soldiers from the Parachute Regiment opened fire on civil rights marchers in Derry, killing thirteen unarmed people. On 2 February angry crowds marched on the British embassy in Dublin and set it alight. In the events that became known as 'Bloody Friday' the IRA carried out multiple bombings in central Belfast on 21 July 1972. The attacks claimed the lives of nine people and injured more than one hundred.

To a middle-class boy like me, Republicans were aggressive young men in pubs selling the Sinn Féin newspaper *An Phoblacht*, a different and dangerous tribe whom we needed no encouragement to shun. In universities and schools we were now being taught a different history. The story of relentless English awfulness – and let there be no doubt, there had been plenty of it – was replaced by a more nuanced narrative in which the past was complex and sometimes confounding.

I realised by the mid-1970s, as the death toll from shootings and bombings in the north moved towards the thousands, that history was a great deal more than the stories my father had told me. It lay in the untold, in the silences that surrounded the killing in which my own family had been involved, and in the Civil War that had divided family members from old comrades. But for all the new spirit of historical revisionism we were not encouraged to ask the obvious contemporary question: What did the violence of our own past have to do with what we saw nightly on our televisions? What made the violence of my grandmother Hannah's time right and the violence of the 'Provos' wrong? Why was Michael Collins a freedom fighter and Gerry Adams a terrorist?

Interrogating these questions did not suit the agenda of the governments that ruled Ireland during the years of modern IRA violence. They were dealing with a secret army that wanted not only to bomb Ireland to unity but overthrow the southern government in the process. Both our main political parties had been founded by men who put bullets into the heads of informers, policemen and soldiers. By the time I was a teenager the last of them was long gone from public life. Their successors, the children of the Revolution, demanded that violence be kept in the past where it could do no harm. In short, we had had enough of that kind of thing.

In this ambition they were enthusiastically supported by the mass of the population. Whatever it took to keep the Provisional IRA and other Republicans in check down south was, by and large, fine with the Irish people. There might be emotional surges after Bloody Sunday in 1972 or the Republican hunger strikes at the Maze prison in the early 1980s, but the guns of Easter 1916 or the killers in the 'Tan war' were not who we were now. The Provisional IRA on the other hand took their cue from the minority within a minority who had declared an All-Ireland Republic with the Easter Rising of 1916, and as long as there was a republic to be fought for they claimed legitimacy for killing in its name. Down south they were hounded and despised, an embarrassing, bearded fringe who occasionally added to the store of public loathing and mistrust by killing a policeman or soldier in the Republic. Any attempt to contrast and compare with the 'Old IRA' was officially discouraged for fear of giving comfort to the Provos.

The northern slaughter helped to shut down discussion of the War of Independence and the Civil War – what we now call the Irish Revolution – in families too. I knew only that my paternal grandmother and her brothers, and my maternal grandfather, fought the 'Black and Tans', the special paramilitary reserve of the Royal Irish Constabulary. Given all we had been taught as children about the old oppressor it was easy for us, who had no knowledge of blood, to accept that the IRA of the War of Independence would shoot the English to drive them out of Ireland. I was not aware that many of those shot were fellow Irishmen wearing police uniforms. In this reading the Old IRA followed in a direct line from the rebels who faced Elizabeth's army at Listowel Castle. They killed the invaders.

Nobody spoke to me of the dead Irishmen who fought for the other side; much less of the fratricidal combat that engulfed north Kerry after the British departed in 1922. In my teens I was not inclined to enquire about the long-ago war. It did not interest me much then. I was already looking abroad to the stories of other nations. In Cork City Library, after my family had moved to Cork from Dublin, I devoured biographies of Napoleon and Bismarck. It was the big sweep of history that had me then. The relentless drumbeat of bad news from the north only pushed me to look further away from all of Ireland.

There was another, more painfully personal reason. When my parents separated in 1972 contact with my father's family, with my grandmother and her people, dropped away. I would see her a couple of times a year at most. Even if I had had the inclination, and she had been willing to speak, there was never the time to ask Hannah the questions. In my mother's family a similar silence prevailed. Although their father had fought in the War of Independence, my maternal uncles and aunts, with whom I spent most of my time, were largely apolitical. They bemoaned the tragedy of the north but felt helpless; their daily lives and ambitions were circumscribed by an attachment to family and to place, to Cork city where we lived a comfortable middle-class existence far from Belfast and its horrors.

It was only much later that I began to ask the questions that had been lying in wait for years. But by then those who might have given me answers were dead or ailing. Paddy Hassett, my maternal grandfather who fought in Cork, was long gone. He had told his own children nothing of his war service. My aunts and uncles knew only slim details of what had happened in north Kerry during the Revolution. It was only thanks to an interview broadcast in 1980, a year after I entered journalism, that I became aware of the darker history that had engulfed my family in north Kerry.

It took an English journalist, Robert Kee, to produce the first full television history of Ireland. Kee interviewed Black and Tans and British soldiers. He spoke with IRA men who described killing informers and ambushing soldiers. The combatants were old men now, sitting in suburban sitting rooms in their cardigans, calmly retelling the events of nearly sixty years before. It was also the first time I had heard any participant speak of what happened after the British left in 1922, and of how those who rejected the negotiated Anglo-Irish Treaty turned on the new Free State government. Men and women who had fought together against the British became mortal enemies.

I remember a sense of shock because the episode on the Civil War focused on an incident in north Kerry where my family had taken the Free State side. I knew the Free State army had carried out severe reprisals for IRA attacks during the Civil War, but the sort of blood vengeance of 'Ballyseedy' evoked the stories my father told me of *English* massacres. Not on the same scale, of course, but with an unsettling viciousness. In March 1923, in retaliation for the killing of five Free State soldiers in a mine attack, nine IRA prisoners were taken from Tralee barracks to the crossroads at Ballyseedy. One man survived the events that followed.

I listened avidly to the story Stephen Fuller told Robert Kee. He began by recalling the moment the prisoners were taken from jail in Tralee:

> He gave us a cigarette and said, 'That is the last cigarette ye'll ever smoke. We're going to blow ye up with a mine.' We were marched out to a lorry and made to lie flat down and taken out to Ballyseedy ... the language, the bad language wasn't too good. One fellah called us 'Irish bastards' ... They tied our hands behind our back and left about a foot between the hands and the next fellah. They tied us in a circle around the mine. They tied our legs, and the knees as well, with a rope. And they took off our caps and said we could be praying away as long as we like. The next fellah to me said his prayers, and I said mine too ... He said goodbye, and I said goodbye, and the next fellah picked it up and said, 'Goodbye lads', and up it went. And I went up with it of course.[15]

The flesh of the butchered men was found in the trees overlooking the road. The interview with Fuller was for me a moment of revelation. He told his story without emotion or embellishment. I had grown up conscious of the bitterness that followed the Civil War. I knew that our main political parties, Fianna Fáil and Fine Gael, had grown out of the conflict and that my own family were 'black' Fine Gael. Die-hard Collinsites. The side that blew up Fuller and the others at Ballyseedy. Now, in the words of Stephen Fuller, I could begin to glimpse the lived experience of the time rather than surmise the truth from the shreds of political rhetoric.

Irish men killed Irish men in the war of 1922–23. They killed each other in the war that went before it: Irish killing Irish with a fury that shocks to read of decades later. Did it shock them, I wondered, when in the long years afterwards they sat and reflected on the war?

The Fuller interview shook from my memory another of my father's stories.

'Watch the ceiling,' he'd say. 'Watch and you will see him.' A man in green uniform would appear and float through the darkness, if I would only wait.

'He is an English soldier and he was killed on the street outside. Wait and he will come.'

The soldier never came. Another of my father's yarns.

But years later I find out that Eamonn was telling a version of a truth.

A man had been killed on our street, shot dead close to the Keane family home. He was killed by an IRA unit that included a family friend with whom my grandmother and her brother had soldiered. The war had been sweeping across the hills and fields around my grandparents' town of Listowel for nearly two years when District Inspector Tobias O'Sullivan, a thirty-eight-year-old married man, an Irish Catholic from County Galway, was shot dead. He was the son of a small farmer, the same stock as my grandmother Hannah's people, and he left a widow and three young children behind. Yet his name was never mentioned. There is no monument to his memory, even though at the time of the killing he was the most powerful man in the locality and it was one of the most talked about events in the area's recent history.

There are many other uncommemorated deaths and events in the journey that forms this book. It is the story of why my own people were willing to kill, and of how people and nations live with the blood that follows deeds – a story that, in one country or another, I have been trying to tell for the last thirty years but not, until now, in my own place. It has been a journey in search of unwilling ghosts. My grandmother Hannah and her brother Mick left no diaries, letters or tape-recorded interviews. What I have are the few confidences shared with their family, some personal files from the military archives, the accounts of comrades in arms, the official histories and contemporary press reports, and my own memories of those rebels of my blood and of the place that made them.

I have tried to avoid yielding to my own collection of biases; however, a story of family such as this cannot be free of the writer's personal shading. When writing of the Civil War I am acutely conscious that I come from a family that took the pro-Treaty side and, later, became stalwarts of the political organization founded by Michael Collins and his comrades. But I have tried to describe the vicious cycle of violence in north Kerry as it happened at the time and as it was experienced by the people of my past, doing so, as much as possible, without the benefit of hindsight, and without acquiescing to the justifications offered by either side. This book does not set out to be an academic history of the period, or a forensic account of every military encounter or killing in north Kerry. Others have done this with great skill. This is a memoir written about everyday Irish people who found themselves caught up on both sides in the great national drama that followed the rebellion of 1916. It is not a narrative which all historians of the period are sure to agree with, or indeed which other members of my family will necessarily endorse: every one of them will see the past through their own experiences and memories. The one bias to which I will readily admit is a loathing of war and of all who celebrate the killing of their fellow men and women. The good soldier shows humility in the remembrance of horror.

I have reached an age where I find myself constantly looking back in the direction of my forebears, seeking to understand myself, and my preoccupations, through the stories of their lives. It is only with the coming of peace on the island of Ireland that I have felt able to interrogate my family past with the sense of perspective that the dead deserve. It felt too close while blood was being daily spilled in the north. 'We return to the lives of those who have gone before us,' wrote the novelist Colum McCann. 'Until we come home, eventually, to ourselves.'[16] Home is where all my journeys of war begin and end.

1

The Night Sweats with Terror

'It is not,' he urged, 'by weak inaction that great empires
are held together; there must be the struggle of brave
men in arms; might is right with those who are at
the summit of power.'

Tacitus, *The Annals*, AD 109

'The freedom of Ireland depends in the long run not upon
the play of politics, nor international dealings, but upon
the will of the Irish people to be free.'

An t-Óglach, Dublin, 29 October 1918

I

It was a January morning of low grey skies. On Dublin's Sackville Street crowds stood in fidgeting silence – street boys, daily paper hawkers, beggars and pickpockets, the old women from the Moore Street market, all gawking at the solemn faces marching up the left flank of the broad thoroughfare. With the cortège out of sight, they turned and went back to that other life of small trades and smaller change. They would have known that this policeman's death was bigger than the usual run. Half the police and army top brass in

Ireland seemed to be there: first came the bands with their sombre music, bands from the Army, the Royal Irish Constabulary, the Dublin Metropolitan Police. Immediately behind them came General Tudor, the most senior British security official in Ireland, along with a phalanx of senior police and military officers. The coffin lay on a gun carriage and was flanked by Auxiliaries marching with rifles reversed. A newspaper reported that some Auxies had taken the hats off men who failed to bare their heads in respect as the cortège passed.

He had been killed down the country, in Kerry, but he came from County Galway in the west. His RIC comrades followed in slow procession beside and behind. The constables of the Royal Irish Constabulary were marching out of history and towards oblivion behind a coffin draped in the Union flag: colours that would vanish from these streets in less than two years. But the marching men could not foresee the end of empire in Ireland. The British imperium stretched from the Pitcairn Islands across the Pacific and the Bay of Bengal, across the Hindu Kush to Delhi, across the Indian Ocean to Arabia and Palestine, through the Strait of Gibraltar until it reached this embattled western frontier, these streets of Dublin, capital of Britain's first colony. The funeral marchers knew of the unravelling in the wider world. Some would have had brothers and cousins still fighting the small wars of peace that erupted after the signing of the Treaty of Versailles.

The Great War was over. But the Bolsheviks were fighting to save their revolution. Churchill had dispatched an expeditionary force to Russia to bolster anti-Communist 'White' forces, in the vicious civil war. As a child I remember seeing a photograph of a soldier, Sergeant Jamesie Harris of the Royal Dublin Fusiliers, crouching in the snow. He was the father of my mother's best friend, Breda, and went to 'fight back the Red menace and collect the shillin' a day'.[1] The Great War irrevocably changed Breda's father. The man in the picture has a wanderlust, perpetually seeking a camaraderie impossible to find in the tenements of Charlemont Street where as many as nine people lived in a single room. More practically the Dublin of escalating guerrilla war was a risky place for an ex-serviceman, unless he was going to offer his services to the Republicans. As long as Jamesie Harris's fellow soldiers were being shot at and grenaded by the IRA, marching across the snows of Russia seemed much the better option.

At the Paris peace talks in 1919 the Irish delegation had been ignored, as had Vietnam, represented by Ho Chi Minh, and T. E. Lawrence with the Arabian commission, who quickly discovered the worth of promises made during war. The treaties of Versailles and Sèvres merely rearranged imperialism. Out with the Germans, Austro-Hungarians and Ottomans and in with the Italians, the Japanese and, greatest and youngest of the looming giants, the United States, a behemoth that oscillated between isolationism and the logic of its expansive energy. The Ottoman Empire, meanwhile, was being devoured by Britain, France and Greece until Turkish nationalism, in the form of Kemal Atatürk, halted their advance. Great armies clashed on the plains of Asia Minor and in the coastal cities of the Aegean. Smoke swirled over the port of Smyrna in 1922 while thousands of Greeks and other Christian minorities were butchered by the Turks.

Versailles did not deliver freedom to the small nation of Ireland. But the future IRA leader Michael Collins surely never expected it would. With his ingrained pragmatism he would have understood the crude realities of power in the post-war world. But they did not daunt him and the other leaders of the Republican movement. In Ireland by January 1921, thousands of regular troops were supporting sixteen thousand regular police and paramilitary forces in the war against the IRA.

Until these past twelve months in Ireland the British had managed to suppress colonial revolt. In the late nineteenth century, countless tribes went down before the machine guns and cannon of imperial armies: Zulus, Xhosa, Ashanti, Matabele, Shona, the Mahdi and his Dervishes at Omdurman. The Boers gave them a fright but ultimately succumbed. The Great War expanded the machinery of terror available to the industrial powers. The Iraqi tribes were crushed with air power and Maxim guns, their villages burned while high explosive shredded and carbonised those bearing arms and those who did not.

In India the viceroy was in the midst of plans to welcome the Prince of Wales, the future King Edward VIII, on a visit during which nationalist agitation was expected. Mahatma Gandhi asked angrily: 'Do the British think we are children? Do they think that parades for the prince will make us forget atrocities in the Punjab or the perpetual delay in granting us Home Rule?'[2] In the House of Lords, Lord Sydenham was worried about the rising militancy of religiously inspired warriors, young men who had forgotten the thrashing handed out to their fathers when they rebelled in 1897 on the North-West Frontier. 'It is always the young tribesmen who are easily accessible to the Mullahs, and they can at any time be led either to attack their neighbours or make raids into British India.'[3] Across Africa, nationalist movements were organising and challenging white rule: the African National Congress was formed in 1912, four years before the Easter Rising.

The new nationalists in Africa, Asia and the Middle East were ruthlessly suppressed. In Ireland alone, from 1920 onwards, the anti-colonial struggle was escalating towards a decisive showdown. The Chief of the Imperial General Staff, Sir Henry Wilson, worried that 'if we have lost Ireland we have lost the Empire'.[4] The funeral of District Inspector O'Sullivan was the latest way station in the decline of British power in Ireland.

The funeral procession passed the ruins of Dublin's General Post Office. How distant the Easter week of 1916 must have seemed now to the marching policemen and soldiers. The war of symbolic martyrdom was over. The poets and dreamers were dead. New leaders imbued with ruthless purpose had emerged to challenge the empire. Michael Collins and his 'Squad' of assassins tracked down police constables, spies and informers. There would be no more heroic failures. This was to be a revolution of steel not poetry. In north Kerry, my grandmother and her brother joined with farmers' children from across Ireland. They fought alongside the hard men of the inner cities and idealistic college students from the middle classes. They were part of a rebel army which would never offer itself up to such easy destruction as had the men and women of 1916. The GPO veteran Collins wrote that the new force would not be 'like the standing armies of even the small independent countries of Europe [but] riflemen scouts ... capable of acting as a self-contained unit'.[5] The concept of the IRA Flying Column was born.

Collins was helping to develop a new form of warfare: assassination and ambush, fast-moving squads of guerrillas – the so-called Flying Columns – would move across the countryside, being sustained by the people. The Boers had tried this with some success, moving across the expanses of the South African veld, before the British burned their farms, rounded up their women and children and stuck them in concentration camps. Such a repressive policy could not be so easily implemented in Ireland, just a few hours' sailing from mainland Britain, and with a watchful press and parliamentary oversight. His approach would pre-date Mao Zedong's seminal *On Guerrilla Warfare* by seventeen years. It would be studied closely by Ho Chi Minh later, as he prepared to liberate Vietnam from French rule, and by many other insurgents, from Algeria to the Far East. But Collins's ambitions for the fall of empire in Ireland did not appear imminently realisable at the start of the conflict.

The British government tried to meet terror with terror. It was brutal enough to push the Irish people deeper into the embrace of the guerrillas. Addressing the Oxford Union, W. B. Yeats condemned 'the horrible things done to ordinary law-abiding people by these maddened men'.[6] He was referring to the paramilitary police who had been recruited to augment the exhausted police. Over ten thousand served in Ireland. Many were veterans of the trenches of France and Flanders.

In Dublin, Nelson still stood on his pillar gazing south across the Liffey; behind him in the Phoenix Park the Chief Secretary for Ireland was still firmly ensconced in the Vice-Regal Lodge. The manager of the Shelbourne Hotel had closed his doors, in deference to the reduced custom occasioned by war, but he could see better days ahead, a return to the normal order, and he ensured that the 'grande old dame' of St Stephen's Green was regularly patrolled by the last remaining porter, upon whom 'devolved the ghostly duty of an inspection tour in the unnatural day-and-night darkness, in the silence piled up floor upon floor'.[7] The past offered some reassurance. There had not been a nationwide rebellion in Ireland for more than a century when the failure of the rising of 1798 led directly to the Act of Union that hobbled Ireland to Britain in 1801.* The most recent outbreak had been a small and failed uprising in 1867, staged by the Fenians, a secret society dedicated to the expulsion of the British Crown from Ireland and to the establishment of an independent republic. In the 1880s the Fenians launched a bombing campaign in Britain, the first major terrorist attacks of the modern age, striking at the London transport system, police stations and prisons, and the dining room of the House of Commons. They even staged an abortive invasion of British Canada.† Their rebellion, in Ireland, had amounted to a handful of skirmishes. But the ideas and organisational structures of Fenianism survived. The movement's short spasm of violence would also allow leaders such as Patrick Pearse to claim an unbroken tradition of armed resistance through the centuries of British rule.

The official name of the Fenian movement was the Irish Republican Brotherhood, and it would recover from defeat in 1867

---

* The rebellion was inspired by the ideals of the American and French Revolutions and led by the United Irishmen, many of them Protestants, who wanted to sever Ireland's connection with Britain. As many as thirty thousand people are believed to have died before the rebellion collapsed after a brutal campaign of government repression. What began, in part, as rebellion to create an Ireland free of sectarian division ended in massacre and deepened alienation between Catholic and Protestant.

† The Fenians enjoyed military victories over mixed Canadian and British forces until the arrival of colonial reinforcements prompted them to return to the United States. The final death toll from the campaign was an estimated thirty-two Canadians, one British soldier and six Fenians.

to shape the political thinking of a new generation of Irish separatists in the early twentieth century. Michael Collins was an IRB man
and steeped in its traditions of secrecy; they would serve him well
in the guerrilla war that erupted in 1919.

It was Collins more than anybody else who forged the war machine
that had killed District Inspector O'Sullivan. He would have been in
Dublin, on the late January day of the policeman's burial; his spies
would likely have been mingling among the mourners and reported
on its progress and on what they overheard. At the top of O'Connell
Street, a crowd of onlookers gathered near the statue of Charles
Stewart Parnell, his arm pointing into the past, towards Home Rule
and peaceful change and all that had been devoured in the age of
revolution. The crowd had their backs turned to the monument and
its chiselled words: 'No Man has a right to fix the Boundary to the
march of a nation.' But the nation was marching after coffins. The
days of Parnell, the Home Rulers and great parliamentary speeches
were over. This new era was crowded with killing.

That same month, a few miles away in Drumcondra the police
captured five IRA men after a failed ambush. An informer betrayed
their position. After courts martial the five were hanged, among
them a nineteen-year-old student from University College Dublin.
The reaction from the IRA was to wait a little. Then, eight weeks
later, the informer was found, abducted and shot. Blood begat blood.
Andrew Moynihan, a married farmer in Ballymacelligott, twenty
miles south of Listowel in County Kerry, was found with incriminating documents by the police. He was shot while trying to escape.
There was a problem with this explanation. A fleeing man would
surely have his back to his pursuers. But Moynihan was shot in the
chest and the face.[8] His killer was a Black and Tan, and veteran of
the war in France. There was a perfunctory investigation but no
charges were pressed. At London's Mansion House, Prime Minister
Lloyd George had confidently declared: 'by the steps we have taken
[in Ireland], we have murder by the throat'.[9]

But in the counties of Ireland murder spat back. It roamed
Dublin, tracking secret agents and killing them where they slept,

smashed into sleeping tenements, coiled in ambush on remote bog roads, ran up the stairs of redbrick Georgian houses in tree-lined suburbs, leaped in flames through the roofs of Anglo-Irish mansions, and always vanished into the sullen, unrevealing faces of the crowd. And murder also wore the uniforms of the British military, Black and Tans, Auxiliaries, regular policemen, and secret agents who dispensed with the law. Yeats captured the mood of the time:

> Now days are dragon-ridden, the nightmare
> Rides upon sleep: a drunken soldiery
> Can leave the mother, murdered at her door,
> To crawl in her own blood, and go scot-free;
> The night can sweat with terror . . .[10]

The police and army filed into Glasnevin cemetery to lay their dead comrade to rest. District Inspector Tobias O'Sullivan was an Irish Catholic and a supporter of Home Rule within the British Empire, the path pursued by the majority of Irish nationalists until the upheaval produced by the rebellion of 1916. O'Sullivan would be buried in the same vast graveyard as nationalist heroes like Parnell, Daniel O'Connell and Jeremiah O'Donovan Rossa. The following year, Michael Collins, the leader of the war that claimed the policeman's life, would be buried here too, shot dead by his former comrades in arms. It was here, six years previously, that Patrick Pearse had delivered the graveside oration for his Fenian friend, Jeremiah O'Donovan Rossa. Pearse's pledge that 'Ireland unfree shall never be at peace' would become the rallying cry for the Revolution to come.

The forces of the Crown stood to attention. Behind them was a group of around a hundred or more mourners. As the Pathé news cameras roll a young boy, a street urchin possibly, suddenly darts forward to pluck something from the ground, just behind the Auxiliaries. What has he found? A dropped coin perhaps. Nobody pays him any attention. And he vanishes out of shot.

Tobias O'Sullivan is buried according to the rites of the Catholic Church. At the grave a woman stands in a mourning veil with two small boys dressed in black coats and caps. These are Bernard and John, the dead policeman's sons. The woman is Mary, his widow, known to her family and friends as May, and she and some others are briefly seen looking away from the grave. That is because Tobias O'Sullivan's daughter, his youngest child, Sara, aged two, is crying, hidden behind the row of larger figures at the grave's edge, and being taken care of by another family member. The two boys look as if they are in a trance. The gravediggers, two young men in shirt-sleeves, stare at the boys. They are in fact young policemen, because the gravediggers are on strike. The film is from the era before sound. But we can imagine the graveside murmur. The stifled cries as earth is piled upon earth. A newspaper reported on 'pathetic scenes at the graveside, the widow and her two young sons weeping pitifully as the police buglers played the Last Post'.[11] Tobias O'Sullivan is buried as an Irish policeman under the British Empire and as such is destined to be officially 'unremembered' in a newly independent Irish state. The only memorials for men like O'Sullivan will exist in quiet homes – a photograph or keepsake on the mantelpiece beside a votive candle; the bloodstained tunic he was wearing when he was shot, kept in a private place ̠ntil his widow has died and eventually it vanishes. These Irishmen who killed and were killed by other Irishmen in the War of Independence are not commemorated or publicly mourned.

An old IRA man who fought in north Kerry remarked wistfully of the War of Independence: 'We didn't handle them properly for their brothers were in the IRA. In August 1920, the RIC were beating up the [Black and] Tans ... we should have been able to pull the RIC our way if we had worked it properly'.[12] The RIC was disbanded after independence. But the wounds of death were not forgotten. Not by those who loved the dead. Or by those who killed them. Tobias O'Sullivan was shot on Church Street in Listowel, near the house where my father grew up. He died at the hands of my grand-mother's comrades in the IRA. Hannah never spoke to me of his death or indeed of her comrades who died at the hands of the police and army. But decades after the killing, the shade of District

Inspector O'Sullivan lingered in the hidden memories of Church Street. The dead have a way of coming back, if they ever went away at all.

II

The day I donned my first uniform was one of the happiest in my life, and I felt that Dublin belonged to me as I swaggered down Grafton Street with my black cane stick, gloves neatly under my shoulder strap and my whistle chain across my breast.[13]

Constable Jeremiah Mee

Tobias O'Sullivan stood at around six feet and was sturdy with wavy dark hair and a thick moustache. A photograph of him in the last year of his life shows him gazing at the camera with a dogged expression. He came from the same Catholic faith and the same rural poverty as his assassins. But he had chosen to defend the existing order and for this his compatriots were ready to kill him.

His family traced their roots to the Gaelic lordship of O'Sullivan Beare, who had fought the English until he was forced into exile in 1603 and was murdered fifteen years later, apparently by an English spy, as he left mass in Madrid. The family believed their ancestors had retreated north-west with O'Sullivan Beare after the battle of Kinsale in County Cork in 1602, when the forces of Elizabeth I defeated a combined Irish and Spanish force, presaging the death of the Gaelic order and the triumph of colonial power. According to family lore, the O'Sullivans fought on and were present at Aughrim in County Galway when their leader Donal Cam O'Sullivan defeated a larger English-led army in January 1603. These were the stories of resilience and hardiness that were told to the young Tobias O'Sullivan. He grew up in this Irish-speaking district believing he had inherited the blood of warriors.

Tobias was one of nine children born in Cornamona, County Galway, of a small farmer whose wife, Tobias's mother, died in childbirth when the boy was just four years old. They lived on twenty-six acres but Tobias's father had known great hardship: he was seven years old when the potato crop failed and the Famine followed. Tobias would have heard stories of the catastrophe.

'The very dogs which had lost their masters or were driven from their homes became roving denizens of this district,' reported an English land surveyor at the time; they 'lived on the unburied or partially buried corpses of their late owners and others, and there was no help for it, as all were prostrate alike, the territory so extensive, and the people so secluded and unknown'.[14]

In fact Tobias's own grandfather, Patrick O'Sullivan, died of cholera during the Famine. He was tending livestock on the Durrus peninsula and, knowing he was dying, sent word back not to fetch him. The O'Sullivans buried him on Inchagoill, a scarred island on Lough Corrib. At the height of the Famine the area also saw a concerted effort to convert Catholics to Protestantism, with considerable sectarian animosity between elements of the two churches. The evictions that accompanied the Famine, and escalated in its aftermath, deepened the alienation. As late as November 1875, ten families were forced off the land near Oughterard, eighteen miles from the O'Sullivans; among them was an eighty-year-old man who died of a heart attack on hearing that he was to be made homeless. When the RIC were called in to enforce the eviction one officer had hot coals poured down his back. Thirty men and women were injured by a subsequent police bayonet charge. By 1880 meetings of the Land League in the area were drawing crowds of more than five thousand people to the slogan 'land for the landless people, land for the children of men'.* An English traveller

* The Irish National Land League was founded in 1879 to campaign for the rights of tenant farmers. It evolved into the biggest mass movement since the campaigns for Catholic Emancipation and Repeal of the Act of Union led by Daniel O'Connell. The confrontation with landlords and the government became known as the Land War. Its leaders were Charles Stewart Parnell and Michael Davitt. It is widely credited with effecting major social change in rural Ireland.

wrote that 'the law was ignored and agrarian crime respected and unpunished'. How can 'this almost universally disaffected tone be changed into one of content and loyalty?' he asked.[15]

The young Tobias would have been aware of the complicated history of the police in the area. The Irish Constabulary were obliged to enforce the law of the land. They took part in evictions. They infiltrated and informed on secret anti-government societies. But Tobias was one among many thousands of Irishmen who signed up to the ranks of the police. Many hundreds of thousands of others joined the Irish regiments of the British Army. Without them, the

Tobias O'Sullivan and his wife, Mary, known to her family as May

writ of Britannia, from Ireland to the empire's most far-flung borders, would have been hard to maintain. It was a choice made by members of my mother's family too, as we will see. The O'Sullivan family had strong police links. Tobias's older brother Bernard spent eight years in the RIC and became an inspector of police in Jamaica. Another brother rose to the rank of lieutenant colonel in the Australian Army. Two of his cousins would become RIC sergeants in Limerick.

Tobias O'Sullivan was an achiever. In the national exams for sergeant in 1910 he came second in Ireland. Growing up, he would have heard stories of the bravery of a local man, John Purcell, who was awarded the Victoria Cross for his actions in the Indian Rebellion of 1857. Neighbours' sons were far more likely to have joined the British Army than a militant nationalist organisation. Besides, the ranks of the Crown forces offered rare escape from rural poverty. The Connaught Rangers regiment recruited heavily from the young men of the region, and throughout the nineteenth century fought in wars across the British Empire.

Why did young men join the police? At home the ranks of the Royal Irish Constabulary offered upward mobility. There was strong competition for positions. Tobias O'Sullivan joined the police with his two brothers and a cousin. My maternal great-grandfather made the same choice with his three brothers. For many young men in rural Ireland the RIC constable was accepted as a pillar of authority and respectability. Even after the upheavals of the Land War the commanding position of the police sergeant in village and town seemed immutable. 'They all went to him for everything,' one officer remarked, 'he was the chief advisor and all.'[16] The police constable's salary was equivalent to that of the bank clerk, the civil servant and the schoolteacher, but the prospects of advancement were better. And while the young schoolteacher and bank clerk would be confined within the narrow space of a classroom or behind a counter, the police constable could get out in the open air, meeting people from town and country. RIC constables had to read and write, and their literacy gave them an additional measure of respectability. There were also other advantages such as the fact that uniforms and boots were supplied free, and married men received a lodging allowance. They were also an armed police force, although in the years before the Revolution they rarely carried their weapons on patrol.

When O'Sullivan joined at the turn of the century the make-up of the force represented the sectarian reality in Ireland: eighty per cent of the constables were Catholic, but Catholics only made up ten per cent of the district and county inspectors. The leadership was dominated by Protestants; the strong Catholic middle class was still excluded from the upper echelons of the state security apparatus. A university education could not break this glass ceiling. No such restrictions existed in the colonies, however. A bright Catholic boy like Michael O' Dwyer, for instance, one of fourteen children of a farmer in County Tipperary, could rise to become Lieutenant Governor of the Punjab, in which role he imposed martial law and defended his subordinate's role in the massacre of between 400 and 1,000 Sikh civilians at Amritsar. (O'Dwyer lost his job and ultimately his life. A Sikh tracked him down and killed him in London twenty-one years later.)

As the twentieth century opened, most Irishmen thought their position within the empire was settled. There was certainly enough consent from the governed for Her Majesty's police to enforce the law largely unhindered. During Queen Victoria's three-week visit to Ireland in April 1900 she had delighted in the 'endless streets full of enthusiastic people' in Dublin and the great fireworks display that lit the skies over the city.[17] Later she entertained 52,000 children to a 'Patriotic Children's Treat' in Phoenix Park.

Irish separatists demonstrated. W. B. Yeats denounced the royal visit and called attention to the plight of the Boers fighting 'an empire that has robbed [them] of their liberty, as it robbed Ireland of hers'. A year earlier, when the colonial secretary Joseph Chamberlain visited Trinity College Dublin, pro-Boer demonstrations turned into full-scale rioting. With a prescience that was generally lacking in Dublin Castle, Under Secretary for Ireland

David Harrel warned that the Boer struggle created 'this idea amongst the younger men of getting the possession of arms'.[18] A cultural revolution was under way, encouraged by Yeats and Lady Gregory who wrote of Irish themes in English, and by Irish language activists seeking to overturn English influence in the cultural sphere. The future first President of Ireland, Douglas Hyde, the son of a Protestant clergyman, deplored the 'constant running to England for our books, literature, music, games, fashions, and ideas'.[19]

But in those days a rural policeman like Tobias O'Sullivan was more likely to be preoccupied with disputes over rights of way and grazing, petty theft, illegal poitín distilling and prosecuting the owners of unlicensed livestock than with the dangers posed by nationalist agitators. By 1907 he was stationed in County Sligo where his name appears in court reports, a constable prosecuting groups of men involved in agitation against dairy farms. They were men of no property who sought fields in which to plant crops; they drove the cattle onto the roads, a symbol of wealth that lay perennially beyond their reach. My maternal great-grandfather, Patrick Hassett, was a thirty-year veteran of the police force by the time Tobias O'Sullivan joined up. A tall, sturdy figure with a piercing gaze, I know Patrick was physically brave. A newspaper report from 1895 refers to him as a man of 'rare coolness and self-possession' and describes how he killed a rabid dog with the stock of his rifle in order to save the life of a young boy.[20]

Yet the politics of the age seeped through. Two court cases from Patrick's service speak of an Ireland more unsettled than the British understood. One afternoon in Cork city, towards the close of the nineteenth century, he, his brother and a fellow constable hailed a horse-drawn cab. They asked to be taken to a police barracks on the western fringe of the city. The driver was the worse for drink and, for reasons unknown, resentful of the police. As soon as they had climbed on board he drove the horse at a furious pace, causing a collision with another cart, carrying lumber. My great-grandfather and his comrades were thrown into the road. His brother John suffered a broken collarbone. But when Patrick Hassett made to arrest the driver a crowd gathered and began to jostle the police. My great-grandfather drew his sword. Then the chanting began: 'Boycott the police!' Constable Hassett emerged unscathed with his prisoner, but the newspapers would later describe how the case had caused 'some stir in the city ... when it was reported that a serious conflict took place between the police and the people'.[21]

Three years later in rural Waterford, Patrick was dispatched to arrest a land campaigner and local Home Rule councillor who had shot at a wealthy Catholic farmer. Patrick succeeded in disarming the assailant who told him: 'God is on my side ... I had every right to do it.'[22] The fight was about land and the big farmer's purchase of ground rented by the poorer man. Land and who lost it, who stole it, who worked it, who gained from it, was the marrow of my ancestors' lives. As I travelled further I would discover in north Kerry, in the fields of my grandmother's people, how nothing was more political than the ground beneath their feet.

My great-grandfather was lucky to have retired from the RIC by the time a choice had to be made about what kind of country he was willing to fight for. In his last years, leading up to the outbreak of the Great War, there was a growing campaign to isolate policemen and their families from the communities in which they lived. The boycott chant he heard in Cork now echoed across rural communities. In 1897 the Gaelic Athletic Association, which attracted hundreds of thousands of young men to the sports of hurling and Gaelic football, banned police and soldiers from membership. Retired policemen faced discrimination in jobs controlled by nationalist town and county councils. When the War of Independence escalated the boycott extended to undertakers who were warned not to transport the bodies of dead policemen back to their home districts.

After the execution of the leaders of the 1916 Easter Rising, many policemen became conflicted about their role. The outbreak of guerrilla war in 1919 put the RIC directly in the firing line of the IRA. The first victims of the IRA were Irish policemen: eighteen were killed before the end of the year. By the middle of the following year more than fifty were resigning every week to avoid the violence. Policemen and their families were directly boycotted. Hundreds of remote police barracks were closed because they could not be defended. Scores of others were burned down.

Tobias O'Sullivan was the sergeant in charge of Athea barracks in County Limerick when it was closed in early 1920 and the police redeployed to more easily defended locations. The village was about eight miles from Listowel where he would be posted the following year. But first he was sent to the County Limerick town of Kilmallock which had a strong barracks in the heart of the town. Twenty years into his police career, O'Sullivan was determined not to be intimidated by the IRA. His resolve hardened in the face of the escalating campaign which branded men like him as traitors. An IRA poster in Cork in March 1920 was explicit in its threat: 'Whereas the spies and traitors known as the Royal Irish Constabulary are holding this country for the enemy ... we do hereby proclaim said spies and traitors, and do hereby solemnly warn prospective recruits that they join the RIC at their own peril. All nations are agreed as to the fate of traitors. It is the sanction of God and man.'[23] Some police cooperated with the IRA. The flow of information from inside police barracks, and from the British administration's head-quarters at Dublin Castle, was instrumental in the IRA's successful targeting of spies and informers. Others looked the other way when confronted with information about IRA operations.

Yet the majority remained loyal. This was partly to do with tradi-tion and discipline, and also the power of the status quo. Every previous rebellion in Irish history had been suppressed and life had always returned to a version of normal. To men like Tobias O'Sullivan the gunmen presented a vision of chaos, threatening the destruction of the more ordered world that had emerged from the anguish of the great Famine and the struggle for land. Late nineteenth-century British governments had been reformist. In the words of Irish chief secretary Gerald Balfour, they set about 'killing Home Rule with kindness'. Still Home Rule within the empire was now promised, a perilous pledge given the obduracy of Ulster Unionists, but a distinct probability in some form in the early years of the twentieth century.

An Ireland run by the armed separatists would probably have horrified O'Sullivan. The British Empire had been shaken by the Great War but in 1920 nothing indicated that it was on the cusp of irreversible decline. Tobias O'Sullivan must have felt he was on the right side of history. His wife May went with him, into the heart of a war she knew could claim her husband's life at any moment. When they married Ireland was already restive. But nobody then antici-pated that revolution was looming. Tobias and May met at the Pattern Fair of Leenane, an ancient saint's festival, held on the last weekend of September between his district near Oughterard and her home in the townland of Aghagower in County Mayo. Nearly twelve years older, he was handsome and would have radiated calm authority. Many years later the policeman's granddaughter Desiree wonders aloud to me if he was reckless, knowing the dangers he faced. Of her grandmother she says: 'She must have lived in terror.'[24]

2

The Ground Beneath
Their Feet

Come all ye loyal heroes wherever you may be
Don't hire with any master till you know what your work will be
For you must rise up early from the clear daylight till dawn
Or else you won't be able to plough the Rocks of Bawn . . .
My shoes they are well worn now, and my socks are getting thin
And my heart is always trembling for fear they might let in
My heart is always trembling from the clear daylight till dawn
I'm afraid I won't be able to plough the Rocks of Bawn

Anonymous ballad, nineteenth century

I

I walk the land in late October. I am coming down past Ballydonoghue church where my grandmother Hannah was baptised and married, where her father and mother were baptised, married and buried, where her brother Mick hid from the Tans, and where my people still farm and course their greyhounds and cheer Kerry's Gaelic football team. The wind is in from the Atlantic and growing stronger as the sun sets on Tralee Bay. It is forty years and more since I last walked these lanes. It has been too long. After my parents' marriage fell apart the trips to Kerry became fewer, and when I did come it was to see my cousins in the town. I keep close to the hedgerow to avoid the gusts. At the end of the hill I turn right towards Lisselton cemetery, which my grandmother would pass on her way to school early in the twentieth century. As the lane curves around towards the graveyard there is a small patch of ground on which lumps of rough-hewn stone are scattered. They are small, each less than the size of a football. There is a sign that reads: 'Don't pray for us/ no sins we knew/ But for our parents/ they'll pray for you.'

This is the Ceallurach, the burial ground of the unbaptised children of the Famine. In Hannah Purtill's time there was no sign here to mark the land. They didn't need one. Everybody knew. My grandmother went to school when there were still living survivors of the disaster. Even then, when people sought every patch of ground to work, the little field was left to become overgrown: outside the burial rites of the church but sacred in its own forbidding, heartbreaking way. Nobody would ever use the land.

I am not a stranger to mass graves. In other places I have seen those mounds bulging out of the earth, the shreds of clothing and shards of bone, and humanity reduced to mulch. I have always seen them as an end result. They have been reached after the sermons of hatred, relentless droughts or the advent of some vast pestilence. But at Lisselton the graves of the dead feel like a beginning. They point me in the direction I need to be going. If I am to understand why my people picked up guns and became revolutionaries some of the answer lies here in these Atlantic fields. On this October evening I begin to walk back into my history. Before leaving I pray for the dead.

Remembrance was private, to be kept suppressed in the heart. For with such immense loss, field after field of it across the county, with so many counting the absences, what could they do but face forwards, lean their shoulders into the work of surviving and hold their grief for night-time, after the quenching of lamps.

Hannah Purtill was born about two miles away from the burial place, in 1901. She was one of four children. The family was small by the standard expectations of the Catholic Church. Perhaps my great-grandfather Edmund Purtill decided he would only rear the number of children his small farm could support.

He laboured for the bigger farmers and worked his own few rented acres. Edmund was poor but not dirt poor. There was food on the table each day and his children went to school. I believe the Purtills came originally out of County Clare where the land was some of the worst in the country. I can find records of them in Ballydonoghue as far back as the 1830s. Rocky, marshy fields that gave nothing back without turning men and women old before their time, or driving their children to America. The Purtills were survivors. Famine had been part of their rural existence for centuries. Those who could work took to their feet rather than starve. Sometimes families followed. At some point in the nineteenth century the Purtills migrated across the River Shannon to north Kerry. The migrants were sometimes called *spailpíns*, meaning labourers. There was a poem we studied at school called 'An Spailpín Fánach' (The Wandering Labourer) about the plight of migrant workers in rural Ireland. The man declares he will give up his life of drudgery and serve with the army of Napoleon:

Never again will I go to Cashel,
Selling and trading my health,
Nor to the hiring-fair, sitting by the wall,
A lounger on the roadside,

You'll not see a hook in my hand for harvesting,
A flail or a short spade,
But the flag of France over my bed,
And the pike for stabbing.

The poem was part of our compulsory school Irish course and I regarded it as a chore. In those days I learned it in Irish, and I had yet to learn a love for the language my father spoke fluently. My Purtill ancestors' world was too distant and I could not then conceive of a kinship with those hard-pressed men and women of the nineteenth century.

The Purtills owned a couple of cows. The dairy cow had a mortal significance for the small farmer. The Famine had taught them not to depend on a subsistence crop that might fail. My uncle, John B. Keane, said that the 'the milch cow was goddess ... beautiful when she is young ... [and] all education, all houses, all food depend on the milk cow, whether we like it or not'.[1] The old homestead was still standing when I was a child. By then the Purtills owned some land and a small herd of cattle. I remember whitewash and thatch and the smell of turf burning on the range and a yard spattered with cow dung after the herd had been brought in for milking. I was allowed to milk one of the more docile cows, my grand-uncle Ned urging me on throughout with a cry of 'Good man boyeen, pull away let you.'

The old cottage was knocked down decades ago and replaced by a modern bungalow. When I last visited, my elderly cousin Willie was in the yard tending to his greyhounds. He lives there alone. As long as Willie can remember the Purtills raced dogs and hunted. There is a shotgun inside his front door for shooting rabbits and foxes, and, I am sure, to deter any intruder who might try and break in. I would call my Purtill relatives 'hardy' people. Willie remembers his parents and grandparents, how 'they worked like slaves' and were never sick. If you wanted a poem written or a song sung then you asked their in-laws, the Keanes. If you wanted work done or men to fight a war, then go to the Purtills.

The townland of Ballydonoghue occupies around eight hundred acres between the north Kerry hills and the Atlantic. The sea is close by; the Purtills could smell it as they led the cattle to pasture and back. In winter it gave them hard weather and flooded the fields and lanes. Across in the Shannon river direction lies the hill of Cnoc an Óir (the Hill of Gold) where, in my father's stories, the star-crossed lovers Diarmuid and Gráinne hid from the pursuing Fianna warriors in the world before history. The beautiful Gráinne was to marry the ageing Fionn, leader of the Fianna, but eloped instead with his younger comrade, Diarmuid, the finest of all the Fianna men. Years later, after they are apparently reconciled, Diarmuid was gored by a wild boar while out hunting with Fionn. All Fionn needed to do, my father explained, was to give him a drink of water from his hands to save his life. But he allowed the water to slip through his fingers. The memory of the old betrayal sent Diarmuid to his grave. Memories were long, said my father.

I revelled in the summer holidays in north Kerry. Legends flickered into life before my eager-to-believe eyes. This world was larger, it was fantastical, and before it my life in the city was reduced to a brittle impermanence. Here a part of my tribe belonged and would always belong. In those days it was not the land-hungry peasantry I saw as my ancestors but, encouraged by my father, a race of warriors and kings and storytellers. My people in Ballydonoghue did not leave behind written accounts of their lives. They passed on stories by word of mouth. They came from a tradition of fabulism. On May eve children were sent to pick up bluebells to place on the hearth to keep away the people of the spirit world who fluttered on the edge of dusk as child-stealers and harbingers of death. It was

Hannah and Bill, my grandparents

considered the worst of luck to plough a fairy fort, usually a mound in the middle of a field in which the people of the spirit world lived, waiting their time to reclaim the earth. Fairies controlled the world of the spirits. To cross them was to invite disaster. Foreshadowings of mortality abounded. My grandmother Hannah's favourite story was about a man who was passing by Lisselton graveyard one night when he heard the sounds of a football match. 'Will you help out?' a player asks. 'We are a man down.' Like any good Kerryman he joins in and scores several goals. At the end he is approached and told 'You will be back next week for good'. Within the week the man was dead and buried.

There were legends that hardened into fact, and hard facts that were softened until they became bearable. I found some local schoolchildren's essays from the 1930s, when Ballydonoghue was little changed from my grandmother's time. Cottages were still being lit by lamps, short journeys were made by foot, longer ones by donkey and cart; the social life of the parish revolved around Sunday mass and other religious devotions, weekend football games, and conversations at the gates of the creamery. There were dances, but these were often frowned upon and sometimes banned by the priests. A matchmaker by the name of Dan Paddy Andy O'Sullivan brought lonely farmers and prospective wives together. He also ran a dancehall, and in his youth he fought in the guerrilla war against the English alongside my grandmother and my uncles.

'The name of my home district is Ballydonoghue,' wrote one of the schoolchildren, eight-year-old Hanna Kelly.[2] 'About fifteen families live there and the population is over a hundred ... some of the houses are thatched and some of them are slated. Most of the houses are labourers' cottages.' Gaelic was no longer spoken as the people's tongue. But in everyday speech the translated forms of the old language infused conversation with a lyric intensity. They were heirs to hedge schools and vanished bardic poets and were natural storytellers with a broad extravagant accent that urbane city folk might mock but whose rootedness they quietly envied. The children's essays noted the departure of young men and women for

England and America, and remarked on the handful of Irish speakers who were left in the area. They wrote about the ruins of an old Yeoman's barracks — a Protestant militia raised during the early 1790s — and about the lost grave of a Dane from Viking times, and of a fort with a pot of gold.

Wide stretches of bog dominated the ground around Ballydonoghue. Willie Purtill used to joke that he graduated from school to the bog at the age of fourteen. Once or twice I footed turf with my cousins. It was backbreaking work for a city boy, and boring for a child who had inherited the Keanes' capacity for dreaming and being easily distracted. But it was made bearable by the promise of sweets and minerals later. The bog stretched towards the Atlantic and I remember how, if you missed your footing, the mulch below sucked your boots off as you tried to walk out, and how once, after rain at Easter, the bogholes glittered like a thousand broken mirrors in the watery sunlight. At the end of the summer bog cotton flowered: to me it looked like snow or the windblown feathers of swans fallen to earth. It could be picked to be stuffed into pillows and cushions.

Over the years there had been attempts to drain part of the bog and create more arable land and pasture. Between 1840 and 1843 the landlord, Sir Pierce Mahony, a liberal Protestant and ally of Catholic Emancipation, obtained more than £600 in drainage grants from the state. But within a year of the last grant the potato Famine had begun: there were more pressing priorities than drainage and the bog endured. The mid-century traveller Lydia Jane Fisher wrote lyrically of the local landscape, where the green and blue flax flower contrasted 'with the golden oats, the brown meadows, and the dark green of the potato — all uniting to make the grand mosaic of Nature particularly beautiful at this season. The foxglove, the heath, and the bog myrtle refreshed our senses.'[3] But a more realistic appreciation was given by James Fraser who saw that 'the soil is generally poor, and still more poorly cultivated. The houses of the gentry are few and far between, and the huts of the peasantry are miserable.'[4] Those who worked the land, like the Purtills, would not have seen any romance. It was the Keanes, their book-loving future in-laws in the town of Listowel, who would be able to rhapsodise to their hearts' content about the joys of spring fields.

I recall listening to my father, Eamonn, and a Purtill relative discussing the subject one afternoon in Ballydonoghue. 'What you have, you hold,' said my father. 'Do you hear that boy?' he said. 'What you have you hold.' Land defined the borders of the imagination. To be a man of substance you needed to own the ground underneath you. My father spoke of a relative who was a middleman at cattle fairs but he had no fields of his own. He was famous for his ability to strike bargains between farmers. To show that he was a man of substance he once pinned a five-pound note to his coat. It might seem a comical gesture until you think about the longing that lay behind it. He had no land and never would have. He would always be the dealer in other people's livestock.

The hunger for land warped men's spirits. It could drive them to acts of malice. If a cow died on your rented acres you might dump it on your neighbour's holding to transfer the bad luck. In her eighties one old woman recalled how a row between two hay mowers at the height of the threshing led to one being deliberately poisoned so that he had acute diarrhoea. 'It was arranged to put something in his tea. In no time he had the runs. There was nothing for it but take off his trousers and work away [for] he was not going to be stopped.'[5]

My uncle, John B, wrote a play called *The Field* about a man who kills an interloper in a dispute over the purchase of a field. The field is invested with a sacred quality whose importance can only be understood by those who work its soil. After the murder, a Catholic bishop addresses locals at mass:

This is a parish in which you understand hunger. But there are many hungers. There is hunger for food – a natural hunger. There is the hunger of the flesh – a natural understandable hunger. There is a hunger for home, for love, for children. These things are good – they are good because they are necessary. But there is also the hunger for land. And in this parish, you, and your fathers before you, knew what it was to starve because you did not own your own land – and that has increased; this unappeasable hunger for land ... How far are you prepared to go to satisfy this hunger? Are you prepared to go to the point of robbery? Are you prepared to go to the point of murder? Are you prepared to kill for land?[6]

The answer is yes. Yes, again and again. Why not when, without it, you are scattered and dissolved? Those whose ancestors had starved to death for want of land, who had been dispossessed at the point of a sword, whose oral history had been embedded in the minds of generations, stressing the shame of being a people without land of their own. Land drove men to blood. It is impossible to understand the War of Independence and the Civil War that followed unless you know the story of the land. It is where the hardest of all memories lay, where the grievance and loss accumulated and became ready to flower into violence.

At one point this part of north Kerry had been notorious for faction fighting. In the middle of the nineteenth century feuds between clans and villages would be settled in battles between groups several hundred strong. Deaths and terrible injuries were common. It was said that some of the bad blood could be traced to the plantation of families from neighbouring County Clare during the age of plantation. But this was local talk. Faction fighting was a feature of rural Ireland in this period, often reflecting communal divisions over land usage, employment and social status. One account from the early nineteenth century described how 'in an instant hundreds of sticks were up – hundreds of heads were broken. In vain the parish priest and his curate rode through the crowd, striking right and left with their whips, in vain a few police-men tried to quell the riot; on it goes until one or other of the factions is beaten and flies'.[7] The fighting stick, the shillelagh, was often sharpened to ensure the scalp was cut or weighted with lead to bludgeon the enemy. Most often the matter was settled once blood had been drawn, and the wounded man would retire from the field. One of the most notorious blood feuds, between the Cooleen and Mulvihill factions, was said to be rooted in an ancient dispute over land. In 1834 it came to a head as more than two thousand people took part in a savage battle of Ballyeagh Strand, close to Ballydonoghue. Men and women, including mounted detachments, set about each other with clubs, slash hooks, horseshoes and guns. Twenty people tried to escape in a boat, which overturned in a swift current. As the survivors tried to reach shore they were pelted with stones and driven back into the waters to drown. Not even the local parish priest would give evidence at the subsequent public inquiry. Silence was the law of the land.

The fighting could be exported across the ocean. In the same year as the battle of Ballyeagh, Irish factions fought each other along the banks of the Chesapeake and Ohio Canal in Maryland and on the rail lines between Canada and Louisiana – but they fought each other here not for land but for jobs.

The violence of the land was threaded throughout the stories of my childhood. About a mile up the hill from the old Purtill home-stead there is a crossroads from where you can see across the plain to Ballyheigue Bay. It was here that An Gabha Beag ('the Little Blacksmith'), the local leader of the rebel 'Whiteboys', was hanged by the English in the early nineteenth century. His name was James Nolan and Hannah used to tell us that he had to be hanged three times because in his forge he had fashioned an iron collar which he placed under his smock to protect his neck. Eventually the redcoats found it and James Nolan was sent to his maker. According to the stories collected by the Ballydonoghue schoolchildren, the landlord responsible for the blacksmith's death was a Mr Raymond, whose family would haunt the later history of the area. In one version the hanged rebel's family come to Gabha's workshop in the dead of night: 'At MIDNIGHT, so the end of this terrible story goes, seven of the dead men's nearest relatives came to the forge and there, by the uncanny light of the fire, cursed Raymond's kith and kin across the anvil. Their curses ... did not fall on sticks or stones.'[8] The Raymonds were to be damned for all time.

The Whiteboys were a cry of revenge against the exactions of landlords and their agents, against parsons and sometimes priests, against those who turned fields where potatoes grew into grazing for cattle, against the men who fenced and enclosed and who demanded tithes and rents. Named after the white smocks they wore in their night raids, they fought for the rights of tenant farmers and against the system of tithes that maintained the Protestant clergy. The tithes could be exacted in cash or kind and provoked bitter resentment among the Catholic poor. The *Topographical Dictionary of Ireland* (1836) recorded that in Lisselton parish, which included Ballydonoghue, the Reverend Anthony Stoughton who, along with his brother Thomas, owned much of the land in the district was in receipt of tithes worth approximately £10,000 in today's money. He also received income from several other parishes in the district. After appeals from the tenants, Stoughton and his brother agreed to reduce their tithe demands, earning gratitude 'for their kind and considerate mode of dealing with us respecting our Tithes; by which one of our heavy burthens has been considerably lightened – and we sincerely regret that all other Proprietors of Tithes do not follow an example which would in a great measure tend to tranquilize the minds of the people at large'.[9] The bigger Catholic landowners, as well as priests who charged for their services at funerals and weddings or condemned the Whiteboys from the pulpit, could also be targets. The raiders maimed and killed cattle, terrorised and sometimes assassinated unpopular landlords and their agents. The founder of Methodism, John Wesley, encountered the Whiteboys whilst visiting County Tipperary and saw how they 'moved as exactly as regular troops and appeared to be thoroughly disciplined'.[10] The violence was episodic but caused widespread terror.

A Whiteboy general, William O'Driscoll, declared: 'We will continue to oppose our oppressors by the most justifiable means in our power, either until they are glutted with our blood, or until humanity raises her angry voice in the councils of the nation to protect the toiling peasant and lighten his burden.'[11] The Whiteboy oath was everything. It gave men a feeling of belonging. And it warned against betrayal. The avenging secret society bound together by oaths became the most powerful force to challenge the established order in early nineteenth-century rural Ireland. 'I sware I will to the best of my power,' the oath-taker would declare, to:

Cut Down Kings,
Queens and Princes, Earls, Lords, and all such with
Land Jobbin and Herrisy.[12]

The English writer Arthur Young, who toured Ireland in the 1770s, wrote about the Whiteboy insurrections and the oppression of the labouring poor. 'A landlord in Ireland can scarcely invent an order which a servant, labourer or cottier dares to refuse to execute,' he noted. 'Disrespect or anything towards sauciness he may punish with his cane or his horsewhip with the most perfect security.' Young, who had travelled all over the British Isles, was shocked to observe in Ireland long lines of workers' carts forced into the ditches so that a gentleman's carriage could pass by. 'It is manifest,' Young wrote of the mounting insurgency, 'that the gentlemen of England never thought of a radical cure from overlooking the real cause of the disease, which in fact lay in themselves, and not in the wretches they doomed to the gallows.' He then added with unsettling prescience: 'A better treatment of the poor in Ireland is a very material point to the welfare of the whole British Empire. Events may happen which may convince us fatally of this truth.'[13]

A landlord in Con Brosnan's home area of Newtownsandes described the situation in March 1786. 'We are so pestered with Whiteboys in this country that we can attend to nothing else.' Landlords were restricted because 'all law ceases but what the Whiteboys like; not a process is to be served, not a cow drove, nor a man removed from his farm on pain of hanging'. The Whiteboys had erected gallows in Newtownsandes, Listowel and Ballylongford with 'their entire aim ... levelled at the tithes'.[14] Traditions of violent resistance were becoming embedded. A decade later a local man, Phil Cunningham, became a leader of the United Irishmen rebellion in County Tipperary. Transported to Australia he died leading a rebellion against the British in 1803.

The fear of a native revolt accompanied by French invasion loomed large in late eighteenth- and early nineteenth-century politics, as the Whiteboy attacks created panic among local Protestant populations. One informer's account refers to a 'meeting of the White Boys at Myre [in Tipperary, where] it was resolved on to burn the houses of the Protestants, and to massacre them in one night, after a landing made by the French, as was expected'.[15]

Government retribution was harsh. Hundreds of rebels or suspected rebels were transported to Australia. Public hangings were often carried out in the rebels' home districts. Con Shine, a local carpenter, recalled an execution by soldiers near Listowel in 1808, as told to him by his family: 'They drove 2 poles in the ground below at the cross and put another pole across they then put him standing in a horse's car put a rope around his neck then pulled away the car and left him hanging there. He was hanging there all day. The soldiers use to come often and give him a swing for sport and leave him swing away for himself. All the doors were shut that day. You would not see a head out the door.'[16]

Around Ballydonoghue the Catholic Church condemned the Whiteboy attacks and pledged 'firm attachment to Our Gracious King and to the Constitution ... we will not enter into conspiracy against the laws of our country'.[17] A priest in Listowel went further and urged his flock to collect £26 as a reward for anybody giving information on those responsible for the burning houses in the parish. The state archives for the period reflect the efforts made by local priests to discourage support for the Whiteboys. The Listowel magistrate, John Church, records parish meetings across north Kerry and praises the efforts of the clergy while noting claims by the church that the disturbances were caused by poverty and poor weather 'more than any political motive as maliciously insinuated in some publick Prints'.[18] By the late 1820s the campaign for Catholic

Emancipation led by Kerryman Daniel O'Connell was on the threshold of success. The church did not want chaos and violence. From the time of the Reformation Catholics had faced a range of restrictions. But in the wake of Cromwellian (1649–53) and then Williamite (1688–91) wars, the repression intensified and a wide range of 'Penal Laws' was gradually introduced, targeting Catholics, as well as Presbyterians and other dissenters from the Anglican order. The laws were meant to ensure the ascendancy of Anglicans, with restrictions on Catholic landholding, worship, education, and even a prohibition on Catholics owning a horse worth more than £5. This last imposition was to ensure that strong swift beasts that would be useful for cavalry were kept out of the hands of Catholics. Enforcement varied in different places and with the passage of time some of the most punitive laws were rescinded, but by the 1820s Catholics were still excluded from Parliament and from being judges or senior civil servants. The effect was to make religion synonymous with the power of the minority. Very soon the reverse would obtain. The campaign to achieve Catholic Emancipation galvanised the Irish poor and gave Europe its first great campaign of peaceful mass protest. By 1829 the battle for religious liberty was won and the confessional demography of Irish life had been asserted. The Catholic Church emerged as the most powerful force in Irish life, a role it would not willingly relinquish for the next century and more. But the Church would struggle to control the unrest which arose from the poverty and injustice of the times.

The Whiteboys were succeeded by the 'Rockites' in the 1820s, inspired by the millenarian writings of Signor Pastorini, the pseudonym for the English Catholic bishop, Charles Walmesley, who predicted the imminent demise of Protestantism. The north Kerry poet Tomás Ruadh O'Suilleabháin saw the coming deliverance of his people from landlordism and English rule:

It is written in Pastorini
That the Irish will not have to pay rent
And the seas will be speckled with ships
Coming around Cape Clear.[19]

The local landlords around Ballydonoghue were frightened by the threats of a Protestant apocalypse. In nearby Tarbert one landowner learned of Pastorini's tract being read 'among the lower orders of Roman Catholics, who ... expect to have the Protestants exterminated out of this kingdom before the year 1825'.[20] An agent working for Reverend Stoughton was battered with stones, stabbed to death and then had his ears and nose cut off and placed on public display by his attackers.[21] The Rockites, like the Whiteboys before them, were suppressed with customary brutality while O'Connell succeeded in diverting the mass of the rural poor into peaceful campaigning. When the Bill for emancipation was voted into effect on 13 April 1829, the people of Ballydonoghue could look up and cheer the flaming bonfire of triumph on top of Cnoc an Óir. Five years later they gathered for the opening of their new church, a stone building that spoke of permanence and where the Purtills still observe the rites of their faith. The campaign for religious freedom awakened people to the power of their numbers. But the hunger and the structural injustices of rural life ensured that violence would come again. Tithes remained a bane of local life and when they prompted an outbreak of agrarian violence a decade later the Stoughtons were targeted.

In January 1833 the *Morning Chronicle* recorded that a bailiff working for the Reverend Anthony Stoughton and his brother Colonel Stoughton of Listowel was murdered by being 'struck on the back of the head with a stone and received about twenty bayonet wounds'.[22] On another occasion a horse belonging to the brothers was cut in two. The so called 'Tithe War' witnessed a familiar ritual of midnight raids but also the politics of highly organised intimidation, not just aimed at the clergy but against those who agreed to pay their tithes. State retribution was harsh, with instances of troops shooting on protesting crowds. But the conflict marked the beginning of the end of the Church of Ireland as the established church and in 1838 the government acted to transfer responsibility for the upkeep of Anglican clerics to the landlords.*

Poverty is not a necessary precondition for civil strife, but mix it with memories of dispossession, in a system based on the supremacy of a minority, and the emergence of groups such as the Whiteboys, and others in years to come, seems utterly logical. They were men and women with nothing to lose and the raw courage of youth. They did not fight for a nation state, or the republican ideals of Wolfe Tone and the United Irishmen. They fought for the ground beneath their feet.

---

* The final phase in the decline of Church of Ireland power came with the Irish Church Act of 1869 which did away with the payment of tithes and replaced them with a life annuity.

3

My Dark Fathers

My Dark Fathers lived the intolerable day
Committed always to the night of wrong,
Stiffened at the hearthstone, the woman lay,
Perished feet nailed to her man's breastbone.
Grim houses beckoned in the swelling gloom
Of Munster fields where the Atlantic night
Fettered the child within the pit of doom,
And everywhere a going down of light.

Brendan Kennelly, 'My Dark Fathers', 1962[1]

I

The Earl was well pleased with his welcome. The gentry had assembled, as had the local clergy, including the formidable Father Jeremiah Mahony, parish priest of St Mary's, who delivered a vote of thanks to his Protestant counterpart, Reverend Edward Denny, 'for his dignified conduct on this, and every other occasion, when called on'.[2] The occasion was a welcome party for the new Earl of Listowel, William Hare, and the language was indicative of something more than the ritual flattery reserved for visits of the mighty. The priest had reason to welcome the Earl, who had been a supporter of Catholic emancipation and provided land for the new Catholic church on the square directly opposite the Protestant St John's. His liberalism on religion put him at odds with several powerful fellow landowners in the area. The formal address urged the Earl to make his visits 'frequent and prolonged' and sought his 'protection and tutelage' for 'a grateful tenantry'.[3] At that moment, seated behind the ivy-clad walls of the Listowel Arms Hotel, among the smiles and handshakes of the men of property, within yards of the Protestant church and its new, taller-spired Catholic counterpart, the Earl might have hoped for a tranquil residence. But beyond the Feale bridge on either side of the road towards Limerick, by the Tarbert road and the road to Ballydonoghue, in every field in north Kerry where potatoes were planted, a catastrophe was taking root.

They were used to hunger. Seven Irish famines of varying extremes had struck since the middle of the eighteenth century. Outside the rapidly industrialising north-east the country was mired in poverty with average income half that of the rest of the United Kingdom. The rural population had grown rapidly, encouraged by the nourishment provided by the widespread cultivation of the potato, and the growing trend to marry young. In the twenty years before the Famine the number of people subsisting in the area increased by nearly two thousand souls.

By the summer of 1839, two years after the new Lord Listowel was welcomed to the town, there were warnings of crisis. At a public meeting in Listowel, the gentry and the clergy (Protestant and Catholic) and prominent townspeople heard reports of the 'increasing difficulties of the labouring classes of this district from the enormous prices which the commonest provisions have reached; agricultural labour, about the only source of employment, has now already terminated'.[4] The meeting noted ominously that the potato crop of the previous harvest had failed. Public works schemes to alleviate the distress of the poor were already under way and 4,000 people each day received rations of oatmeal. The novelist William Makepeace Thackeray passed through Listowel in the same year and saw a town that 'lies very prettily on a river ... [but] it has, on a more intimate acquaintance, by no means the prosperous appearance which a first glance gives it'.[5]

The writer, at best a condescending witness to Irish travails, went on to record the poverty of the scene, the numerous beggars (their number undoubtedly swollen by the growing hunger in the countryside), the appearance of 'the usual crowd of idlers round the car: the epileptic idiot holding piteously out his empty tin snuff-box; the brutal idiot, in an old soldier's coat, proffering his money-box and grinning and clattering the single halfpenny it contained; the old man with no eyelids, calling upon you in the name of the Lord; the woman with a child at her hideous, wrinkled breast; the children without number'.[6] The following year the *Kerry Evening Post* recorded the failure of the potato crop in the north of the county. A landowner near Ballydonoghue noted in his journal: 'we were concerned to hear many complain of a dry rot appearing more extensively than hitherto ... The farmers are very apprehensive of it.'[7] In early February the first of the destitute were admitted to the workhouse in Listowel.

The Purtills and their neighbours watched as a vast withering engulfed the fields of north Kerry in the late summer of 1845. The land agent, William Trench, gave a vivid account of his first encounter with the blight:

The leaves of the potatoes on many fields I passed were quite withered, and a strange stench, such as I had never smelt before, but which became a well-known feature in 'the blight' for years after, filled the atmosphere adjoining each field of potatoes. The crop of all crops, on which they depended for food, had suddenly melted away, and no adequate arrangements had been made to meet this calamity, the extent of which was so sudden and so terrible that no one had appreciated it in time, and thus thousands perished almost without an effort to save themselves.[8]

Soon the smell of the rotting crop was thick around Ballydonoghue. It would be followed soon enough by the smell of corpses.

The newspapers of Kerry and Cork provide us with a picture of deepening distress over the Famine years. There was relief, but never enough. Concern by some landlords, but indifference and cruelty from others. In August 1846 the correspondent of the *Cork Examiner* reported that the potato crop 'was not partially but totally destroyed in the neighbourhood of Listowel ... the common cholera has set in there without a particle of doubt'.[9] By autumn desperation had given way to rage. In November a crowd of up to six thousand came to Listowel 'shouting out "Bread or Blood" and proceeded in the greatest state of excitement to attack the Workhouse ... with the intention of forcibly helping themselves to whatever provisions they might find within the building'.[10] They were stopped by the intervention of a popular priest.

North Kerry was devastated. The *Tralee Evening News* of 16 February 1847 described how: 'Fever and dysentery prevail here to a frightening extent.' The 'bloody flux' reduced its victims to hopelessly defecating shadows who squatted and lurched in roads, lanes, fields, market squares, on the seashore and riverside, reduced by the mayhem of disease, covered in their own waste, uncared for, and, when they died, often left unburied. 'Men women and children [are] thrown into the graves without a coffin,' reported the *Kerry Examiner*, 'no inquests inquire as to how they came by their death, as hunger has hardened the hearts of the people. Those who survive cannot long remain so – the naked wife and children staring them in the face – their bones penetrating through the skin.'[11]

A parish historian recorded the deaths of eighty people in 1847, nearly half of whom were buried without coffins.* Kerry had the second-highest rate of recorded deaths from dysentery during the

---

* The local historian John D. Pierse has published figures showing a fall of 481 in the number of residents in the district in the years 1841–1851 – nearly 22 per cent of the population.

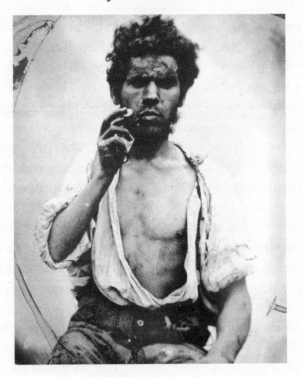

Rural labourer in Famine era

Famine. Starvation and disease would take the lives of around 18,000 people in just a single decade.

Thousands fled, emigrating to Britain and further afield. Taking ship to escape poverty was an established feature of life in the area and the expanding frontiers of North America offered opportunity. Garret and Mary Galvin from Listowel arrived in Canada with only meagre belongings but within a few years were farming thirty-six acres in Ontario, with twelve cattle, two horses, seventeen pigs and forty sheep. That was in 1826. Two decades later conditions were unrecognisably worse: the government logs of passengers do not even list their names. A few entries picked from the records of the year 1851, hint at the great migration:

18 July: twenty-eight from Listowel make the crossing to
  Quebec on the ship *Jeannie Johnstone*.
29 August: sixty-five from Listowel board for Canada on the
  ship *Clio*.
26 September: thirteen from Listowel sail on the *John Francis* ...[12]

Passengers were often selected by their landlords, being of no further economic use on the land, or by the guardians of the work-houses, and sent away to North America with just the price of their fare.

At Quebec the immigrants disembarked at Grosse Isle in the St Lawrence archipelago. Five thousand were buried there, the major-ity killed by typhus. A priest who went on board the arriving ships left an account of desolation:

> Two to three hundred sick might be found in one ship, attacked
> by typhoid fever and dysentery, most lying on the refuse that
> had accumulated under them during the voyage; beside the sick
> and the dying were spread out the corpses that had not yet
> been buried at sea. On the decks a layer of muck had formed so
> thick that footprints were noticeable in it. To all this add the
> bad quality of the water, the scarcity of food and you will
> conceive but feebly of the sufferings that people endured during
> the long and hard trip. Sickness and death made terrible inroads
> on them. On some ships almost a third of the passengers died.
> The crew members themselves were often in such bad shape
> that they could hardly man the ship.[13]

A report from the government in Quebec noted that those 'sent out by their landlords were chiefly large helpless families, and in many instances widows and their children' and that they 'were generally very scantily supplied ... The condition of many of the emigrants, I need not inform you, was deplorable.'[14] A priest gave the last rites to the dying. 'I have not taken off my surplice today,' wrote Father Bernard McGauran, 'they are dying on the rocks and on the beach, where they have been cast by the sailors who simply could not carry them to the hospitals. We buried 28 yesterday, 28 today, and now (two hours past midnight) there are 30 dead whom we will bury tomorrow. I have not gone to bed for five nights.'[15]

The Listowel passengers on the ship *Clio* were told to expect a sum of money from the Listowel Union on arrival. Nothing was sent and they were left 'entirely without means'. The colonial government moved them on to where they might find work.

In the same period Scots Highlanders were also being shipped out by their landlords. A Colonel Gordon sent his entire tenantry – 1,400 people from the islands of Barra and Uist – to Canada. But to those Irish who were forced into migration, and to those left behind, what mattered was their particular circumstance. Even if they had been aware of the sufferings inflicted on the Scottish and English poor it would not have ameliorated their sense of loss, or the accumulation of grievance that the Famine caused. Nor would it have disposed them to think more highly of the government and the landlords. The wider context is everything until it is nothing at all.

My grandmother Hannah and her brother Mick and their friends were brought up with stories of the Famine as passed on by their grandparents. Moss Keane from Ballygrennan outside Listowel recalled his grandfather's memories: 'The families used to get sick and die. The fever was so bad in the end they used to bury the people by throwing their mud houses down on them; then they were buried. The English could relieve them if they wished ... Many a person was found dead on the roadside with grass on their mouths.'[16] As always the spirit world was invoked in memory of the dead. People told of meeting them along the road.

They were in the ground but walking still.

One story relates how a prosperous landowner came to gloat at a starving old woman. She was so ashamed of her plight that she boiled stones in the pot and pretended they were potatoes. 'But when the time came, she found flowery bursting spuds in the pot.'[17] Another tells of a great fiddler from the locality who was buried in a mass grave and whose music could still be heard on certain nights.

I found out that there had indeed been such a man, a famous dancing master who died of exposure in Listowel Workhouse.*

I met a woman walking past Ballydonoghue church one evening who turned out to be a family friend of the Purtills. Nora Mulvihill was born and reared here and came from a line that went back to the nineteenth century. Nora was middle-aged with grown-up children, and most evenings she walked the local roads to keep fit. Drive the roads of rural Ireland any evening and weather and you will see women like her, heads down and arms swinging. She knew the land and its stories.

We drove to Gale cemetery where the dead of the Famine from Ballydonoghue were buried. 'Do you know about the doctors that were here?' she asked. I assumed she meant the medics who visited the workhouse during the disease epidemics. But no, Nora had another story. I would leave without knowing how to interpret what I was told. Maybe it was just a story, like so many of the others told over the generations by the old people, a story with some truth maybe or none, or maybe entirely true. But it was a story that lasted. 'There was a house above in Coolard where there were doctors,' Nora told me. 'I don't know who they were or what they were doing there, whether it was the one family or whatever. But at any rate they lived there through the hunger. At the time there was a lot of dead bodies lying around the place. People were falling on the roads. So the doctors sent their servants out to bring in bodies to them and they had a room upstairs in the house where they did experiments. When they were finished with them a man would come with a cart and take the corpses to the graveyard here.' The man was known locally as 'Jack the Dead'.

---

* The writer Catherine E. Foley, an expert on Irish dancing tradition, unearthed the death certificate of 'Muirin' in her research on the effects of the Famine on the music and dance culture of the rural poor. She describes him as being fifty-five at the time of his death. 'Step dancing was seen as a skill to be mastered,' she writes, 'a skill that showed individuals had control and mastery over their minds and bodies.' See Catherine E. Foley, *Cultural Memory, Step Dancing, Representation and Performance: An Examination of Tearmann and The Great Famine*, in Traditiones (Llubljana 2015).

A local historian, John D. Pierse, found an account of a 'Dr Raymond [who] used to buy bodies for a couple of shillings from the local people ... he'd come at the diseased part of the body and examine it ... they used to do that wholesale.'[18] The county archives showed that Dr Samuel Raymond was living in this area in 1843, on the eve of the Famine, and was still serving as a magistrate in 1862. It may have been that he was carrying out sample autopsies on behalf of the government. But in the memory of the place he is a ghoulish exploiter to whom the bodies of the dead were mere biological material.

The stories offered the poor a promise that their suffering would be remembered, if not by individual names, then at least the manner of their death, a series of accusing fingers pointing out of the past at the English, the landlords, the big Catholic farmers who had food on their tables every night ... at the whole army of their 'betters'.

The Listowel Workhouse was the repository of the doomed. Those who ended up in this cramped, disease-ridden barracks had lost all hope of survival on the outside. A doctor treating smallpox sufferers found that 'three or four fever patients are placed in beds that are unusually small'. He witnessed two children die soon after arriving 'probably being caused by the cold to which such children were exposed to on account of being brought in so long a distance'.[19] The doctor found the body of a newborn baby in the latrines. A record for the 22 March 1851 documented the deaths of sixty-six people in the workhouse, of whom forty-nine were under the age of fifteen.

Out of this misery grew an ambitious scheme. A report at the height of the Famine quoted the Listowel Workhouse master as saying 'the education of the female children appears to be very much neglected ... very few could even read very imperfectly. Only one or two make any attempt at writing.'[20] The remedy to illiteracy and the prospect of death from starvation or disease was to pack thirty-seven girls off to Australia. They were among 4,000 Irish girls selected to find new lives in the colonies. Most ended up marrying miners or farmers in the outback. In the great departures that followed the Famine, some of my own Purtill relatives took ship for America, settling in Kentucky and New York, and bringing with them a memory of loss to be handed to the coming generations. Their children would learn that as many as half a million people were evicted from their homes during the Famine; that the government failed the starving when it might, through swifter action, have saved hundreds of thousands; they learnt that the poor were damned by the incompetence of ministers and by their rigid ideological beliefs, the conviction that the market was God; that the poor should learn a lesson about the 'moral hazard' of their own fecklessness; that too much charity would weaken the paupers' determination to help themselves – and that all of this was part of God's plan. It was not genocide in the manner I have known it. Genocide takes a plan for extermination with a defined course set at the outset. But it was a moral crime of staggering proportions.

The Famine changed the world around the Purtills. But they survived. How? Were they tougher than others? I will never know. There is only one narrative of the Famine when I am growing up. This is of English infamy, the clearances and evictions and the workhouse. But it is not the whole story. The story of survival and its psychological costs is not told: how some of the bigger Catholic farmers also evicted tenants, how the vanishing of the labouring class created the room for bigger farms, and how the Famine set in train the destruction of the landlord system. Hunger begets desperation, begets fierce survival strategies, and these beget shame which begets silence.

I find myself going back to Brendan Kennelly's 'My Dark Fathers'. I do so because I believe there are parts of history only the poets can convey, the deeper emotional scars that form themselves into ways of seeing things that inhabit later generations. Brendan told me he had written the poem after attending a wedding in north Kerry. A boy was called upon to sing. He had a beautiful voice but was painfully shy. So he turned to face the wall and in this way was able to perform. Kennelly was transfixed. He saw in that moment the shame of survival that had stalked his ancestors and mine.

Skeletoned in darkness, my dark fathers lay
Unknown, and could not understand
The giant grief that trampled night and day,
The awful absence moping through the land.
Upon the headland, the encroaching sea
Left sand that hardened after tides of Spring,
No dancing feet disturbed its symmetry
And those who loved good music ceased to sing.

Since every moment of the clock
Accumulates to form a final name,
Since I am come of Kerry clay and rock,
I celebrate the darkness and the shame
That could compel a man to turn his face
Against the wall, withdrawn from light so strong
And undeceiving, spancelled in a place
Of unapplauding hands and broken song.[21]

Writing twenty years after the Famine, the lawyer and essayist William O'Connor Morris visited Kerry and found that 'the memory of the Famine, which disturbed society rudely in this county ... has left considerable traces of bitterness'.[22] There is an entry in the diary of the landlord Sir John Benn Walsh which recalls a dinner held by the workhouse guardians. It is towards the end of the Famine. Benn Walsh is shocked to find that there are 'three Catholic priests and a party with them who refused to rise when the Queens health was drunk and a cry was raised of "long live the French Republic" ... this little toast shows all the disloyalty in the hearts of those people'.[23]

The bitterness curdled across the Atlantic into the Irish ghettos of America's east coast, where hatred of England grew into a revolutionary political force that would return to Ireland, reaching back to the eighteenth century for its defining theme: only total separation from England could cure the ills of Ireland. The lives of the Purtills were transformed in the decades after the Famine but not through armed struggle in a quest for national sovereignty. It was the campaign for land that showed the Purtills and their like what it meant to win.

II

The Landlord and his agent
wrote Davitt from his cell
For selfishness and cruelty
They have no parallel
And the one thing they're entitled to
these idle thoroughbreds
Is a one-way ticket out of here
third class to Holyhead.

Andy Irvine, *Forgotten Hero*, 1989

Tenant farmers like Edmund Purtill had few guaranteed rights before the land campaign of the late nineteenth century. Although the rate of evictions had declined considerably, they endured in the collective memory. Joseph O'Connor lived six miles outside Listowel on the lands of Lord Listowel and described his family's eviction at Christmas time in 1863:

> They came on small Christmas Day [6 January, the Feast of the Epiphany] in January 1863, bailiffs, peelers an' soldiers, an' had us out on the cold bog before dawn. They burned down the houses for fear we'd go back into them when their backs were turned and took my father and the other grown up men to the Workhouse in Listowel with them. They did that 'out of charity' they said because Lady Listowel wouldn't sleep the night, if the poor creatures were left homeless on the mountain. They left me and my brother Patsy to look after ourselves. We slept out with the hares, a couple o' nights, eatin' swedes that had ice in the heart o' them an' then we parted. He went east an' I went

west towards Tralee. I must ha' been a sight, after walkin'
twenty miles on my bare feet an' an empty belly.[24]

Cast into destitution by the landlord, Joseph turned to the only
means of lawful survival open to him and joined up with the very
Crown forces that had turned out his family. In his early teens,
O'Connor became a soldier with Her Majesty's 10th Regiment of
Foot. The British Army saved him from starvation.

But these were the last years of the old landlordism. Sixteen years
after the O'Connors were driven onto the roads of north Kerry, the
rest of rural Ireland was gripped by an agrarian revolution that, for
the most part, eschewed the gun in favour of civil defiance. By the
time the Land League was formed in 1879 the whole edifice was
ready to topple. The Famine had wiped out the rents on which many
landlords depended. Rates became impossible to pay. Bankruptcy
stalked the landed gentry. 'An Irish estate is like a sponge,' wrote one
lord, 'and an Irish landlord is never as rich as when he is rid of his
property.'[25] Gladstone had already begun the process of strengthen-
ing tenants' rights in 1870. Reform created its own momentum. The
Land League would take care of the rest.

Charles Stewart Parnell and Michael Davitt were second only to
Michael Collins in my father's pantheon of greats. It was Parnell,
Eamonn said, who gave people back their dignity. Parnell and Davitt
were very different men, in temperament and background. Parnell
was a Protestant landowner, liberal and nationalist, a brilliant political tactician and leader of the Irish Party at Westminster. His fellow
MPs knew him as a man of 'iron resolution ... impenetrable reserve
[with] ... a volcanic energy and also a ruthless determination'.[26]
Michael Davitt was the child of an evicted family from County
Mayo, brought up in the north of England where he went into the
mills as a child labourer, losing his arm at the age of eleven in an
industrial accident. Davitt began his political life in the Fenians and
in 1870 was sentenced to fifteen years' hard labour for treason. He
was twenty-four years old at the time and endured a harsh regime
as a political prisoner. Yet Davitt emerged from jail convinced that

violence would never achieve a complete revolution. In this he fore-shadowed by a century the experience of the IRA prisoners in the Maze prison. Davitt became an internationalist in prison, seeing the Irish farm labourer as part of the worldwide struggle of the oppressed. Passionate, approachable, he provided the organisational genius of the Land League.

My father occasionally spoke of him, but always the doomed glamour of Parnell, Pearse and Collins shut out the light. Yet Michael Davitt did more than anybody to change the lives of my forebears. I only came to appreciate him in later life – this internationalist and socialist and campaigning foreign correspondent, who made the journey from revolutionary violence to a true people's politics.

In later life, as a journalist, he revealed the horror of the anti-Semitic pogrom at Kishinev in the tsarist empire in 1903. He arrived in Kishinev 'a striking figure with a black beard, armless sleeve, and trilby hat', and set about interviewing the survivors and witnesses.[27] His journalism seethed with righteous indignation but was always supported by a meticulous attention to the facts. Davitt came across a house where a young girl had been raped and murdered: 'The entire place littered with fragments of the furniture, glass, feathers, a scene of the most complete wreckage possible. It was in the inner room (in carpenters shed) where … the young girl of 12 was outraged and literally torn asunder … the shrieks of the girl were heard by the terrified crowd in the shed for a short while and then all was silent.'[28] His reporting created an international outcry.

He also went to South Africa as a correspondent during the Boer War, where he felt conflicting emotions as he encountered British prisoners of war: '[I felt] a personal sympathy towards them as prisoners; a political feeling that the enemy of Ireland and of nationality was humiliated before me and that I stood in one of the few places in the world in which the power of England was weak, helpless and despised.'[29]

In Ireland, Davitt had started the Land League campaign with the alluring slogan: 'The land of Ireland for the people of Ireland'. Huge meetings were held across the country during the late nineteenth century in support of what became known as 'the Three Fs': Fixity of Tenure, Fair Rent, and Free Sale. Predictably the agitation brought a return of violent customs in the north Kerry countryside. The targets were not only the old Protestant landlord class. Rural Ireland now had a large body of Catholic bigger, or 'strong', farmers, who became targets of the League.

At the height of the land agitation, in the crucial years 1879–85, the colonial government was forced to install a permanent military garrison in Listowel. A bad landlord, a greedy big farmer, might expect retribution in the form of boycott, or a visit from 'Captain Moonlight' or the Moonlighters – agrarian raiders who hocked cattle and burned hay barns. Catholics who rented land from others who were evicted or who paid rent in defiance of a boycott were frequent targets. The French writer Paschal Grousset met a man in north Kerry in 1887 whose ears had been mutilated and whose cattle had had their tails docked. The man's crime was to have accepted work on a boycotted farm. 'Let a farmer, small or great, decline to enter the organisation,' wrote Grousset:

> or check it by paying rent to the landlord without the reduction agreed to by the tenantry ... or commit any other serious offence against the law of the land war, he is boycotted. That is to say he will no longer be able to sell his goods, to buy the necessities of life; to have his horses shod, corn milled, or even exchange a word with a living soul within a radius of fifteen to twenty miles of his house. His servants are tampered with and induced to leave him, his tradespeople shut their doors in his face, his neighbours compelled to cut him ... people come and play football in his oat fields, his potatoes are rooted out: his fish or cattle poisoned; his game destroyed.'[30]

And if he refused to accede to the threats? Grousett put it starkly: 'Then his business is settled. Someday or other, he will receive a bullet in his arm, if not in his head.'[31]

Another man, who had shaken the hand of a hated landlord, was forced to wear a black glove on that hand. A seventy-two-year-old writ-server had his left ear sliced off. The land agent S. M. Hussey was forced out of the area after his home was destroyed by dynamite in 1884. There were sixteen people in the house at the time. Miraculously no one was hurt. 'To show how matters stood,' he wrote, 'one of my daughters reminds me that I gave her a very neat revolver as a present, and whenever she came back from school she always slept with it under her pillow.'[32] Hussey aroused particular loathing because of a rent rise intended to pay for a £100,000 mansion for one of his landlord clients, and the burning down of several evicted tenants' houses. The land agent for Lord Listowel, Paul Sweetnam, evicted the O'Connell family at Finuge for non-payment of rent, as a contemporary report described.* 'When Mr O'Connell came on the scene the eviction was almost completed ... He had no place to shelter himself or his family. He came into town and asked the agent for a night's lodging in the home from which he was evicted. The agent refused.'[33]

The bigger Catholic farmers watched the violence with alarm. The attackers were nearly always the 'men of no property', the rural underclass made up of the sons of small farmers or farm labourers. The land campaigners promised them a stake in the soil they worked. Land would be redistributed. By the beginning of 1880 worsening agricultural prices and poor weather reduced many of the peasantry in the area to destitution. The horror of famine loomed once more. A letter from the organisers of hunger relief in Ballybunion, about five miles from the Purtills, described how the 'surging crowds of deserving and naked poor who throng the streets every day seeking

---

* Sweetnam came from a Protestant farming background in west Cork. He was an unpopular figure with many in the locality because of his work instigating prosecutions for non-payment of rent for Lord Listowel, and newspapers recorded instances where men who tried to intimidate him ended up in court. In 1899, long after the Land War ended, he appeared in court seeking to evict a Mary Brennan from a caretaker's house on Lord Listowel's lands. He would also appear dramatically in the story of District Inspector Tobias O'Sullivan.

relief show unmistakably that dire distress prevails in the locality and that unless immediate relief be given and held on for some time there can be no alternative but the blackest Famine ... the state of our poor is hourly verging on absolute destitution and the condition of the poor children attending our schools deplorable'.[34]

Once more a network of secret groups sprang up across the countryside to mete out the people's justice. Informers were despised. A parallel system of justice with its own courts was set up to adjudicate on land disputes. Ominously, in parts of north Kerry the Royal Irish Constabulary were increasingly identified as the landlord's enforcers. 'They have thrown the whole thing on the police,' a report noted, 'who for the past six months have acted more in the capacity of herds[men] than policemen and the result is the men are becoming completely worn out, disgusted in their duty and demoralised'.[35]

The hour of the night raiders was back.

The Moonlighters roamed the country in disguise. They raided to exact retribution and to arm themselves with seized guns. The Catholic farmer John Curtin, a senior local figure in the Land League, was murdered in 1885 in south Kerry. One of the attackers was shot during the raid and Curtin's daughters gave evidence that led to the conviction of some of the Moonlighters. As a consequence, the family was damned. They were booed and jeered when they drove on the local roads. All their servants left. An old man who had herded their cattle for thirty years was too afraid to remain. When they went to mass 'a derisive cheer was raised by six or eight shameless girls ... believing that the police won't interfere with them'.[36] The parish priest 'never uttered a word in condemnation'. They were again assailed outside the church. The priest, Father Patrick O'Connor, explained that on a previous raid Curtin had surrendered a gun and 'that if he had given up a gun they would not have hurt a hair on his head'.[37] The following week the daughters were accompanied by twenty-five policemen and a representative of the Land League. But the presence of the man from the League made no difference. Stones were thrown. When he tried to address the crowd he was shouted down and afterwards said he owed his life to the police. A group of women ripped out the Curtin family pew and destroyed it in the church grounds. Curtin's widow could neither sell nor leave. The sale was boycotted. Any prospective buyer was threatened with death. 'I cannot live here in peace but they won't let me go,' she wrote. But the mother of one of the convicted men showed no compassion. 'As long as I am alive and my children and their children live, we will try to root the Curtins out of the land.'[38] The words have an obliterative violence, as if she were speaking of the destruction of weeds. The Nationalist MP John O'Connor sounded a note of hopelessness when he remarked that if the Curtin family was to be protected from the annoyances, to which he regretted they had been subjected, 'it would have to be by other means than public denunciations of outrages'.[39] Not for the last time in Irish history, political condemnations would mean nothing. After eighteen months of hostility the Curtins sold their farm for half of its value and left the area. Nobody, not the police, not the gentry, not the government, could change the minds of their neighbours.

Near to Ballydonoghue, sixty-year-old John Foran was murdered in 1888 for renting the farm of an evicted man. The teenage Bertha Creagh, whose father acted as solicitor for several landlords, saw his killers planning their attack as she went for a walk. 'I remarked on their evident seriousness to my brother,' she wrote. Foran was a successful farmer and had gone to Tralee to hire extra help. When on his way home with his labourers and fourteen-year-old son, an assassin appeared out of the woods at a bend in the road and 'fired from a six-chambered revolver, and lodged bullets in succession in Fohran's [sic] body ... the terrified boy, having waited to lay his dying father on the grass at the roadside, drove on to Listowel'.[40] The murdered man was a survivor of the Famine and a contemporary account describes him as 'being brave even to rashness – that the people of his district had a wholesome dread of himself and his shillelagh'.[41] He had also endured four years of harassment – with police protection that had only recently been withdrawn at the time of the murder.

The investigation followed a familiar pattern. There were arrests and court hearings but nobody was convicted. The witnesses kept to the law of silence. In the time of my grandparents, the IRA would draw on those old traditions of silence and communal solidarity.

The Land League was denounced and Parnell and Davitt accused of fomenting violence. The League leaders knew how rural Ireland worked. Violence was not a surprise to them. Davitt condemned the murders but stressed the responsibility of history. 'The condition and treatment of the poorer tenantry of Ireland have not been, and could not be, humanly speaking, free from the crime which injustice begets everywhere,' he declared. 'For that violence which has taken the form of retaliatory chastisement for acknowledged merciless wrong, I make no apology on the part of the victims of Irish land-lordism. For me to do so would be to indict Nature for having implanted within us the instinct of self-defence.'[42]

With tough anti-coercion laws, and a gradual resolution of the land issues, violence abated. The Land War wound down. Parnell led a new campaign for Home Rule before he was destroyed by scandal. Davitt went off to become a journalist and then took a seat in the House of Commons. He dreamed of nationalising the land of Ireland but misunderstood entirely the character of rural Ireland. Only the land a man held for himself offered any security. By 1914, seventy-five per cent of Irish tenants were in a position to buy the land which they rented. They were assisted by British government loans. Labourers were helped by the building of cottages, each on an acre of land. The Purtills bought their own land. In time the sons of the family would move out and buy their own farms. When my cousin Vincent Purtill sold his 400-acre farm and retired he felt agitated. Without the land who was he and where was he? Eventually the stress got the best of him. He went and bought a small farm of twenty-four acres. 'I need only walk out the door and I am walking on my land. I do it every day,' he said.

By the early years of the twentieth century, Listowel seemed at peace. Violence was present but contained. It flared occasionally and just as quickly fell away. Tenant farmers used the law to challenge landlords. One case from the Ballydonoghue area in March 1895 shows how dramatically rural life had changed. George Sandes, a descendant of Cromwellian planters, was one of the most powerful landowners in the area. The town of Newtownsandes, about five miles from the Purtills, was named after his family. During the Land War, Sandes was such an unpopular figure that locals attempted to rename the town after one of the Land League leaders. He was a resident magistrate during those years

But in the new rural world forged by Parnell and Davitt, Sandes was no longer free to evict at will. When a farmer went to court to challenge his eviction Sandes lost and was ordered to pay damages.

Constitutional politics were again on the march and Home Rule was promised. My great-grandfather, Edmund Purtill, was listed as donating 1 shilling and sixpence to the cause of the Irish Party at Westminster. Enclosing a cheque for £32 from the parish, the Very Reverend John Molyneaux assured the party treasurer in London that there was not 'in any parish in the South of Ireland a people more willing and anxious to generously support any movement which has for its object the interests of religion, and the happiness and prosperity of the people'.[43] It may have been that Edmund Purtill harboured more radical sympathies and was donating money out of a desire to please the parish priest. But it is more likely that he believed Home Rule within the British Empire was the surest guarantee of stability. The Purtills were still poor but they had a stake in the land. At that point in history, directly on the turn of the century, the majority of Irish Catholics took the same view. The area returned Home Rule MPs at successive elections. The Catholic hierarchy and most of the priests preached cooperation with the government. Nothing in the immediate circumstances of my grandmother's childhood would have made her or her brothers likely converts to revolution. But there was a desire for change brewing in Ballydonoghue and across Ireland and Europe. The times were about to be disturbed by restless nationalisms that would usher in the end of the age of empire, from the Danube to the River Feale, and make rebels of my forebears.

4

Revolution

Soldiers are we whose lives are pledged to Ireland ...

Peadar Kearney, *The Soldier's Song*, 1907

I

To approach a man near his home where his wife and young children are waiting for him, to fire enough bullets into his head and chest to make sure he is dead, and to do this when you have never killed before, and to live with this for fifty years and more and never speak of it: how does a man, a man like you, live with this? Others in Ireland will tell war stories. They will boast of their exploits. Not you. There will be annual parades to attend. You will become part of the national myth of origin that cries out for heroic deeds. But you are remembered as a modest, decent man.

Con Brosnan: hero of the good clean fight against the evil of the Black and Tans. But you know how it really was. It is all there in memory, whenever war comes back: his face down in the space between the cart and the footpath, the blood thickening in the gutter, the children crying. You were brave in the Revolution and a man of peace when it was needed after the Civil War. You were well loved by your own people. For you the act of killing was no lightly taken enterprise. It stays locked inside you for nearly thirty years until the men from the Bureau of Military History came calling.* What you told them was true: you were following orders that came all the way from headquarters in Dublin. But what was the story you told yourself down the years? You were good friends with my uncle Mick Purtill and his sister Hannah. You lived in a neighbouring village, shared the hardship of the Tan war with them, fought on the same side in the Civil War, and after that war you once threatened to shoot a man who had cursed the name of Mick Purtill. 'The Purtills and Brosnans were fierce close' was how your son put it.[1]

A neighbour of yours, the poet Gabriel Fitzmaurice, told me that every day you went to church to pray for the souls of the men you killed. The District Inspector will not be the only killing in which you play a part. It reminded me of something a friend of mine, a Special Forces soldier, a man who killed at close quarters, told me once. He would never let his son join the army, he said. 'I would never want him to see the things I keep locked up in my head.'

Cornelius – 'Con' – Brosnan and Mick Purtill were members of the Irish Volunteers. My grandmother would join the women's wing, Cumann na mBan, which had been founded in 1914. I believe Hannah was nineteen when she joined; Con Brosnan was the same age when he joined up in 1917.

Like the Purtills, Con had grown up on a scrap of land, the son of a small farmer who also ran a small public house in Newtownsandes, now called Moyvane – the 'small, sleepy straggle of a village about seven miles from Listowel in north Kerry, and off the main road'.[2]

---

* Between 1947 and 1957 the Irish state collected the testimony of 1,733 witnesses and participants to the revolutionary period. The aim was to create an oral history of the period leading from the foundation of the Irish Volunteers in 1913 to the signing of the Truce in 1921. The interviews were carried out by army officers and civil servants working for the Bureau of Military History established by the Department of Defence. The statements were locked away until the last of the witnesses passed away in 2003. The material has helped to transform how Irish people view the period.

Con Brosnan, revolutionary and footballing legend

To get there from Ballydonoghue I drove the long, straight small roads across the plain. I saw the smallness of the killing zone and how the flat terrain with its sparse woodland offered no decisive advantage to guerrillas. I imagine how I would read this land as a war correspondent; the habit is ingrained in me now, a perverse filter through which topography is measured for the cover it provides and the menace it conceals.

There are no steep mountains, plunging valleys; there are no acres of trees or dense scrubland that come up to the roadside for mile after mile. I think of the long drives I have made through ambush zones around the world, my mouth dry and stomach knotted knowing the killers could be as close as the high grass brushing the side of the car. Once in Rwanda I saw them, armed with AK 47s, standing in the middle of the road, surprised by us as we came around the corner of a jungle track. There was a split second when they might have turned on us but they ran into the bush, the element of surprise lost. We turned around and went back, survivors by the grace of chance. So often in armed convoys in guerrilla territory I have strained to see who might be hiding in the passing treelines, or to hear the first shot that would signal an ambush; I have spent fruitless hours calculating whether it was safest to travel in the front, middle or end of a convoy. With enough ambushers and a mine in the road the chances of escape are pretty small, as good friends of mine have found out in Africa, the Balkans and Iraq. Here in north Kerry there was a lot of hiding in plain sight for the men of the IRA. It was in the homes of the people that they found their hiding places, and in barns and dugouts meticulously camouflaged under turf and ricks of hay.

The Brosnan family pub sits in the middle of the town, on a corner beside the road that runs down the gradually levelling land towards Listowel. Con's son Gerry still lives here and his grandson is a farmer nearby. The flags of the Kerry football team and the Irish Republic hang from stands on the pub's gable wall. The colonial name of Newtownsandes has been erased. Today the village is called Moyvane – from the Irish for the 'middle plain'. In his deposition to the military historians, Con Brosnan still referred to it as Newtownsandes. He was born there in 1900 and went to the local national school and then to secondary in Listowel. His schooling ended when he was sixteen, the summer after the Easter Rising.

There was no one reason why Hannah and Mick and Con Brosnan took up arms against the British Empire. Youth was part of it, as was the extraordinary moment in world history when they came of age. They lived in one of those periods when history had slipped its bonds. The impossible became imaginable and then possible and they saw a chance of belonging to something larger than themselves. Events propelled them forward until they became agents of change themselves. It was part politics of the moment and in part the resurrection of long-buried sentiment ignited by the Easter Rising and the events that followed. By 1913 a branch of the Irish Volunteers had been set up in Listowel. The Volunteer movement was a broad coalition that included militant separatists as well as constitutional nationalists devoted to Home Rule. A nationalist private army on such a scale might never have existed but for a dramatic escalation in tensions in Ulster.

By 1910 the dream for which my great-grandfather Edmund Purtill had contributed his shillings seemed to be coming to fruition. The Irish Party held the balance of power in Westminster and Home Rule was the price of their support for the government.* The possibility of nationalist advancement provoked a furious reaction from northern unionists whose response was to threaten civil war. They were encouraged by the leader of the Conservative Party, Andrew Bonar Law. His words are worth remembering, coming as they did from the leader of Her Majesty's Most Loyal Opposition. In July 1912 he told a rally at Blenheim Palace in Oxfordshire that he could 'imagine no length of resistance to which Ulster can go in which I should not be prepared to support them'. This was no rush of blood to the head. A year later, on 12 July, the anniversary of the Battle of the Boyne, Bonar Law again threatened treason when he told Ulster Protestants: 'Whatever steps you may feel compelled to take, whether they are constitutional, or whether in the long run they are unconstitutional, you have the whole Unionist Party, under my leadership, behind you.'³ The Tory leader knew he was adding fuel to the growing fire. Anti-Home Rule agitation had a bloody history. When the first Home Rule bill was introduced in 1886 around fifty people were killed in Belfast, hundreds injured and scores of homes burned. In addition, Bonar Law and the government were well aware that the Ulster Volunteer Force, formed in 1912, were arming and drilling to fight Home Rule.

I doubt that my relatives in Ballydonoghue thought much about the north before then. It was far away on a long train journey or by miles of bad roads. But the rise of the Ulster Volunteers electrified

---

* Two previous Home Rule bills, in 1886 and 1893, had been defeated by Unionists and their allies, first in the House of Commons and then the House of Lords. The removal of the Lords veto power enabled Prime Minister Herbert Asquith to present a third Home Rule Bill in April 1912. This could now only be delayed by the Lords for up to two years, making the parliamentary passage of Home Rule appear inevitable.

separatists in the south. They watched the British state do nothing to stop the import of weapons by the UVF. If the Ulster Protestants could have a militia to fight Home Rule the Irish nationalists should have an equal right to defend it. The formation of the Irish Volunteers in late 1913 created a second private army on the island. That December, in Listowel, the first meeting of the Irish Volunteers heard Mr J. J. McKenna, a local merchant, urge the locals to follow the example set by the Unionist leader, Edward Carson: 'He has been going around so far preaching what some called sedition,' said McKenna. 'At all events he had been preaching the rights of the people of the North to defend what he called their rights, but whether they were rights or whether they were wrongs, he was urging on them to defend them in the way that God intended.'[4] Another speaker said the Irish Volunteers wanted 'no informers … no cads or cadgers [but] true, manly men'.[5] Afterwards men and boys queued to place their right hand on the barrel of a gun and swear allegiance.

From the outset the Irish Volunteers meant different things to different factions. The Home Rulers led by Parnell's successor John Redmond wanted a force ready to defend the new devolved government when it came into being and hoped the drilling and marching would take some of the steam out of more militant nationalists. But the militants were ahead of him and gradually infiltrated the Irish Volunteers. The Irish Republican Brotherhood – the IRB – sought complete independence rather than Home Rule within the empire.* Separatist ideas in culture and sport had been growing since the end of the previous century.

---

* The IRB was the official name of the Fenians who had maintained their secret structures since the failure of the rebellions of the nineteenth century. It drew considerable organisational and financial support from the Irish diaspora in America. Its members dominated the leadership of the Easter rebels and the IRA during the War of Independence. Its tradition of secrecy created divisions in the Republican movement during the war against the British administration in Ireland. The Civil War of 1922–3 exposed the depth of internal resentments and the organisation disappeared from the political scene.

In the rural areas like north Kerry the appeal to 'de-Anglicise Ireland' provoked a strong response. Music, dancing and language lessons sponsored by the Gaelic League became popular.* My grandfather Bill Keane was a member of the Gaelic League in Listowel and passed on a love of the Irish language to his children. But he was by nature a moderate who disdained cultural exceptionalism. He taught students who went on to join the British Army and those who joined the IRA and he could understand the motivations of both. I believe it was this which kept him from being involved with the more militarily 'advanced' nationalists who were organising in and around Listowel. Those with memories of the Fenian rebellion of 1867 held discussion groups with younger men and women. The Gaelic League sponsored essay competitions in Irish, with the Listowel branch asking for entries on subjects such as 'Tillage over Grazing', an innocent enough-looking topic until you remember the bitterness of the small tenant farmers who saw their plots taken over by the big cattlemen in the decades after the Famine. Violence on the land still flared sporadically. In 1909, the *Kerry Sentinel* reported a 'shooting affair of an extraordinary nature' near Ballydonoghue, after a group of around twenty turf cutters were fired on by armed and masked men.[6] The workers were 'scattered . . . in all directions, some of them in their wild stampede falling into bog holes'.[7]

The general sense of unease would have affected young men like Mick Purtill and Con Brosnan. For both, sport was a likely route into a more militant nationalism. They were enthusiastic Gaelic footballers in a county where a good player was the hero of his locality. The Gaelic Athletic Association banned anyone who served

---

* The Gaelic League was founded in 1893 with the dedicated aim of promoting Irish as a spoken language and encouraging the growth of a national literature in the vernacular. The movement was open to all faiths and, in theory, was meant to be non-political. But from the outset it was home to a significant number of militant nationalists. The majority of the signatories of the 1916 Proclamation were members of the league.

the Crown from joining and was heavily infiltrated by separatists.*
At least two prominent Listowel GAA figures were also leading
members of the local Irish Volunteers. A Listowel delegate to the
GAA County Board urged that rifle clubs should be affiliated to the
organisation. He appears to have been listened to. 'Kerry, true to its
traditions, has made a good start,' an article in the *National Volunteer*
declared.[8] The separatists reached into Listowel's schools for
recruits. At St Michael's College, where Con Brosnan went to school,
at least four boys were sworn into the ranks of the Irish Republican
Brotherhood.

By the spring of 1914 the crisis around Home Rule was threatening to escalate into armed conflict. In March, in response to
reports that the military would be used to suppress a Unionist
rebellion, officers at the Curragh camp outside Dublin declared
they would refuse to enforce Home Rule, a stance supported by
senior generals. The following month the UVF imported more than
20,000 rifles and ammunition without any government action to
stop them and all, according to the *Belfast Telegraph*, 'accomplished
with celerity, yet without fuss or splutter, because it was done in
pursuance of a well-formed plan, executed as perfectly as it had
been preconceived'.[9] The membership of the Listowel Volunteers
rose dramatically in the aftermath. From a few dozen men and boys
at the outset, the organisation now numbered around two hundred.

At the end of July 1914 nationalists landed weapons at Howth
outside Dublin. British troops who had been called out to seize the
weapons fired on a hostile crowd in Dublin, killing four people. The
island was slipping towards civil war.

Across Europe the old bonds that guaranteed peace between
empires were fraying, as alliances that had once maintained a balance
of power confronted each other. Young men were rallying to the

---

* The Gaelic Athletic Association is the most powerful cultural and sporting
organisation in Ireland. It was founded in 1882 to promote the games of football,
hurling, camogie and handball. The GAA has over 500,000 members. It banned soldiers
and policemen from membership until 2001.

banner of national self-determination from Bohemia to Tralee Bay. From vastly different national standpoints writers such as Rupert Brooke and Patrick Pearse employed a language of redemptive blood sacrifice. In Ireland the exhumed animosities of generations – territorial, sectarian, social, cultural, economic – simmered until all was placed in abeyance by the opening shots of cataclysm in Sarajevo on 28 June 1914. Imperial armies mobilised. Home Rule was postponed and the UVF marched off to fight in Flanders.

The immediate threat of civil war between nationalist and loyalist armies abated. In north Kerry, as in the rest of the country, the war split the Irish Volunteers. Men from Listowel marched off to the front in the uniform of the Royal Munster Fusiliers, urged on by John Redmond, who declared that the 'interests of Ireland – of the whole of Ireland – are at stake in this war ... undertaken in the defence of the highest principles of religion and morality'.[10] As Redmond framed it, the best means to secure Home Rule was to convince the Unionists that southern Catholics could be as loyal as they were. Militant nationalists were immediately scornful. Redmond reckoned on a swift Allied victory, not the butchery that, by 1916, had brought so much anguish to the homes of those who marched off to war at his urging. It would be his undoing and the death knell of the constitutional project.

Far more men from around Listowel and Ballydonoghue died fighting in Belgium, France, Gallipoli, Egypt, Jutland and Salonika than would die in the war against Britain that was to come. Out of the 147 north Kerry men killed in action in the Great War, six were neighbours of the Purtills in Ballydonoghue and sixty-three hailed from Listowel, including Edward Stack, who lived near the Keanes on Church Street and who died two months into the war, and the youngest of the north Kerry dead, Peter Flavin, just sixteen when he was killed in Belgium. The Revolution would sweep them all from public memory. The Listowel writer Cyril Kelly, whose grand-father was an RIC man based in the town, recalled family memories of the tensions of the period when Volunteers and Britannia competed for the loyalties of young men:

The time, 1914, when North Kerry was beginning to ferment, when unrest was growing restless, when indigenous forces of sedition were becoming insidious, like fairy thorn; resinous roots snaking into the surrounding hinterland, places with unpronounceable names, Currachatoosane, Knockanasaig, Gortagleanna, places where – according to intelligence reports – men were being inducted into the Irish Republican Brotherhood.

Hadn't Ernest Blythe, a full time organiser of the Volunteers, brazenly visited Listowel, exhorting the local company to resist the Redmonites, resist the RIC, those shoneens who threatened that old-age pensions would be withdrawn from relatives of anyone parlaying with civil disobedience?[11]

II

For Ireland, for Ireland, for Ireland all,
Our ranks we band in might:
From her four seas we at Ireland's call
In Ireland's cause unite,
And march to the hosting of Gael and Gall,
To claim our Freedom's right.

Thomas MacDonagh, 'Marching Song of the Irish Volunteers', 1913

An IRA man from close to where my grandmother lived recalled that when 'John Redmond called on the Volunteers to defend the shores of Ireland there was a split in the company which soon after ceased to exist'.[12] Militant nationalists had no interest in defending the shores of Ireland by fighting in France. But for two years nothing much happened on the home front. Patrick Pearse and his comrades were a minority within a minority of advanced nationalists, but were already planning an insurrection. Early in 1916, the Irish Republican Brotherhood began to secretly prepare, though the plans for armed action were kept secret from many senior figures in the Volunteers. A friend of Mick Purtill, who later fought alongside him in the IRA, recalled how the IRB came to his village 'seeking men who would go into action at short notice in the event of a rebellion'.[13] Drilling began again. But in the run-up to the Easter Rising no instructions came for the Ballylongford company to take part. Republican strategists kept their plans a closely guarded secret, which led to some of the subsequent chaos. To facilitate a national insurrection, a German ship would land arms in Tralee Bay. A train would disperse rifles to Volunteer units from Kerry through Limerick, Clare and to Galway. In Listowel, the rebels planned to seize the town and cut all communications. But the plans went wrong. The German arms ship was seized by the Royal Navy and scuttled. Sir Roger Casement landed at Banna Strand near Tralee, but was captured almost immediately. Irish Volunteers leaders who had been excluded from the rebel plan had recently learned of it and were now committed to stopping what they considered a suicidal folly. They issued a countermanding order to units across the country. In Munster a north Kerry man drove desperately across the counties to try and stop mobilisation. Michael O'Rahilly from Ballylongford was a key figure in the national organisation of the Volunteers but he was not a member of the IRB or the faction that had planned the rebellion. His mission to call off the rebellion was a failure but he felt honour bound to join the rebels in the GPO in Dublin, declaring the whole enterprise as 'madness but ... glorious madness'.* 'The O'Rahilly', as he was called, was one of three local men killed fighting at the GPO in Dublin in 1916.

In Dublin the Rising lasted for six days and cost the lives of 485 people, the majority of them civilians, before British shelling and overwhelming numbers forced the surrender of the rebels. The

---

* Michael O'Rahilly was a son of the Irish middle class educated at the Jesuits' Clongowes Wood College and then in New York where he studied to become a doctor. He was drawn to the idea of national rebirth implicit in the Cultural Revival. He gave himself the title 'The O'Rahilly' in emulation of those used by ancient Gaelic chieftains.

capture of the arms ship meant there would be no new weapons for the Volunteers in Kerry or neighbouring counties. In Listowel the mobilised Volunteers were sent home. The Irish Volunteers were damned from the pulpits and told to go home to their families. The Bishop of Kerry warned of the dangers of civil war. Nineteen Kerry prisoners were sent to England. Nobody rioted in response to this. But then the British made their first great mistake. Fifteen leaders of the Easter Rising were executed. The echo of the firing squads was heard across north Kerry. On 11 May 1916, with executions still under way in Dublin, the prominent Home Rule MP, John Dillon, rose to his feet to excoriate the government of Herbert Asquith. It is one of the most prescient and powerful speeches in Irish history:'We are held up to odium as traitors by those men who made this rebellion, and our lives have been in danger a hundred times during the last thirty years because we have endeavoured to reconcile the two things, and now you are washing out our whole life work in a sea of blood.'[14]

The following day the British executed the leader of the socialist Irish Citizen Army, James Connolly, who was so badly wounded he faced his firing squad strapped into a chair, and Seán Mac Diarmada, who had long argued for a blood sacrifice to revive Irish separatism.

A year after the Rising came a significant indication of the political upheaval that had been unleashed. Across the Shannon in County Clare, Éamon de Valera of Sinn Féin won a landslide victory in a by-election caused by the death in Flanders of Captain Willie Redmond MP, the brother of John Redmond, leader of the nationalist MPs at Westminster. De Valera, who had campaigned on the slogans 'A Vote for Ireland a Nation, a Vote Against Conscription, a Vote Against Partition, a Vote for Ireland's Language', and 'for Ireland's Ideals and Civilization', had only escaped execution after the Rising because his court-martial came at a time of growing public and international criticism. The constitutionalists had held the seat for over thirty years. To celebrate de Valera's victory, Republicans marched in Ballybunion, a few miles from the Purtills' homestead. A stone thrown through the RIC barracks window there was met with a volley of fire. More stones were thrown and the ensuing police volleys killed a local member of the Volunteers. Sinn Féin sent a prominent lawyer from Dublin to investigate but the policeman involved in the fatal shooting escaped justice. 'This Ballybunion episode was the first manifestation of real savagery by the police,' concluded Charles Wyse-Power, 'and there is no doubt that it was the East Clare election that brought this out in them.'[15]

Hannah and Mick Purtill felt their world changing. In those days, said my father, Hannah 'couldn't be bested. When her mind was set it was set.' She may have been influenced by her childhood neighbour May Ahern who became an active Republican in 1917 and first drew attention to herself by stealing the bicycles of two RIC men attending a Gaelic football match in Ballydonoghue. In the beginning, before the first fighting between Republicans and the state, the teenagers organised 'dances, raffles and plays for funds'.[16] But the founders of Cumann na mBan believed women were meant for tougher work than making tea and sandwiches for the men. In her memoir of the period, the veteran activist Mary Colum wrote how the women 'would collect money or arms, we would learn ambulance work, learn how to make haversacks and bandoliers ... we would practise the use of the rifle, we would make speeches, we would do everything that came in our way – for we are not the auxiliaries or the handmaidens or the camp followers of the Volunteers – we are their allies.'[17]

The Revolution challenged authority in many forms. The Catholic Church would find that while Volunteers adhered to its rites, they could easily ignore condemnations and later, during the Civil War, the threat of excommunication. For parents who had lived a lifetime in the United Kingdom, the period from 1912 onwards was a challenge to certainty and authority. It has been the same in every revolution and civil conflict I have ever reported. It is not truth but 'parental control' that is the first casualty of war. According to the great memoirist of the period, Ernie O'Malley, young women like my grandmother had a chance to revolutionise their place in society.

'The girls too developed and broke away from strict parental discipline,' he wrote. 'This to my mind was the greatest innovation.'[18]

By the time the Volunteers were ready to launch a guerrilla war, Hannah was working for the prosperous Listowel draper Ned Moran and already moving away from the farm life of her parents and grandparents. Con Brosnan joined the Irish Volunteers in 1917. He recalled that there were only about twenty men in the Volunteer company in Newtownsandes at the start. 'We had no arms at that time but we drilled and paraded all that year.'[19] Relations with the police deteriorated drastically across that year. In October 1917 hundreds rioted in Listowel following a confrontation with the police during the annual Listowel horse races. There had been Volunteer drilling in Ballybunion on the previous day, and the arrest of an army deserter in Listowel added to the atmosphere of tension. Prominent Sinn Féiners faced off with the police on street corners. It began with the exchange of curses and descended into a furious assault at William Street. Surrounded, the RIC faced a continuous volley of stones. District Inspector M. J. Molloy described how his men became trapped in the centre of town. 'The police were hit – scarcely any men escaped and most men were struck several times,' he said. 'Constable Delaney was wounded on the forehead by a stone and was knocked down and kicked by the mob ... our only chance of escaping defeat and probably being murdered was to charge into the Lower William Street mob and take possession of the small square.'[20]

A second detachment of RIC was surrounded at the railway station and barricaded themselves into the waiting room there. Those in William Street fired repeated volleys above the heads of the rioters but they would not disperse. Several were wounded. The parish priest intervened along with some local merchants and tried to persuade the police to retreat to the barracks. 'I refused to comply to that,' D.I. Molley reported.[21] But the scale of the fury shocked him. 'I have very long service in the police (27 years) and I have witnessed very many riots, but I must say that I have never seen any disturbance nearly as great as the one I am describing.'[22] The crowds could not reach the British rulers at Dublin Castle or the government in Westminster, so they turned their fury on the green uniformed representatives of the state on the streets of their town.

Opinion had already well hardened when the British committed a colossal blunder. Ignoring the warning signal of de Valera's election, and the growing evidence of public sympathy for Irish separatism, a compulsory military service bill was passed by the House of Commons in April 1918. With this the Cabinet proposed to force the men of Ireland into the charnel house of the Western Front. The hierarchy of the Catholic Church in Ireland warned that 'between mismanagement and mischief-making this country has already been deplorably upset, and it would be a fatal mistake, surpassing the worst blunders of the past four years ... to enforce conscription'.[23] The bishops ordered a solemn novena. The Home Rulers railed in Parliament and eventually boycotted it. The trade unions organised Ireland's first general strike. And the IRB got to work recruiting and preparing for revolution. Membership of the Irish Volunteers alone jumped to more than 150 in Con Brosnan's village. The same was true in Ballylongford, where it was said that 'all the men in the locality joined the Volunteers'.[24]

The British stepped back from enforcing conscription. But the damage was done. In the 1918 general election, held just a month after the Armistice, the separatists of Sinn Féin won a decisive victory, destroying the Home Rule politics that had dominated nationalism since the time of Parnell, and resurrecting the ideal of complete independence in the form of a republic.

Guerrilla war came in Ireland not because the people demanded it, but because they were ready for it. The executions, the plan to introduce conscription, melded with older resentments to create a growing mood of national alienation. The Leader of the Opposition, Lord Asquith, encapsulated the situation during a Lords debate. Resentment of the government had grown 'greatly during the last few years' Asquith declared:

partly due no doubt to the war; partly due to disgust; partly to anger at the state of affairs which arose in the North of Ireland, anger at their own arms being stopped when they thought that the arms of that other portion of Ireland had been allowed to go in; anger at the vacillation and changes which took place over Conscription and over Home Rule; treating of Home Rule as 'a broken treaty'. There the thing is. How is it to be met by the British Government? These incidents have been attributed to the British Government; the vacillations and changes have also been attributed to the British Government. I am not blaming particularly the present Government over this matter; it is unfortunately the fact that, owing to our Party system, we never have any continuity of Government in Ireland. There is vacillation first to one policy and then to another; and even during the career of one Government there is vacillation because the Government of Ireland is carried on by a small coterie of men in Dublin Castle, and the policy they carry out largely depends on who is the most dominant person and how long he is in office.[25]

If the British were constantly indecisive on Ireland they faced an emerging enemy with clear goals and increasingly sophisticated organisation and intelligence-gathering. Sinn Féin refused to attend Westminster and instead set up its own parliament in Dublin, Dáil Eireann, to which the Irish Volunteers swore allegiance, increasingly becoming known as the Irish Republican Army. The Dáil set about forming a parallel administration with its own ministries and bureaucracy, with the shadow state's writ enforced by the IRA. The constitutional road to devolved government mapped out by Parnell and then John Redmond had vanished.

A teenage recruit to the IRA, Seamus O'Connor, was powerfully impressed by the changed attitude of the people in north Kerry as Republican prisoners were gradually released after the Rising: 'The Ireland they left was a puzzled Ireland, incapable of understanding the glory of what had happened; the Ireland they came back to, received them with welcoming processions and blazing bonfires throughout the country.'[26] A Listowel soldier, home on leave from the British Army, described how the 'IRA came to me and informed me that if I rejoined the army it would mean instant death, so through fear I never did.' He deserted and never received 'a penny gratuity or anything else'.[27]

Arms were being stockpiled around the district. They were mostly shotguns and a couple of rifles, including one that its owner had used in the South African War while fighting for the Boers. In November 1917, the Irish Volunteers in Ballylongford had been visited by their local organiser to discuss obtaining arms. A Catholic priest went to Manchester with £75 raised locally and purchased and smuggled back rifles. Visits were made to farmhouses and twenty-five weapons, mostly shotguns, were seized. The organiser was a Gaelic teacher named Liam Scully. His name will recur and become a crucial element in the unfolding violence. He was originally from south Kerry but moved to Ballylongford to run the Gaelic League in the north of the county. By the time the first shots were fired in the revolutionary war he was already a trusted Volunteer leader.

The Republicans were under close police surveillance. Local leaders were rounded up under the Defence of the Realm Act. The Listowel bookshop owner, Danny Flavin, a great friend of my grandfather, was arrested for possession of seditious literature and jailed for three months.

Danny was there when the Volunteers staged their first big confrontation with the state in May 1918. Some locals, including several Volunteers, wanted to plant crops on land belonging to Lord Listowel. The case was complex. The lord had rented the land to two Catholic tenants, who used the ground for grazing. Armed only with hurleys, several Volunteer units from the district and at least two brass bands marched through Listowel to the lord's field. The two cattlemen had wisely relinquished their rights to the land in the weeks before the march. But Lord Listowel's agent was less inclined to give way. Soldiers with machine guns backed up the considerable police contingent. 'A strong force of military was present,' one IRA man testified, 'but they did not interfere when informed the tenants had agreed to forgo their claim to the land.'[28] The British officer in charge reportedly told the land agent that soldiers had no right to interfere in a matter that belonged in the courts. The gates were smashed open and the Volunteers marched with bands, plough horses and hundreds of excited locals. There was no choice in the matter. The law belonged to the men willing to use their muscle and who were beginning to gain popular legitimacy. At a public meeting afterwards a Sinn Fein campaigner praised the Volunteers 'who had done a noble day's work for the people of Listowel by assuring them of a plentiful supply of food, none of which would ever find its way into the corn stores of England'.[29] Danny Flavin and several others ended up serving a month in jail for the land invasion, but the sentence would only have enhanced their reputation as defenders of the people.

Later in the conflict local agrarian grievances could become militarised. A dispute between two creameries resulted in boycott and bombing. The privately owned creamery in Ballymacelligott was targeted by supporters of a new cooperative. Anybody trying to buy milk from the private creamery faced attack. A horse was shot, milk churns were emptied into the ditches, an old man had his whiskers cut off and forced down his throat. Class rivalries and the old unresolved tensions over land boiled to the surface. Just across the Limerick border in Abbeyfeale, a feud erupted when a creamery manager sacked some labourers and gave their jobs to farmers' sons. 'It was common practice for one or other of the two parties to come out at night and fire a few shots through the windows of their opponents' houses,' IRA man James Collins recalled.[30] When the farmers formed their own 'vigilance committee' and began patrols with the police, the IRA stepped in and disarmed them. 'By 1st June, every farmer in the area, including those attached to the vigilance committee, had joined the IRA.'[31]

Mick Purtill and Con Brosnan belonged to a class of people whose lives had improved since the Land War. They were not rich but they came from families who had a stake in the land. In the conditions of war against the government they forged a common patriotic cause with the sons of farm labourers. But the tension between farmers and labourers, between those hungry for land and those who already had a stake, would re-emerge when the British left.

There were a few returned soldiers with experience of the Western Front who joined the IRA. They directed the training but local leaders were chosen by their comrades, and had to earn their trust. Paddy Kennelly from Ballybunion was wounded at the Battle of Messines in 1917 and his life was saved by a fellow north Kerry man who saw him bleeding in no man's land. Within a year of his return from the Western Front, Kennelly would be preparing men to fight Britain. Officers were often elected because they were popular with their comrades. It was a long way from Dublin and the war would be defined by local initiative. Collins might send orders but the daily conduct of the war was left to the men on the ground. As far back as the mid-nineteenth century there were some militant nationalists who saw the impossibility of meeting the British in fixed battles. The Rising had been a political success but an expensive military failure of a kind that could not be repeated. The rebel leader Fintan Lalor had advocated guerrilla war in the 1840s, urging militants to adopt the tactics which would attack their enemies discipline.* 'You cannot organise, or train, or discipline your own force to any point of efficiency,' said Lalor. 'You must therefore disorganise, and untrain, and undiscipline that of the enemy, and not alone must you unsoldier, you must unofficer it also; nullify its tactique and strategy, as well as its discipline; decompose the science and system of war, and resolve them into their first elements. You must make the hostile army a mob, as your own will be.'[32]

Con Brosnan and Hannah and Mick Purtill stood on the verge of actions that would change their lives in ways for which they were

---

* James Fintan Lalor, Mar 1807–Dec 1849, was a leader of the *Young Irelander* movement which organised a brief rebellion in 1848. As a Republican theorist his writings profoundly influenced generations of nationalists.

utterly unprepared. But local involvement in acts of revolutionary violence was gradual. The first ambushes were small. There was no one cataclysmic event. In April 1918, the IRA raided the police barracks at Gortatlea, about twenty miles south of Listowel. This was the first armed engagement of the war in Ireland and was meant to deliver a haul of rifles. It was a disaster. An IRA man was shot through the head. Another was wounded and died a day later. Men who had never experienced fighting saw how 'in less than a minute the barrack room floor was covered with blood'.[33] When an IRA volunteer asked the leader of the raid if he should shoot the prisoners, he was told that men with their hands up could not be killed. The survivors fled without weapons. In 1919 as the IRA began to stage more ambushes fewer than twenty soldiers and policemen were killed. But the rules would change as the IRA became more ruthless and efficient.

III

Policemen would be ambushed on patrol, but also hit walking to and from home. In the first half of 1920 forty-four soldiers and police were killed in Ireland. The numbers jumped to 334 in the following six months. In the same period the IRA losses went from thirty-two for the first six months of 1920, to 228 up to the end of December.

In every village and town eyes watched and recorded the movements of the police. Times were noted, and patrol numbers assessed. Women like my grandmother carried the information to the IRA. In Listowel one of Hannah's comrades, a forty-year-old mother of four, spied and smuggled guns from within the RIC barracks where she worked as a clerical assistant. 'She got out about six revolvers,' remembered a neighbour of the Keanes on Church Street.[34] Hannah's childhood friend and comrade, May Ahern, later revealed the extent of the danger they risked. Some of the women were told to ingratiate themselves with the Black and Tans. 'They used to tell me to be very friendly with the Tans,' May remembered, 'and I knew a couple of them and I once got a copy of the "Hue and Cry" [the list of wanted men] ... I had one who told me that if they were ever raiding about the place he would fire a shot and let me know.'[35]

On another occasion May was sent to collect luggage which had been packed with revolvers and ammunition and placed on a train to north Kerry from Dublin. The bag had been waiting for collection at Kilmorna station. On the way she passed roadside crosses erected to the memory of comrades recently shot by Crown forces. 'I could guess what her thoughts were when she landed at the station,' recalled one of the IRA men involved in the operation. As luck had it, the mail train that day was held up and the station was filled with police. May was told by the IRA to leave at once. But she waited, steeled herself and went to recover the luggage. 'Just imagine,' said the IRA commander, Thomas Collins, 'walking through a platform filled with Tans holding on to two bags filled with guns, ammunition and Mills bombs.'[36]

The IRA and the police both depended on local intelligence. Informers were hunted down mercilessly. Often the evidence for either side only needed to be anecdotal. Later in the war an eighty-year-old 'tinker called Old Tom O'Sullivan' was seen talking regularly to the Black and Tans. It was enough for him to be killed. His body was then used to lure the police into a bog near Rathmore on the border with Cork in 1921. They were ambushed when they tried to reach it and eight were killed.

Bodies began to appear on country roads with the words 'Spies Beware' hung on cards around their necks. Informers had been the bane of every Irish rebellion before this. Michael Collins now sent orders to target the British spy network in the countryside, most notably the officers and men of the RIC, both serving and former constables, who might still keep links to the force. 'Without her spies England was helpless,' he said. 'Without their police throughout the country, how could they find the men they wanted?' The north Kerry IRA man Seamus O'Connor recalled how 'for the first time in Irish history the spy had no place. Drastic punishment was so certain and so imminent that it was as much as a man's life was worth to utter a discordant note, let alone give information to the enemy'.[37]

The reference to 'discordant' notes also applied within the north Kerry IRA. An IRA man who helped kill a local ex-serviceman known to be friendly with the police spoke of him being 'tried, found guilty and sentenced to death'.[38] But where was the evidence? How did the prisoner plead? Was anybody allowed to speak for him or defend his case? We are not told, but his death was probably decided before he was ever arrested. A guerrilla army had neither the time nor resources, nor very often the desire, to mount trials that would satisfy the most elementary standards of justice. There were numerous such cases across the country. The IRA volunteer who described the execution was one of six men involved. Another of the group had been regarded beforehand as a suspect 'as he had on several occasions discussed IRA matters in the presence of strangers and generally talked too much about IRA activities'.[39] For this reason he was made to take part so that 'having carried out the execution himself he would have to remain silent about it'.[40]

The government responded to the violence by banning Sinn Féin, the IRA, Cumann na mBan and the Gaelic League. Like tens of thousands of other Irish people, my grandmother and her brother and their friends now belonged to proscribed organisations. The move only deepened their resentment of the British.

Hannah smuggled weapons and messages, brought food and clothes to men hiding in dugouts and observed the movements of the police and military. The guns she hid were meant for killing: smuggled messages could be the first step in a chain that ended with a man's brains spilt on a rural road. I picture this teenager with her long raven hair tucked under a scarf, a solid young countrywoman of medium height, her gabardine belted against the hard weather, crossing the winter fields, climbing over ditches, and up narrow tracks on the move to or from where the fighters hid out, or at work in the town smiling at the police and the military so they wouldn't suspect she was part of a machine devoted to their destruction. Hannah lived the lie of loyalty because that was what

My great-uncle Mick Purtill in his
Free State army uniform

the war demanded. I remember once she remarked that the British Army – the regular army – were polite, a 'better class of men', who didn't swear or get drunk in public. It was no great trouble to be civil to such men. But later when the reinforcements, the Black and Tans and the Auxies, arrived, she would struggle to contain her temper. By now she knew that her work had one purpose: to inflict as much damage on the British until they gave up and left Ireland.

Her brother Mick fought in the countryside. He lived off the land, depending on the welcome of country people, hiding in dugouts and hay barns. The privations of life on the run ensured that this was a young man's war. After an icy winter downpour, men might lie hidden under bushes for hours while the police and military searched the fields around them, or shiver in earthen dugouts, unable to light a fire for fear of giving away their positions. Most dugouts held no more than four men. The more comfortable had a corrugated iron roof with a hole for ventilation, camouflaged with sods of turf. Exhaustion overcame discomfort. 'To fall asleep and remain so was always the least of our troubles, no matter where we were,' remembered Seamus O'Connor; 'no sooner did we lay down than we fell asleep and remained so until morning'.[41] The men preferred to sleep in hay sheds because they were 'warm and comfortable ... apart from an occasional attack of hay insects which seemed to frequent some hay barns'.[42] But they became too dangerous as searchers began to prod them with bayonets or to fire bullets into the stacks at random.

Searching the military archives I find the first record of my uncle Mick Purtill in action. On 13 March 1920 he and Con Brosnan and another boyhood friend, Con Dee, were sent to take part in an attack on Ballybunion RIC station. There were around sixty men and they met in a field outside the town. Later on they would be careful never to gather in such a big group near a town centre. Most were carrying shotguns or pistols. There were only four rifles. But there was a homemade mine which was to be used to blast an entrance to the barracks. A commander went through the ranks and divided the men up into five sections and sent them off to surround the barracks. Listen for the blast of a whistle, they were told. 'That is when you fire. Not before. Two blasts means ceasefire. Three blasts means retire.'

Con Brosnan was sent to block roads around the town and forestall the arrival of Crown reinforcements. Mick Purtill and Con Dee went with one of the sections attacking the barracks. The novice gunmen were given an early example of how the war would affect civilians. A family living next to the barracks was 'moved to safety' so that the homemade mine could be used to blow down the wall between their living room and the barracks.[43] How long had they been living there? How did they react? There is no further mention of them in the official account. In the end the bomb failed to explode, but the signal to fire was given anyway. Soon the IRA could see Very lights being blasted into the sky from the direction of Ballydonoghue police post. But they stayed where they were, shooting at the barracks until their ammunition was exhausted. It was the action of men with more courage and luck than military sense. They escaped before reinforcements could arrive. Con Dee remembered how 'these barracks were but eight miles from my home [and] I had to be on the run from that time on'.[44]

Up to now the RIC in Listowel town had not been attacked. One constable recalled how they 'did the usual routine police work and carried arms only at night. There was no interference with the people who went about their business and did not show any active animosity towards the police. There were no military in the town and no necessity for them.'[45] Yet the men read the morning newspapers. They listened to the accounts coming in of killing elsewhere in the country. It was a matter of time before blood was spilled.

It would happen near Ballydonoghue, about a ten-minute walk from the Purtill homestead. On 3 May 1920, an RIC sergeant and two constables were cycling back from court in Listowel. Several IRA volunteers from Ballydonoghue were lying in wait behind the ditches on either side of the road. Mick Purtill is not named as being among the attackers but the men were all close comrades of his and it is highly likely he was present. Jack Ahern, the brother of Hannah's childhood friend, May, was there and May herself acted as a lookout.

Sergeant Francis J. McKenna, a thirty-nine-year-old married man with three children, was making a journey he and his constables had made many times before. They were three Irishmen passing the time of the day in the spring weather, trusting still that the people of the area had no reason to want to kill them.*They came along the

---

* A few years earlier McKenna had given evidence against men who had been jailed for illegal military drilling. But the sentences were short – drilling was not a high offence at that stage in the conflict – and the men were quickly released. This day, however, McKenna and his constables were more likely to have been targeted for their weapons. It is also possible they were attacked because they had taken part in court proceedings. The IRA was attempting to disrupt normal courts. The Republican movement ran its own 'Sinn Féin courts' as part of the strategy of creating a parallel state ready to supplant the British.

road, past a steep tree-lined bank, walking for the last time as country policemen, sure of their ground. According to one IRA man, the police were called on to surrender but 'refused and attempted to draw their revolvers'.[46] There were no witnesses to prove this one way or the other. The Ballydonoghue men opened fire at close range. McKenna was hit in the face by a shotgun blast, a hideous wound that obliterated his features and caused massive damage to the brain. He died at the scene. The two constables were wounded but survived; one of them managed to inflict a light wound on an attacker. May Ahern remembered that 'going back I met my brother and I took a revolver and handcuffs from him'.[47] These belonged to the dead sergeant.

There had been no killing on these rural roads of north Kerry since the Land War. But blood would now follow blood. The shooting of Sergeant McKenna brought searches and threats. A local priest, Father Curtayne, known to be an active Sinn Féiner, received a threatening letter telling him: 'Prepare for your death, Black hand gang'.[48] The letter was from the police who suspected the priest was in league with the killers.

Hannah Purtill was working in Listowel as a draper's assistant. Besides providing a useful income the job gave her cover for moving between the town and country. Every day she cycled the four miles from her home in Ballydonoghue to work. The policemen on the roadblocks got used to her comings and goings, morning and evening.

One day she was walking around a corner in Listowel when she bumped into a studious-looking older man who smiled warmly and apologised. He had dark hair and eyes 'full of devilment' and she was lost to him in that moment – or so she told her daughters decades later. Bill Keane was a schoolteacher who had recently returned home from County Tipperary to take up a job near Listowel.

A few days later he got a message to her, asking if she would walk out with him – an invitation which meant exactly that and no more in this conservative rural community. They walked by the River

Feale and through Gurtenard Wood. Hannah was taken by his courteous manner and his way with words. This was how their courtship
developed. With words, a fine spring torrent of them, as Bill
declaimed poetry, they followed the lazy course of the Feale upriver.
They walked and laughed. He seemed to know everything about the
town and he joked about the residents and their foibles as they
passed the houses on Church Street, a long meandering thoroughfare of shops, public houses and private homes which ran parallel to
open fields and woodland on one side, and the heart of Listowel on
the other. Hannah was taken to meet his family, into the house on
Church Street where Bill's parents and his brother and sister lived,
and where he would continue to live even when he and Hannah got
married. Cheek by jowl. This was the way and Hannah knew she
must accept it.

She could tell the Keanes were very different people to her own.
They were different from most people. Out in Ballydonoghue there
was always work to be done. The Purtills were constantly on the go,
fixing and patching, labouring, digging and sowing, tending the livestock. The Keanes worked hard too. But they liked to talk. They
were fond of drink and storytelling and there was an eccentric
streak in them that could flower into wildness. They were what the
country people might, affectionately, call 'half-cracked'. Bill had a
stock of books that he kept in a cupboard in the kitchen. His brother
Dan lived up in the attic, accompanied, my father told me, by a tame
jackdaw. He worked as a cattle jobber, a go-between who made deals
with farmers bringing their livestock to market. His skills were
much in demand but the revolutionary war was disrupting his business. Their sister, Juleanne, showed no inclination to leave the house
on Church Street for marriage. She was a good-looking woman but
rebuffed the advances of all callers. Both siblings were wary of the
newcomer in their brother's life, but Hannah Purtill was too preoccupied with the war and her love affair with Bill to pay too much
attention to the personal dynamics on Church Street.

The Keanes lived close to Listowel police barracks, about one
minute's walk out the front door to the right, close enough to hear

any commotion and to be kept awake at night by the distinctive noise of the Crossley Tender engines of the RIC and military. This proximity would not have escaped Hannah's attention and she and her comrades in Cumann na mBan kept up the flow of weapons and messages to the IRA. They hid men on the run, like Liam McCabe, who had been injured fleeing from an ambush. McCabe had blood poisoning and needed to be treated in hospital. The women managed to smuggle him into Listowel hospital under cover for three months. They were helped by the nuns who ran the wards and whose militant piety would have daunted the most determined searchers. McCabe remembered that when more than a hundred Crown forces men surrounded the hospital, two nuns 'helped me from my bed to a part of the hospital already searched and from there to the back of the Altar in another part of the hospital'.[49] He was then spirited out to a safe house.

The local RIC were under relentless strain. During May the empty police hut near Ballydonoghue was set on fire. The vacated barracks at Lixnaw was burned down a few days later. So it went on across the county. Remote stations were being given up without a fight and trains going between Limerick and Tralee were held up. A company of troops from the Loyal North Lancashire Regiment was deployed to Listowel, but the government still held back from flooding Ireland with troops or launching a military offensive. To do so would be to acknowledge that revolutionary war was under way. Instead they sent in paramilitary police, offering their enemies a propaganda gift which would keep giving long into posterity.

5

Tans

And heedless of churches
and dead men's bones
With an armoured car leading
And massed in vans
Come the 'devil-may-cares'
Called the Black and Tans

RIC propaganda ballad, 1920

I

If you believed my father, they were the sweepings of Britain's jails: to a man they were murderers, cut-throats and rapists in the long inglorious line of Elizabeth I's pillagers, Cromwell's butchers and the gibbet-bearing redcoats. The Black and Tans could match them all for cruelty. I knew my father was given to hyperbolic declarations but he was only reflecting a national orthodoxy from which no substantial strain of political opinion demurred. My grandmother Hannah, in one of her rare comments about the war, called them 'bad hoors' who 'treated us like peasants'. They were intended as ready to fight reinforcements for the exhausted Royal Irish

Constabulary and many among the ten thousand who served were recruited from the ranks of military demobbed after the Great War. The name Black and Tan came from the fact that the police had insufficient supplies of the RIC uniform and so the new recruits were dressed in a mismatch of police dark green and military light khaki, a blend that reminded some Munster wit of the coats of a pack of hunting dogs named 'the Black and Tans'.

The first of them arrived in March 1920. Very soon after there were reports of drunkenness and abuse of civilians. Even British troops regarded the Tans as men to be avoided. Private Arthur Robinson from the East Yorkshire Regiment went into a pub with a comrade only to be confronted by a drunken Tan. 'He was drunk and he fired between us . . . we went for him and he cleared off . . . he was a big man. Some of them had big heads. That was their attitude.'[1] In British Army accounts there is a consistent theme: the temporary constables in the Black and Tans operated outside the rules; they were 'a pretty rough and tough lot' whose culture was 'to shoot first and ask questions afterwards'.[2] Horace Todman was a teenage bugler with the South Wales Borderers when he was sent to Ireland as part of the army. On his first night in the country a body was brought in to the barracks, 'very grey, a man of about thirty in ordinary clothes [with] a very neat little bullet wound in his head'.[3] Because of a lack of space, Todman spent the night in the same room as the corpse. He remembered the Tans being 'really hated by the local people . . . [and] our own people didn't like them'.[4]

The Black and Tans were followed in July by a self-contained paramilitary force recruited from among ex-officers. An advertisement in the London *Times* appealed to former army officers who had 'Courage, Discretion, Tact and Judgement' to join a new 'Corps d'elite': the Auxiliary Division of the Royal Irish Constabulary. They were offered £1 a day and generous leave. A high proportion of this new force were men who had risen through the ranks of the military during the Great War. Unlike the Tans, the 'Auxies' were meant to bring the war to the IRA. In theory they were a division of the RIC but in practice they operated as an independent strike force.

Tans in Dublin

They were the first of the counter-insurgency forces of the colonial wars of the twentieth century and many would go on to serve in Palestine during the Arab revolt. The public tended to regard them with the same contempt as the Tans. The IRA learned to fear them.

One regular British officer, who served in Ireland and later commanded former Auxiliaries in Palestine, called them 'a bit rough' but 'a magnificent crowd of men' who had resorted to harsh measures after seeing awful sights such as 'friends murdered and stuffed down a drain'.[5] Brigadier John Rymer-Jones was a veteran of the Western Front himself and conceded that it was a mistake sending men who had been immersed in the horror of the trenches straight into a war of ambush among civilians. 'I think the trouble is that when you have had a war like that,' he later reflected, 'you should avoid if at all possible putting those same people into a position where they are being attacked by Sinn Féiners ... or IRA ... If you have been through a long war ... you take it as an insult if people are attacking you.'[6]

IRA action could bring fierce reprisals against civilians. This deepened the alienation of the public from the government, a truth that would in time prove as enduring in the Mekong Delta and the Casbah of Algiers as in the hills of north Kerry. In Listowel tensions grew quickly between the Tans and some of the regular police. In 1921, Constable John McNamara told an American inquiry into conditions in Ireland that he had heard Black and Tans boast of killing and torturing prisoners. 'It is their practice to break into public houses and saloons and confiscate the liquor there,' he explained. 'They use the vilest imaginable language on all occasions and no man who respects himself would be associated with them. It is their practice to steal food, fowl and other farm animals at night on raids which they conducted dressed in civilian clothes and with blackened faces. None of the officials in charge of the barracks reprimand them for these raids.'[7]

The IRA offensive against the police drove Dublin Castle to redeploy its forces. On 16 May 1920 the RIC in Listowel were told that most of their number were to be sent to remote posts. The army was to move into the barracks. Constable Jeremiah Mee, who was the proudest of men when he first marched down Grafton Street in his police uniform, gathered his comrades for an emergency meeting. Mee left behind a detailed testimony. His address to his comrades, if taken at face value, was strikingly clear-sighted:

> I pointed out that in a war one of two things must happen. We had either to win or lose. I assumed that we would win the war with the assistance of the British military. When we had defeated our own people, the British military would return to their own country and we would remain with our own people whom we had, with the assistance of the British Government, crushed and defeated. That would be the best side of our case. If we lost the war, the position would be still worse.[8]

Mee and his men decided to refuse transfer and any cooperation with the British military. On 17 May, he presented an ultimatum to the District Inspector. It contained an incendiary paragraph: 'When we joined the police force, we joined with characters second to none, and we refuse to cooperate or work in any capacity with the British military, men of low moral character who frequented bad houses, kept the company of prostitutes and generally were unsuitable and undesirable characters.'[9] This last reference was more likely aimed at the Black and Tans and was hyperbolic; there was as much likelihood of finding a brothel in Listowel as snow in the Congo. In fact, Mee had earlier commended the army commander in Listowel as 'a tall handsome British military officer who kept his men under good control'.[10] Captain John Bidwell Watson of the Loyal North Lancashire Regiment was a veteran of the Great War, most of which he spent in a prisoner of war camp in East Africa after being captured at the battle of Tanga in November 1914. In custody he learned the value of patience. It would prove critical in the months ahead.

On the nineteenth, two days after the initial police revolt, the top brass of the RIC descended on Listowel. They were led by Lieutenant General Henry Tudor, veteran of the Boer War, veteran of the Great War, a friend of Winston Churchill from India days and now the effective chief of police in Ireland. But Tudor said nothing. His mere presence was meant to awe the rural constables. It was given to Lieutenant Colonel Gerald Brice Ferguson Smyth to address the men. He was another old India hand and much-decorated veteran of the Western Front whose left arm was paralysed by wounds. As Mee remembered it, both Tudor and Smyth were wearing full-dress uniform with the attendant complement of medals. They were accompanied by around fifty military and police escorts. 'This display of force was no doubt intended to terrorise our little garrison,' said Mee. 'And I will admit that I never felt less cheerful.'[11]

However, the officers had not come to chide them. Smyth, the divisional commissioner, appears to have misunderstood the mood completely. Rather than threaten sanctions, or reverse the transfer decision, Mee claimed Smyth offered the men unfettered licence to kill. By Mee's account his orders were draconian:

Police and military will patrol the country roads at least five nights a week. They are not to confine themselves to the main roads but take across country, lie in ambush, take cover behind fences, near the roads, and, when civilians are seen approaching, shout 'hands up'. Should the order be not immediately obeyed, shoot, and shoot with effect. If the persons approaching carry their hands in their pockets or are in any way suspicious looking, shoot them down. You may make mistakes occasionally and innocent persons may be shot, but this cannot be helped and you are bound to get the right persons sometimes. The more you shoot, the better I will like you, and I assure you that no policeman will get into trouble for shooting any man.[12]

This appeared to contradict a general order Smyth would issue the following month, on 17 June – to specifically shoot IRA members who failed to surrender when ordered. In the same order he warned against reprisals saying, 'I will deal severely with any officer or man concerned in them.'[13]

Mee's reported account was explosive and easy to accept for a population suffering under the terror of the Tans. Later Mee claimed Smyth's words had been written down within an hour of his hearing them, and that he had fellow constables read and sign the document to affirm its veracity. In Mee's description there was uproar after the Smyth speech. He called Smyth a murderer and surrendered his belt and gun. Tudor attempted to calm things down and promised to scrap the transfers. The Listowel barracks had become a nest of subversives, with the British beginning to wonder if their Irish comrades would turn their guns on them.

After a few weeks Mee and three other constables deserted with their weapons. The story of 'the Listowel mutiny' was picked up by the press and nationalist propagandists and soon spread abroad. Mee's comrades backed him up and some gave evidence to an American commission of inquiry the following year. In the House of Commons, the Nationalist MP Joseph Devlin pressed for a debate: 'Is not the House entitled to have this matter discussed in view of the intense passion that the statements have aroused in the country and the possibility of serious and immediate bloodshed in consequence?'[14]

On 14 July 1920, Colonel Smyth was questioned by the Chief Secretary for Ireland, Sir Hamar Greenwood, during which he repudiated Mee's version as a 'distorting and wholly misleading account of what took place'.[15] Smyth opened a libel suit against a newspaper that published Mee's account. In his description of what happened he does no more than stress government policy on reprisals and repeat the order about shooting armed men, or men thought to be armed, who refused to surrender. He also advocated the commandeering of houses and turning the inhabitants onto the streets if an RIC barracks was burned. The houses of Sinn Féiners were preferable but not imperative. Smyth covered himself carefully against allegations of a general shoot-to-kill order, but he knew police were already operating well beyond the bounds of legality and were steadily alienating the civilian population.

The controversy ensured that Smyth became a marked man. The following July he was in Cork city when IRA men burst into the Cork and County Club, where he had been playing billiards, and shot him dead. Smyth's body was taken back to the north of Ireland where he was born. After his funeral there were reprisals: the homes of Catholics were attacked in the town of Banbridge and Catholic workers driven from their jobs in a three-day-long rampage. The killing of Gerald Smyth begat another tragedy for his family. His brother Osbert came to Ireland from a military posting in Egypt to seek vengeance on the IRA and was killed by them in Dublin, less than three months after his brother.

The war kept growing, feeding ravenously on rage and fear, killing an innocent man here, destroying a family there; it dispatched death with whispers and nods, on scraps of paper with scribbled addresses in city suburbs, provincial towns, remote farmsteads; it was a war of enemies real and guessed at, a war of a kind that will recur often in the century ahead as the old world of empires is convulsed by men and women who understand the power of propaganda and popular mobilisation. In this war the brutality of your enemy becomes a weapon to be turned against them. The Auxies tortured and killed, often with impunity but rarely without exposure, as they carried out some of the most notorious reprisals. In December 1920 my maternal grandmother witnessed a red glow over her home city of Cork. She was ten years old and her family was politically uninvolved. The war did not reach their genteel suburb.

On the night of 11 December, in retaliation for an ambush just outside Cork which killed one Auxiliary and wounded several others, the Auxiliaries, assisted by Black and Tans and soldiers, burned part of the city's commercial district, the city hall and library, and prevented the fire brigade from responding. Civilians were beaten and robbed. Businesses were looted. Several people were shot. My grandmother remembered being petrified. Her father was in the city, where he worked as a book-keeper for a firm of biscuit-makers. He had not come home for tea and so she waited up all night with her mother and sister listening to the sounds of shooting echoing from the valley below. The following morning a key turned in the lock. Her father was home and unharmed having gone to the pub after work and, seeing the disturbance, retreated to the house of a friend nearer the city centre.

From the outset there had been reprisals, officially disavowed but privately supported by the government. Reprisal raids were sometimes ordered and led by senior officers. They most frequently happened when men wanted to avenge attacks on comrades. The County Inspector for Limerick, John M. Regan, wrote after the war that the 'police quickest to avenge the death of a comrade were Irishmen and men of an excellent type. Black and Tans, having drink taken, might fire out of lorries indiscriminately, loot public houses, or terrorise a village but the Irishman would avenge his comrade when absolutely stone cold sober and on the right person. It required a great deal of courage to do so as if detected he ran a serious risk of being hanged.'[16] The last sentence is disingenuous. Regan knew that the state took a more than lenient view of such reprisals committed by police. It was complicit in them. The Auxiliaries were already in the habit of tying men to the front of vehicles as human shields while travelling through dangerous territory. Security force death squads were becoming an established phenomenon.

The case of the Black and Tan Thomas Huckerby illustrated the complicity of the RIC command in covering up such crimes. Huckerby was the son of Methodist missionaries, born in the Caribbean and of mixed race, a former RAF cadet and then sailor in the Royal Naval Reserve. He arrived in Ireland in July 1920 at the age of nineteen and was posted to the west Limerick/north Kerry borderlands. A few weeks after arrival he and another constable were held up by the IRA and stripped of their uniforms and made to walk back to barracks through the village of Shanagolden. That night the Tans raided the village and burned the creamery. Killings began soon after. A local pensioner, John Hynes, was shot dead. Nobody was charged, but Huckerby was suspected by locals. He was moved about fifteen miles to the larger town of Abbeyfeale, directly on the Kerry border. By now he was on the IRA's target list. In September the IRA ambushed a patrol and killed two constables, believing Huckerby was present. He was in fact off duty that night.

Two days later Huckerby shot two innocent men claiming they looked suspicious and had tried to run away from him. He was transferred again, this time to Limerick city. Clearly feeling that his time was running out, he left Ireland at the end of the year without facing any charges over the killings.

Occasionally the violence of the police paramilitaries provoked a military intervention. A week after the attempt on Huckerby's life, a joint force of Tans and Auxies descended on Abbeyfeale and seized the eighteen-year-old brother of a local IRA leader. He was tied to a bush and beaten while being interrogated in full view of the people passing through the town square. Within the next hour a frantic drama was played out as the parish priest pleaded with the District Inspector of the RIC to intervene. The senior police officer was apparently so intimidated by the Tans that he called for military reinforcements. The victim's brother, local IRA leader James Collins, gave a detailed account of what happened next:

> When the military arrived, the Auxiliaries and Black and Tans protested at their interference. They held on to Michael and would not hand him over. An argument then developed between the two parties and was becoming serious when the Tans and Auxiliaries released him and tied him by the legs to their lorry. Preceded by the military, the Auxiliaries dragged him through the town towards Newcastlewest. When they reached Barna, about six miles away, the military halted and again remonstrated with the Auxiliaries and Tans. By this time, he was unconscious. His head and body were battered and bruised. At last, they untied him and threw him into a dyke and left him for dead.[17]

It is an extraordinary testimony, revealing not just the scale of the brutality meted out to civilians, but the tension which could erupt between different forces of the Crown. Reprisals became official government policy in January 1921. In the government's *Weekly Summary*, Sir Nevil Macready, the general officer commanding, wrote that because 'the machinery of law [has] broken down, they feel there is no certain means of redress and punishment, and it is only human that they should act on their own initiative'.[18] Shops and garages were razed to the ground in many parts of the country. In another foreshadowing of the punishments of later colonial wars, the family homes of some of those suspected of attacks were demolished. Shots were fired at groups of young men in the streets. Prisoners were given savage beatings. Any civilian captured with a weapon could expect to die.

The official line was that Republican violence was being caused by a minority. But in Listowel there was enough of a quiet majority behind the rebels to keep the war going. Con Brosnan and Mick Purtill were honing their skills as guerrilla fighters, and my grandmother Hannah was becoming bolder in her gun-running and spying. The state pledged to restore order but from the first burnings and killings it had lost its moral authority. There would be no going back to the Ireland of the Viceroy and the Loyal Children's picnics.

6

The Abode of Wolves

Here once the pride of princely Desmond flushed;
His courtiers knelt, his mailed squadrons rushed.

Aubrey de Vere[1]

I

It was the place where his life turned. Tobias O'Sullivan came to Kilmallock in County Limerick in his late thirties. He arrived as a diligent but ordinary police officer. He would leave as a decorated and swiftly promoted hero – and as a marked man at the highest levels of the IRA.

It is possible that had he been sent to Dublin Castle or Belfast, or to a small station in the midlands, somewhere that did not offer the same challenge or opportunity, he might never have become such an important target. But I believe that would be to misread the man. His character was of a kind made for war. He would have found the front line. Such men find the action because it is where they test themselves. I have known men like the District Inspector. Under fire they are the last ones standing between survival and the chaos of defeat. It is what happens under his command in Kilmallock that sparks in me this recognition. Ireland

After the siege of Kilmallock, Tobias O'Sullivan (centre)

would not be willingly handed over to the IRA by a man like Tobias O'Sullivan.

He was transferred to Kilmallock from Athea as the guerrillas were stepping up their attacks on remote posts. He arrived with his wife, May, his sons Bernard, aged six, and John, aged four, and the one-and-a-half-year-old baby Sara.

Throughout 1919 the atmosphere had been changing in rural towns and villages. Police and their families had become vulnerable. Backs were turned and conversations stopped when policemen's wives entered shops. In dormant areas, the IRA sent outsiders as organisers to escalate the conflict. One of them, Liam Scully, former schoolteacher, had been sent from north Kerry where he trained men like Mick Purtill and Con Brosnan. Scully was popular with the men back in Ballylongford, where he was a captain with the IRA, and he came to Kilmallock with a reputation as a man of action.

*   *   *

In the 1920s, Kilmallock was a small market town set in the rich pastureland of south Limerick. It had retained a strategic significance from the time of the Elizabethan conquests, commanding the main road between the east and west of Munster, creating a block-ade against the perpetual fear of invaders from the Atlantic coast. Back then order was imposed with customary savagery. Sir Humphrey Gilbert, coloniser, half-brother of Sir Walter Ralegh and decapitator of the peasantry, could boast that the conquered territories were 'so quiet that I have but to send my horseboy for any man and he will come'.[2]

In 1573 the Irish rebel Sir James Fitzmaurice and his army torched Kilmallock, creating 'a black thick and gloomy shroud of smoke about it, after they had torn down its houses of stone and wood', so that in the description of one chronicler the town 'became the receptacle and abode of wolves'.[3] Fitzmaurice was the first to define, for reasons of conviction and convenience, a national identity that melded 'Faith and Fatherland', or what James Joyce would centuries later call 'Christ and Caesar hand in glove'.[4] A tenacious and resourceful commander, Fitzmaurice ran the English ragged, much as the IRA Flying Columns would some four hundred years later. One contemporary chronicle described him as a 'brave and gallant gentleman, witty, learned, circumspect ... not much given to the pleasures of Bacchus or Venus'.[5] This view would change as Fitzmaurice stayed at large, his liberty a taunt to the English administration. He was eventually captured and offered a pardon if he submitted to the authority of the Crown. Fitzmaurice would have felt he had little option but to submit. The alternative was a gory traitor's death on the scaffold, designed to impose maximum humiliation on the defeated lord. He had a halter placed around his neck and was led like a farm animal before Sir John Perrot, the president's sword pressed against his chest. In front of the assembled nobility of Munster, Fitzmaurice recited the words written for him by the English, but spoken in both Gaelic and English: 'This earth of Kilmallock, which town I have most traitorously sacked and burnt, I kiss, and on the same lie prostrate, overfraught with sorrow upon the present view of my most mischievous past.'[6]

In Kilmallock the outline of the Irish struggle with the English could be traced in the ruins of the ancient moss-bewigged walls, in the roofless and abandoned Dominican priory, sacked by Cromwell's forces in 1648, and in the contours of deforested lands ploughed into fields of grain and barley, the pastures dotted with the grazing cattle of the planters. In the colonists' telling, the wilderness had been transformed by English organisation and discipline. It was to be seen in their promotion of laws and businesses, in the markets and the spires of new Protestant churches; more poignantly it could be heard in the music of itinerant harpists who once played for Gaelic chieftains and now blended the English and continental forms with the native music. They earned their coins and keep in the Ascendancy mansions where, in less than a generation, a rugged soldier from Worcestershire could become lord and master of vast lands, his Catholic tenants kept firmly in hand with the threat of eviction and consequent destitution.

By the nineteenth century the colonists' mark was also to be seen in the town's broad main street with its abundant life of commerce, the regular market days, the creameries and coach-building facto- ries, the thriving public houses, and the omnipresent patrols of 'Peelers', the Irish Constabulary in their dark green uniforms who kept order from a sturdy police barracks.

Political violence occasionally simmered. Three decades before Tobias O'Sullivan arrived, the Kilmallock barracks was attacked by the Fenians. About twenty men advanced in a military formation more suited to the massed ranks of the recently ended American Civil War, in which several leading Fenian commanders had served. A handful were armed with guns but the majority clutched only pikes to face volleys of fire from the well-prepared police defenders. The Fenians were routed with ease. After the attack, the police received an unexpected honour from Queen Victoria who, accord- ing to the Unionist *Irish Times*, 'had been graciously pleased to command that the force should thereafter be called the "Royal" Irish

Constabulary and that they should be entitled to have the harp and crown as badges of that force'.[7]

But the core tenet of Fenianism – the belief that Britain could only be driven from Ireland by force – retained a powerful hold among a small circle of revolutionaries in the area.

By the time Tobias O'Sullivan arrived in Kilmallock in May 1920 he found a troubled town and mounting IRA violence in the surrounding countryside. It was still prosperous with numerous grocers, public houses, a pig market and four hotels. The finest of the hotels was Clerys, 'near the railway station, at which best horses and cars attend all trains'.[8] Clerys was located opposite the barracks of the Royal Irish Constabulary.

The previous month, the IRA had hit the RIC garrison at Ballylanders, about ten miles away. Very lights – illumination flares fired from pistols – filled the night sky in bright coloured streaks, a desperate call for assistance from the occupants. But the IRA had blocked all approach roads to the town to delay reinforcements. Heavy iron weights were used to smash the barracks' slate roof and petrol was poured in, followed by bombs. Faced with being burned alive the seven-strong police garrison at Ballylanders surrendered.

The man leading the attack was one of the most formidable IRA figures of his day. Seán Forde was hard-headed and clinical in his decision making.* He had fought in the Easter Rising and shared a cell with one of the leaders, Seán McDermott, the night before he was executed. When Prime Minister Herbert Asquith visited IRA prisoners in Dublin after the Rising, Forde was among those who refused to stand up when he entered their quarters. Asquith was unperturbed and listened patiently to a lecture from Forde about the men's demand for prisoner-of-war status. 'I said if we were

---

* Forde's real name was Tomás O'Maoileoin, from Nenagh in County Tipperary. However, it was as Forde that he was known and hunted by the government forces throughout the campaign.

prisoners of war our leaders – our officers – would not have been executed.'[9] Forde was exceptionally brave in the field, single-handedly attacking a lorryload of troops at close quarters. 'I remember myself emptying an automatic pistol into one of the lorries,' he said, 'and throwing a little haversack full of bombs into it as well. From what I could see stooping over, all the military in it were bleeding and hanging out of the lorry in various attitudes.'[10] Yet when his men captured soldiers in another ambush the wounded were well treated and a Church of Ireland minister was found to console the most seriously hurt.

Forde had been sent to the Kilmallock area by Michael Collins with instructions to 'get those Limerick men into the fight'.[11] Like Collins, Forde understood that realism was the essence of guerrilla warfare. No fights were to be picked unless there was a chance of winning. Martyrdom by hunger strike or on the gallows had value in creating public outrage. But with the new revolutionaries it was a tactic not a creed. Since Forde's arrival the local units were better coordinated and more aggressive. After Ballylanders the highly motivated guerrillas wanted a bigger target, and eyed the RIC barracks in Kilmallock. 'We had done so well at Ballylanders,' Forde recalled, 'that we said at some of the meetings: "Why not attack the big one and do it properly!"'[12]

Kilmallock was better defended. Set back from the main street, the barracks was sandbagged, steel-shuttered and surrounded by barbed wire. Local Volunteers noted that it was overlooked by Clery's hotel and had a number of neighbouring houses and small shops which could be taken over without much difficulty. Breaching the roof was possible but Forde would need help from IRA men in the region. The word went out for men, guns and ammunition across Limerick and Cork, Clare and Tipperary. Units began to converge on safe houses around Kilmallock.

At the RIC barracks there was always a general expectation of attack, but no specific warning of the inferno that was about to be unleashed by the IRA. The newly arrived Sergeant O'Sullivan had suffered a serious failure of his local intelligence network.

II

There can be no covenants between men and lions, wolves and
lambs can never be of one mind, but hate each other out and
out and through. Therefore there can be no understanding
between you and me, nor may there be any covenants between
us, till one or other shall fall.

Homer, *Iliad*

The men infiltrated the town in ones and twos. It was the last Friday
of May and Kilmallock was thronged with farmers and townspeople. The guns were hidden in a dump on the western approaches
to the town, the explosives and paraffin placed on the eastern side.
One man posing as a commercial traveller was sent to book rooms
on the top floor of Clery's. If the manager guessed what was being
prepared, he had the wit to say nothing. Two volunteers were sent
to take over Mr Carroll's shop next to the barracks. They bought a
bottle of whiskey from the terrified owner. 'The poor man got a
great fright at first but after a little talk became calm,'[13] one IRA
man recalled. By nightfall there were thirty gunmen in place for the
direct attack on the base. Around forty others were deployed to cut
off any attempt by the police to break out into surrounding lane-
ways. Beyond the town, other contingents barricaded roads, severed
telephone and telegraph wires and tore up railway tracks.

By midnight Kilmallock was totally cut off. The local bank
manager, Cyril Andrews, who lived above the premises adjacent to
the barracks, was woken by 'armed men who appeared mysteriously
in my bedroom'. They allowed him, his wife and children to dress
before escorting them to a local hotel. 'I asked them not to unduly
alarm my wife ... [they] were all the time most courteous to my
wife and myself.'[14] Like many bank managers at the time, Andrews
was a Protestant and might have feared that the IRA would see him
as a loyalist spy.

By now the men in the barracks were aware that an attack was imminent. They had heard men clambering onto nearby roofs. But with no communications, Sergeant Tobias O'Sullivan and the six men under his command had few options. They could have tried to leave but would almost certainly have been mown down on the street without cover. They could have surrendered and hoped for mercy, or they could choose to fight it out and hope to survive until the army in Limerick was alerted, about an hour away. Given the humane treatment afforded the Ballylanders garrison, surrender might have looked a better option. But O'Sullivan was constitutionally unsuited to surrender. He would stand and fight.

On the roof of the house nearest the barracks Seán Forde edged forward with a flash lamp. The men in their attacking positions waited for his signal. Complete fire discipline was maintained. One of the attackers remembered that 'suddenly from the roof top three flashes of light winked out into the night and were instantly answered by the roar of thirty rifles'.[15] As at Ballylanders, lumps of cast iron weighing fifty, sixty, pounds were then hurled onto the roof of the barracks. Each crashed through the slates. 'Into this opening our leader, from the roof, hurled bottle after bottle of petrol.'[16] Mills bombs, homemade grenades and rifle fire were directed at the breach to ignite the fuel. When nothing happened, more bombs and paraffin were poured in. A horse-drawn petrol pump was brought up and more fuel funnelled in through the roof. The fire was soon blazing. IRA men would remember a street hazed in red, the remorseless crack of rifle shots and their own hoarse voices singing the revolutionary anthem 'The Soldier's Song'.

We'll sing a song, a soldier's song,
With cheering rousing chorus,
As round our blazing fires we throng,
The starry heavens o'er us;
And as we wait the morning's light,
Here in the silence of the night,
We'll chant a soldier's song.

123

After two hours of fighting a 'cease fire' order was given. Seán Forde called out for the police to surrender. 'No surrender' came the reply, accompanied by sustained rifle and grenade fire. The grenades brought bricks and dust crashing around the attackers. One IRA account published in the 1950s claims that O'Sullivan asked about surrender during a lull in the fighting but was refused and 'continued a most valiant defence'.[17] As the main barracks became an inferno, O'Sullivan and his men retreated to an outbuilding. 'They fought the fight of heroes,' one IRA account recalled, 'and although we were engaged in a life and death struggle with them, we readily acknowledged the magnificent stand they made in the face of an utterly hopeless situation.'[18] This was some acknowledgement from an organisation which officially regarded the men of the Royal Irish Constabulary as traitors. Another volunteer remembered his personal admiration for those 'who grimly refused to surrender even when the building which they held was consumed and in ruins around them'.[19] There was an echo of the rebels in the blazing GPO in 1916, but separated by a vast chasm in loyalties.

On occasion, in the heat of furious battle, the IRA attackers began to falter under the fierce response from the police. A fire broke out in their rooftop room and was answered with a bucket of water thrown by Seán Forde. The water turned out to be paraffin. Men screamed and cursed. Frantic smothering with wet sacks brought the fire under control. One parched attacker was offered a bottle of water to drink. This too was paraffin. He threatened to kill the man involved.

For five hours the police held out. Two wounded constables who failed to escape to the outhouse were burned to death. But O'Sullivan still refused to give in. He may have hoped that reinforcements would inevitably arrive, particularly as the morning approached. Towards dawn, Liam Scully, the IRA captain from Kerry, stepped into the street in the belief that all the police had withdrawn or were dead. A marksman caught him instantly, the bullet entering his head just below his ear, killing him immediately. The reverberations from his death would be felt back in north Kerry.

With dawn rising and ammunition low the IRA retreated. Kilmallock had held out against a large, well-coordinated IRA attack led by one of its best commanders. The defiant police sergeant O'Sullivan and his surviving men advanced into the street with bayonets drawn. They were spotted by a party of the IRA covering the retreat. A shot rang out and one of the policemen doubled over, struck in the stomach. The attackers vanished.

The stricken Scully was retrieved from the firing line and taken to the bank-cum-dressing station where he was given the last rites. It was thought too risky to take his body home to Kerry, so the next day he was taken to Templeglantine in County Limerick, a few miles from the Kerry border. His brother Bertie was with an IRA unit nearby and remembered being called to a safe house. 'It was bright moonlight but the house was lit up. I hid near the house, expecting a raid, but Chris was watching out for me and called me. I went in. Seán Forde, Paddy Kenneally and another chap were inside. When they told me Liam had been killed the night before in the Kilmallock barracks attack I don't think it surprised me.'[20] Bertie Scully knew the times, and he knew his brother. Forde told him that the death was to be kept secret, probably to keep the Crown forces guessing. It was futile, though, and word reached north Kerry quickly.

Bertie was taken to a farmhouse and followed the others into a kitchen where he saw his brother's body on the table. It was the first time he had seen a dead man. Some volunteers were making a coffin. Bertie was given a tricolour and the contents of his brother's wallet, including a bloodstained map which his brother had used to plan the Kilmallock attack. 'I think it was T. Crowley of East Limerick who afterwards said that "only for him the Barracks would never have been destroyed". This gave me to understand that he had a good deal to do with the planning.'[21] The men had come to the point where death was accepted as part of their days and nights. If they were killed, the burial would most likely be in secret. The rituals of Catholic burial in this part of the country – the wake, the neighbours coming, the crowds at the removal and mass – were forsaken in the interests of safety. Still, for Liam Scully around fifty IRA men converged on Templeglantine cemetery, where he was buried hours after the May evening light went down over the Mullaghareirk mountains. At midnight, after prayers led by three priests, his coffin was lowered into the grave and a volley fired into the air.

Afterwards Bertie Scully took it into his head to go and see the place where his brother had been killed. He made his way across county to Kilmallock, a distance of about twenty-five miles – probably off the main roads, cutting through fields and fording streams to avoid detection. When he reached Kilmallock the local IRA took him to a dugout where he met one of his brother's old comrades. 'I offered to stay with the East Limerick Flying Column but he laughed and said, "We don't want the second one of ye to get killed here".'[22] The man with the friendly advice was killed soon afterwards himself.

The Unionist *Belfast Telegraph* reported the barracks attack in detail, with predictably rapturous praise for the police and a denunciation of the 'devilish work' of the IRA, and describing how a thousand spent cartridges had been found in one house alone, how a rosary had been found next to the burned body of a policeman, and how Sergeant O'Sullivan had survived only because a pocket book above his breast stopped a bullet from entering his heart. A photograph of the surviving police contingent shows Tobias O'Sullivan standing in the centre, his exhausted men on either side. It is tempting to read in a man's expression the effect of traumatic experience. But Sergeant O'Sullivan does not look harrowed in the photograph. Exhausted certainly. But his is the face of a dogged man, one to be feared in battle, a man who had decided he would not take a step backwards in fighting for the Ireland in which he believed.

There are a few lines in one account of the attack which indicate how the IRA came to view the sergeant at Kilmallock. They are significant because they come from one of the most thoughtful of IRA veterans, speaking years afterwards to the military historians. By the time he was interviewed, Seán Moylan was Minister of Education in Éamon de Valera's Fianna Fáil government. His memories of Kilmallock and Tobias O'Sullivan were still vivid. 'His experiences of that fierce night in May seemed to develop in him a mania for vengeance,' said Moylan. 'Shortly afterwards he appeared in Kilmallock with a group of police and soldiers, burned a number of houses and ill-treated a number of townspeople. It was reported to me that he passed between Cork and Limerick with a military party on a number of occasions and many times I lay on that road awaiting him and his party.'[23]

There is no other recorded claim of this alleged incident or of Tobias O'Sullivan abusing civilians in Kilmallock. But in the files of the Bureau of Military History I found evidence of another plot to kill him before he left County Limerick. In the wake of the Kilmallock attack, O'Sullivan published a list of fourteen names wanted for complicity in the operation. One of those, Nicholas O'Dwyer, remarked that 'the RIC Sergeant Sullivan [*sic*] was more responsible than anyone else for the formation of the East Limerick Column which I believe the prototype of all the Flying Columns. When he published the list of fourteen names ... we had no option but to band ourselves together on the run, and take enough ammunition for self-defence from the people who had it – the British Forces.'[24] The quest for vengeance led O'Dwyer and Seán Forde to plan the killing of Tobias O'Sullivan but by the time they had made their plan he 'had been moved on'.[25]

In the House of Commons Lloyd George praised the defence of Kilmallock barracks. The surviving constables were awarded the Police Medal for bravery and Tobias O'Sullivan was promoted to the rank of District Inspector. The defence enhanced his reputation as a fearless leader of men. Where better to send him afterwards than a place where morale had collapsed so much that the RIC had mutinied. In the autumn of 1920 District Inspector Tobias O'Sullivan set out for Listowel determined to face the IRA.

7

Sunshine Elsewhere

If Ireland did not accept them, they did not know it —
and it is in that unawareness of final rejection,
unawareness of being looked at from some secretive,
opposed life, that the Anglo-Irish naive dignity
and even, tragedy seems to me to stand.[1]

Elizabeth Bowen

I

I drive through the half-yellowed trees of October. Moyvane, home parish of Con Brosnan and his descendants, is across the fields to the north. Tarbert and the Shannon are beyond that again, and the Limerick and Cork borders ahead to the east. There are handsome houses along the road, a garden with football posts, a children's trampoline. I drive towards where Kilmorna once stood, five miles east of Listowel: the site of burnings and death during the Civil War. The road here is narrow. There has been no cause for widening in the years since independence. It is a road that still leads to small villages and to other small roads. Not far away is the spot where Mick Purtill saw his friend Mick Galvin shot dead beside him in the spring of 1921, when they ambushed the military. Mick was lucky to make it out alive that day, racing across the fields with the Tans and soldiers close behind.

My people had the comfort of knowing that they belonged to a majority. They had struggled to assert their right to own the land and to establish their country as an independent nation, and they were reassured in their struggle by the strength of their numbers and the teaching of their schoolmasters and priests who declared them the true indigenous Irish: the Gaels who carried the true faith through centuries of oppression. It was a certainty that had grown as the eighteenth century progressed and the fortunes of the Anglo-Irish ebbed ever more swiftly. A community that had survived rebellions, agrarian violence and rapidly changing economic fortunes would be fatally diminished by the aftermath of the Famine and the consequent rise of a strong Catholic landowning class. The war that swept through north Kerry after 1919 foreshadowed their final dispersal.

The first time I visited Kilmorna, it was with my father, and nearly fifty years after the terrible events that occurred there. We walked into a place where newly planted fields, patches of weed, had erased the Anglo-Irish past. Where, my father swore, the Irish crown jewels were hidden but would never be found because the house's owner, Sir Arthur Vicars, had done such a good job of concealing them.

In the beginning Vicars had not been a target of the IRA. To the locals he was just a 'harmless craythur', as my father described him. In 1921, Vicars had been living at 'the Great House' at Kilmorna for over a decade. He was the son of an Indian army officer but had no military inclination himself, being bookish, slightly eccentric and fatally trusting.

As a boy Arthur developed a consuming preoccupation with heraldry, having been convinced that his mother's family lineage stretched back to the earliest Kings of Ireland. He spent his school holidays at the Irish homes of his half-brothers, the Gunn-Mahonys, Protestant landowners with strong nationalist sympathies who had lived at Kilmorna since the mid-1820s. The family's nationalist credentials stretched back to the days of Daniel O'Connell and the campaign for Catholic Emancipation. Later in the century they were closely allied with Charles Stewart Parnell and the Home Rule campaign.

From 1893, Vicars had served in Dublin Castle as Ulster King of Arms, a role which gave him responsibility for the security of the Irish Crown jewels. These were composed of Brazilian stones, diamonds, rubies and emeralds and were the regalia of the Sovereign and Grand Master of the Order of St Patrick – the monarch when they were present, the Lord Lieutenant in their absence. Unhappily for Vicars, on 6 July 1907, just four days before the King and Queen were due to visit Dublin, the jewels vanished.

Sir Arthur Vicars in better days when keeper
of the Irish Crown Jewels

The theft caused apoplexy at Buckingham Palace and scandalised Edwardian Britain. There were rumours that a group of homosexual men were meeting and throwing wild parties in Dublin Castle and that these included Vicars's deputy and friend, Francis Shackleton, brother of the Polar explorer, Ernest, who, in the fullness of time, would be exposed as a scoundrel of extravagant proportions.* Francis Shackleton was almost certainly the thief but the police could never prove it. Vicars was negligent but nothing more – despite claims made in the *Daily Mail* that he had passed a key to the woman reputed to be his mistress. Vicars won the subsequent libel suit against the *Daily Mail* but by this stage he had already lost his job.

Vicars tried in vain to clear his name and would express his resentment at king and government in his last will and testament. 'I might have had more to dispose of,' he wrote bitterly, 'had it not been for the outrageous way in which I was treated by the Irish government over the loss of the Irish crown jewels in 1907, backed up by the late King Edward VII whom I had always loyally and faithfully served.' He claimed to have been scapegoated 'to save other departments' and to shield 'the real culprit and thief Francis R. Shackleton (brother of the explorer who didn't reach the South Pole). My whole life and work was ruined by this cruel misfortune and by the wicked and blackguardly acts of the Irish government.'[2]

To denounce the King was out of character but it reflected the deep personal hurt. There is a hint of Vicars's somewhat other-worldly character in the closing statement of his will where he writes that he had 'hoped to leave a legacy to my dear little dog Ronnie, had he not been taken from me this year – well we shall meet in the next world'.[3]

Vicars loved Kilmorna, with its ivy-covered walls and woodland paths that belonged to a childhood world of fantasy he had never left behind. The house was a mix of faux knight's castle and country

---

* Francis Shackleton was convicted of fraud in a separate case in 1913 and sentenced to fifteen months' hard labour. He subsequently retired to Cheltenham where he worked as an antique dealer.

mansion, composed of three interlinked lodges and set in 600 acres of farmland and forest through which the River Feale flowed on its journey towards the Atlantic. By the time he arrived to live in north Kerry, he was forty-eight years old, still a young man in terms of public service but with no hope of government employment again. He had been rusticated to the country house far earlier than planned: an exile from the Dublin imperial establishment that left him a figure of ridicule. Vicars had neither private wealth nor government pension and, with his wife, depended largely on the munificence of his sister who now owned Kilmorna.

Arthur Vicars may have been broken in spirit but, according to his Irish valet, he was 'a thorough gentleman who always mixed freely with the tenants on the estate'.[4] In 1917, the fifty-five-year-old had married Miss Gertrude Wright, daughter of a County Wicklow Anglo-Irish family. It was a late and childless marriage which seems to have been happy. His wife kept fox terriers and whenever one died, so the local story goes, Lady Vicars would insist 'the workmen dress in black and look solemn'.[5] In the folk memory Vicars is depicted as a kindly man, as evidenced in the recollections gathered for a local magazine more than sixty years after his death:

> There were over 100 local people employed directly or
> indirectly by Sir Arthur, who paid them wages above the
> average for this backward area of Ireland. The old people of
> Kilmorna in my childhood still remembered the huge party that
> was organised for the local children by Sir Arthur at Christmas.
> He loved to ride about the neighbouring farms on horseback.
> He owned the only car in the district and, once or twice a
> week, he would drive to Listowel, handing out produce from
> the Kilmorna gardens and orchards to needy families,
> Protestant and Catholic alike.[6]

He also busied himself in the life of the Protestant Church, helping to restore an historic chapel associated with the nationalist rebel leader Robert Emmet, executed for treason in 1803. Vicars had sympathy with the land and people of Ireland. He also remained, despite his harsh treatment by the late King, an empire loyalist. He did not see a contradiction between an instinctive sense of Irishness and the obligation of loyalty to the monarchy. Well after the outbreak of the War of Independence, Vicars continued to welcome parties of young army officers to Kilmorna to fish for salmon and trout in the River Feale, which flowed through the estate.

Perhaps because he was an outsider to Kerry, a summer visitor schooled and largely reared in England, Vicars was probably not as sensitive as local Protestants to the dangerous possibilities of the revolutionary war. For the established families of north Kerry, mostly descendants of English settlers who had arrived with the Elizabethan and Cromwellian conquests, the IRA hinted at ancestral terrors. These 'Anglo-Irish' had supplanted the old Gaelic lordships and the so-called 'Old English', descendants of the Norman settlers of the twelfth century who had long ago gone over to native ways and held to the Catholic faith, and by the mid-eighteenth century the plantation was securely established. The Trinity-educated doctor, Charles Smith, wrote an account of his travels in the area in the late eighteenth century, a volume of sharply observed social commentary and vivid descriptive prose written from the vantage point of a social improver and aesthete. At Lixnaw, the ancient seat of the earls of Kerry, Smith visited the house of a lord on whose walls were painted copies of 'the celebrated cartoons of Raphael at Hampton Court'.[7] He marvelled at the reproduction of the lame man healed by the apostles Peter and John, with 'figures larger than life'. Elsewhere in the mansion he saw busts of Homer, Virgil, Milton and Pope. To Smith the land of my forebears was waiting to be turned into a paradise for landlords and workers alike. In his words, though expressed in more liberal terms, was the old planter's dream of making Ireland a land fit for English civilisation, the perfect ordered land of those Elizabethan warriors who had carved their bloody way through my childhood stories:

This barony besides the ocean and the River Shannon, hath the advantage of the rivers Feal and Cashin to export and import commodities to and from almost every part of it ... the soil is so naturally rich in most places that it would take but very little manure of any kind to bring it to produce corn ... No people in Europe can have a better opportunity of employing the poor, and improving their country than the gentlemen of estate in Ireland. When they are at their feats every object that presents itself may remind them of these designs: their houses being removed from the tumults of cities, afford them the best opportunity and freedom of observation how their lands may be improved ... and how their tenants are employed, not only among the labouring men, but also among the women, and children, in whose young hands industry ought to be planted, in order to its thriving and taking root the better.[8]

By the time the English traveller Arthur Young arrived in north Kerry in 1762, it was possible to detect a sense of an eclipse fore-told. 'Left Ardfert, accompanying Lord Crosbie to Listowel,' he wrote. 'Called on the way to Lixnaw ... but deserted for ten years past, and now presents so melancholy a scene of desolation, that it shocked me to see it. Everything around lies in ruin and the house itself is going fast off by thieving depredations of the neighbourhood.'[9]

To a people whose footing in the land was insecure, the 'big houses' they built were of paramount psychological importance. They proclaimed the conviction that this Protestant version of Irishness was no alien hybrid to be eradicated, but deep-rooted and enduring. Like Shelley's Ozymandias, the decline of a great house like Lixnaw was a reminder of the transience of all greatness, though not in those days a possibility entertained by the mass of the north Kerry gentry.

Passing through Ballydonoghue, the hinterland of my Purtill fore-bears, Arthur Young went on to the coastal town of Tarbert, which sits where the River Shannon enters the Atlantic. Here he found an altogether more pleasing demesne, the home of Edward Leslie, a liberal Protestant who hosted Benjamin Franklin during his visit to Ireland in 1771, and who supported the cause of Catholic Emancipation. Later visitors to this Arcadian retreat included Charlotte Brontë and Winston Churchill. Young described a house 'on the edge of a beautiful lawn, with a thick margin of full grown wood, hanging on a steep bank to the Shannon, so that the river is seen from the house over the tops of this wood ... The union of wood, water, and lawn forms upon the whole a very fine scene.'[10] Young saw this enlightened Anglo-Irish demesne as the model for Ireland. He marvelled at the atmosphere of industry around Tarbert with one hundred boats bringing turf to Limerick from the bogs of north Kerry and Clare.

II

In my family lore, the Anglo-Irish around Listowel lived in draughty houses, sent their children to boarding schools in England and read the King James Bible. The eldest sons inherited the estate; the younger usually made their way into the army or the imperial civil service, and then there were the inevitable ne'er-do-wells for whom no career could be constructed and who provided a ready supply of gossip for the servants. Protestant Bertha Creagh, who wrote of fin de siècle Anglo-Irish life in the area, recalls one neighbour who was encumbered with the following epitaph: 'He was handsome, a good shot, inoffensive and popular – but whiskey was cheap and there was little else to do.'[11] Writing in the middle of the previous century, William Makepeace Thackeray encountered some of the county bucks on a journey through north Kerry, observing on his coach 'a company of young squires ... and they talked of horse-racing and hunting punctually for three hours, during which time I do believe they did not utter one single word upon any other subject. What a wonderful faculty it is.'[12]

The local Irish that Bertha Creagh encountered on the family estate were usually kindly maids, or ex-soldiers retired from the colonial wars now employed as stable grooms and farm labourers. There would be jolly parties when the Royal Artillery would stop overnight on their way south for gunnery practice, the air filled with the sound of their bugles and the jangling of spurs. Bertha's childhood was dappled and carefree. Her memories evoke a childish wonder at the customs of the Catholic world. Her Irish nurse blessed her with holy water when thunderstorms approached and fell to her knees to pray when the Angelus bell rang. 'Little streams played about and made a happy, gentle music,' she remembered. 'One nursery maid who took me there as a small child told me that if I was not good "Biddy-Bark" who lived behind he trees would carry me off ... there were few things we did not attempt, playing tennis before breakfast which we felt was a "grown up" thing to do, was one of our escapades ... we were allowed to wander about and do what we liked apparently, as long as we kept to ourselves.'[13]

There were exceptions to this exclusivity. The clergyman, Reverend George Fitzmaurice, married his Catholic servant and had twelve children. Winifred O'Connor was nineteen years old and pregnant with his child when they were betrothed. On Sundays he would leave his wife at the Catholic church for mass before going on to take the Protestant service. Years later, a Catholic neighbour would remember the Fitzmaurice family as 'good people even though they were Protestant'.[14] The writer Cyril Kelly could recall his Ulster Protestant grandfather, who married a County Limerick Catholic and came to Listowel as a constable in the RIC, living at 88 Church Street an 'intensely private Protestant man'.[15]

Looking back, it is clear that the age of Protestant supremacy was in a state of terminal decline from around the 1830s, and even earlier there were warnings from the more perceptive observers of the age. Henry Grey Bennet, lawyer and politician, wrote of Irish Catholics in 1803, two years after the Act of Union, that it was 'fallacious to say they are satisfied, because they do not rebel; nor is it true, that the Catholics have always continued quiet and contented ... If ever there were a time in which it became the interest, as it always is the duty, of governments, to watch over the welfare of their subjects, it is surely that in which we live.'[16] Sadly Bennet was a minority voice in the early nineteenth century and he was to leave the scene too early, distracted by grief over the death of his only son and one of his daughters. His career was ruined by a later scandal over claims he tried to seduce a male servant.

The remaining anti-Catholic laws which guaranteed Protestant supremacy were ended. Pressure from Daniel O'Connell's Catholic Association and Repeal movements had led to the disestablishment of the Church of Ireland, while the Irish Land League and relentless economic pressure drastically reduced the size of many Anglo-Irish estates and opened the way for a new Catholic elite.* My Purtill family would have seen the physical decay of the local Protestant church at Lisselton, which by 1917 had been reduced to a simple tower. A visitor remarked on how a 'bonfire having been made of the remains of old coffins inside of the tower, much of the ivy was burned to the obvious improvement of the tower, which stands out as a landmark'.[17]

No longer a political elite, the Protestants of north Kerry were becoming an increasingly marginal social caste. They lacked the Calvinist certainty of the northern Presbyterians, and the crucial numbers and working-class muscle that made the Protestants of Ulster such a formidable foe.

---

* The rise of a powerful conservative Catholic middle class is the most striking feature of the first half of the nineteenth century. It also sets the tone for the future Irish state and its preoccupations. The sons of small businessmen and strong farmers steadily encroached on traditionally Protestant centres of wealth and power. In the cities they moved into business and, gradually, the public service, so that by the middle of the 1860s, Catholics held nearly half of the judges posts in the Irish Supreme Court as well entrenching themselves in the management of public utilities and banks. The stronger farmers were also the main beneficiaries of the breaking up of struggling Anglo-Irish estates in the aftermath of the Famine. For more see Roy Foster, 'Protestant Magic: W. B. Yeats and the Spell of Irish History', Chatterton Lecture, Dec 1989.

One of those who lived through the Anglo-Irish twilight near the Purtills was Horatio Herbert Kitchener, avenger of Gordon of Khartoum and future field marshal. His father had purchased land that became vacant due to the bankruptcy of an Anglo-Irish land-lord and, according to an early account of Kitchener's life, it included 'a little village depopulated by the potato Famine'.[18] Kitchener's father Henry was a man on the make among the embattled estates of the old Anglo-Irish world. The rural hinterland of Listowel offered the prospect of a gentleman's life at a fraction of the cost in England. The Kitcheners arrived in 1850 while the Famine was still killing in north Kerry. They were outsiders. They could trace no lineage to the Elizabethan or Cromwellian plantations. But Anglo-Irish society welcomed them by virtue of their Protestant faith, and the social status incumbent upon Henry Kitchener's former rank of lieutenant colonel. His son Horatio was born at Gunsboro near Ballydonoghue the year they arrived. It appears that the family came under attack from agrarian raiders at some point in the 1850s. A fawning article in the local press, published half a century later, described how the brave lieutenant colonel had single-handedly fought off the gunmen. 'Mr. Kitchener during his residence at Gunsboro was most popular in the district,' wrote the *Kerry Evening Post*.

He may have been less popular with his son, at least as a young boy. Horatio was remembered with pity by locals because of his strict rearing. Bertha Creagh recalled how the young Kitchener was forced to walk his father's cattle to market, an unusual and humbling requirement for the offspring of the landholding class. A local story has it that the owner of the Listowel Arms was instructed by Kitchener Senior not to provide his son with breakfast until all the cattle were sold. On another occasion Horatio is reputed to have used his cane to strike a farm labourer. The youth then knocked Kitchener from his horse with a blow. It was remembered, to his credit in the locality, that he did not have the young man sacked or prosecuted.

Another story, collected by my grandfather, reflects the easy co-mingling of Catholic beliefs and the spirit world of pre-Christian

Ireland. In the tale, Kitchener's mother is reviled for her alleged anti-Catholicism and put under a spell which moves her ear to her mouth and vice versa. Although the family left north Kerry when Kitchener was fourteen, his papers in the National Archives in London reveal a continuing connection. There is a poignant letter from the daughter of the famous soldier's old nurse, Elizabeth Fitzgerald. The family was near destitution as the grand demesnes around Listowel shrank after the Land War and so the demand for labour decreased. The poorly written missive sits among bundles of letters of congratulation, telegrams from maharajas, pashas, princes, aristocrats, town councillors and fellow officers. The tone of the letter is frequently ingratiating but, in Miss Fitzgerald's words, there is also an air of due entitlement. After detailing the sickness and unemployment that plagued the family she writes that she 'expects a favourable reply by Christmas'.[19] Kitchener's response is not recorded. He returned only once, in 1910, when he walked the grounds of his father's old estate at Crotta between Listowel and Tralee.

The church at Aghavillen, where he was baptised, had already fallen into ruin. Would the great warrior of empire have seen in this fading community any hint of a wider imperial faltering? Probably not. It is only with hindsight that we can see how the long Irish revolution, from mass campaigning around religion and land in the nineteenth century, to the hour of the gun in the twentieth, represented the beginning of the end of empire. The soldiers of the Edwardian age still saw a red splendour splashed across the frontiers of the globe.

Yet the Anglo-Irish would be the first of the former elites in the modern British Empire to feel history turn away from them, and like others who would follow them many felt alienated from the land of their distant English ancestors, many feeling they were accepted neither in Ireland nor England.

The best days were gone. As the novelist Elizabeth Bowen, a Protestant from County Cork, put it, the old days were 'like sunshine elsewhere or firelight in an empty room'.[20]

Southern Irish Protestantism was more complex than a morality tale of a stranded monolithic elite. There were working-class Protestants in Dublin, like the playwright and Republican socialist Seán O'Casey, the middle-class W. B. Yeats who defined the Revolution in poetry, and the novelist turned gun-smuggler and Republican, Erskine Childers, whose mother was Anglo-Irish and who had himself fought in the Boer War and Great War, one of the many Protestants who, over centuries, lived in and imagined a very different Ireland. In west Cork communities of smaller Protestant farmers would have confounded any attempt to define them as an elite, and in west Limerick, with some straggling over the border into north Kerry, the descendants of German Palatines lived a frugal rural life that differed little in substance from their Catholic neighbours.*

But in the north Kerry countryside of the War of Independence the families who had once formed a genuine elite – the people of the 'big houses' – faced a choice that allowed no nuance: they could support a republic when weapons or supplies were demanded, or be regarded as enemies. To display loyalty to the Crown invited attack. To their more militant co-religionists in the north of Ireland, the Protestants around Listowel would have been regarded as soft Unionists, unwilling to risk their lives by fighting to defend a British Ireland. The local demographics dictated extreme caution. There were never more than a few hundred Protestants living around Listowel, not sufficient to form an entrenched political bloc, much less paramilitary units like the Ulster Volunteer Force that would have fought against the IRA or threatened Britain with rebellion.

---

* The Palatines were German Protestant refugees from the European wars of religion of the early seventeenth century. Around 3,000 came to Ireland, although two-thirds are estimated to have subsequently returned. They were welcomed by Protestant landlords who saw them as industrious tenants and a potential bulwark against the Catholic majority. The largest area of settlement was around Rathkeale in County Limerick, with some families moving also to north Kerry, among them the Hoffmans whose descendant Frank fought with the IRA and was killed by the Black and Tans in 1920.

There was no working-class Unionist muscle toiling in the lands of north Kerry, or charismatic leaders like Edward Carson urging the Protestants to follow a course of resistance.

Most Protestants in the area would probably have been privately loyal to the existing order. During the Great War many had relatives serving with the British Army. To many of these Irish people, the Rising of 1916 was an act of betrayal and they had no reason to believe the flare-up of violence would not end like the others. There would be outrages, but in due course order would be restored and a peaceful political settlement with moderate Home Rulers could be achieved. Despite the evidence of the 1918 election, the Sinn Féiners continued to be dismissed as trouble-makers who would be sorted out in due course.

At Kilmorna, Sir Arthur Vicars carried on with life as in pre-war days. Young army officers continued to cycle out from Listowel to his estate to fish the waters of the Feale. He was glad of the company. But then Vicars made what would prove a fatal miscalculation. In May 1920, the IRA arrived at Kilmorna looking for guns. Vicars refused to open his strong room. The IRA suspected that he was holding a stockpile of weapons for local loyalists: why else would he need such a powerfully built safe and refuse to admit them? They would remember his obduracy.

8

Assassins

In the morning I shall part from all that is human.
I shall follow the warrior band;
Go to thy house, stay not here,
The end of the night is at hand.

Kuno Meyer, 'The Tryst After Death', translated from
the ancient Irish, 1911[1]

I

The special correspondent of the *Yorkshire Post* remembered him as a 'big, bluff, hearty Irishman, with a bucolic face which radiated good nature ... [who] might easily have been unsuspected of any subtlety of thought'.[2] He also remembered that 'since his exploits at Kilmallock Barracks', O'Sullivan 'knew he was a marked man'.[3] Later that same day the reporter dramatically changed his mind about O'Sullivan's lack of mental subtlety. O'Sullivan had taken a lift in the direction of Limerick with the journalist and his colleagues, driving in a touring car along the main road leading west. Outside Newcastlewest the car skidded and crashed into a deep ditch and the 'shattered windscreen and the thorny hedge inflicted some rather severe cuts and scratches on the hands and faces of the occupants'. It was a close thing. Had the car overturned, the Inspector and his fellow travellers might have died. What transpired next puzzled the English journalist. The policeman looked in the car mirror and declared that he would return to Listowel.

'If I go into Limerick in this state the news will go round like quickfire that Inspector O'Sullivan's been seen bleeding, and that there's been an attempt on his life. It doesn't do to suggest such a thing, and to let the people round here realise that you're human, that you're vulnerable, and that you can bleed.' O'Sullivan flagged down a passing police lorry and began his journey back to Listowel 'with a laughing farewell'.

O'Sullivan arrived in the late autumn of 1920 as the war around north Kerry was descending into a cycle of ambush and reprisal.

The British correspondent Hugh Martin visited Listowel in October and recorded evidence of attacks by the Black and Tans on local civilians. A girl from near the town had had her hair cropped by the IRA for the crime of 'keeping company' with the Tans. In

Rose McNamara, a captain in Cumann na mBan,
in uniform

retaliation the Tans staged night raids on the homes of the suspects. 'In return for the cropping of one girl's hair,' wrote Martin, 'they cropped the hair of four others, beat six young men with the stocks of their rifles till they were black and blue, burnt several ricks and set a creamery on fire.'[4] His reporting would bring death threats, with the Tans reportedly seeking him out at local hotels. Martin was a journalist of considerable courage. From Listowel on 28 October he wrote: 'The touring season is over. Otherwise you might find tourists returning from the South-West of Ireland in a mood that might shock even the Chief Secretary. For to pretend that there is no general police terror there is sheer hypocrisy. Why not admit at once that circumstances have made it expedient to employ terror as a form of government, and have done with furtive humanitarianism.'[5]

Around Listowel, the women of Cumann na mBan were increasingly active. A lone country girl like Hannah Purtill could easily smuggle a revolver through roadblocks, since at that time the police did not employ female searchers. The gun that killed could be smuggled past several police and army posts within an hour of the attack. But with the Tans and the Auxies deployed in the town, Hannah's activities became ever more dangerous. Towards the end of 1920 Cumann na mBan ordered its members to carry out 'detective work' for the IRA. The British intercepted this dispatch. They now knew that women were infiltrating the communications networks, with one intelligence officer complaining that the 'postal and telegraph services were corrupt, and the telephone services equally so, whilst instances of Government services and members of the Crown Forces giving information to the enemy have, unfortunately, not been lacking'.[6] My grandmother told one of her daughters how she transported communiqués and other information hidden in her underwear. The IRA operated without the field telephones of regular armies and few households had telephone lines installed. Plans, lists of personnel, names of suspected informers were committed to paper and sent by courier. For the British, such documents captured from the IRA could be vital intelligence.

One notorious Tan named Darcy took a particular interest in Hannah. He would come into the draper's shop where she worked and flirt with her, calling her his 'Maid of the Mountains'. Each evening when she passed the roadblock he invariably stopped her. Hannah Purtill, engaged to be married to Bill Keane, was a conservative rural woman, but she could not afford to antagonise a Tan. She was polite in the face of his advances but nothing more. Darcy persisted. When she emphatically refused him he pulled a gun and placed it to her forehead. Years later she told one of my aunts what transpired. 'He said: "If you don't get out of town you will be killed". But she didn't go. Later the IRA targeted Darcy. He was badly wounded and it was he who ended up leaving Listowel.

Fearful and disunited, the RIC were being increasingly asked to operate like an army but without the protection afforded by well-defended military bases or the mandate for offensive action granted to soldiers in war. They were still required to observe the fiction of being a civil police force acting with the support of the people, but with every reprisal such public support as existed drained away. The RIC was by now a messy amalgam of Black and Tans, Auxiliaries and Irish constables, the latter sometimes the fiercest supporters of reprisals against men who killed their comrades. Senior officers thought to be resistant to harsh counter-measures were retired.

The Republicans did not need wholesale defections of RIC men who disagreed with the Crown's policies in Ireland. A handful of figures in key posts in Dublin Castle and the major barracks could compromise police and military operations with devastating effect. Men who were dismissed or resigned in sympathy with the rebels were offered financial support by the underground government. Some were set to work fomenting instability in the ranks. After the Listowel mutiny, Jeremiah Mee fled to Dublin and made contact with the IRA. He then made a secret trip back to Listowel with two colleagues, under instruction from Michael Collins to try and instigate a mass walk-out of Irish police from the barracks. Four of the original mutineers were still stationed in Listowel but, as a form of punishment, were 'invariably detailed to go with the Black and Tans on midnight raids which involved the burning of farm buildings, creameries and homesteads, and the beating up of civilians'.[7]

In his memoir Mee made much of the drama of his return to Listowel: he was now a mutineer and a deserter and was sure of rough treatment if captured. At their initial meeting in July 1920, Collins had told him that the remaining four mutineers should be instructed to form an underground force within the Listowel RIC, supplying intelligence to the IRA. Three men agreed and the secret conduit was apparently successful until two of the men were suspended and told they would face court martial. Confidential police files had been found on an IRA man near Listowel and the mutineers were natural suspects. If an escape plan was not possible, Mee was to pass on a message from Collins that 'in any sacrifice they might be called upon to make they would have the sympathy and support of the nation'.[8] Some small comfort when being caught could mean facing the gallows.

At Listowel railway station, Mee saw a police patrol monitoring passengers and managed to evade detection with the help of a sympathetic porter. Next he went to a pub near my grandparents' house on Church Street to meet his IRA contact. The pub was full of Tans and RIC, but newcomers mostly, so Mee's brief appearance was not noted. He was led upstairs to safety. The plan to form a police underground unit came to nothing. Word came back from the recently suspended District Inspector (the man replaced by Tobias O'Sullivan) that Jeremiah Mee 'should leave Listowel at once' because if he were arrested he 'would be shot like a dog'.[9]

Mee left Listowel on 31 October. Years later, he would remember the lowing of cattle arriving at the market in the early morning as he prepared to set off. The calm was illusory. North Kerry was about to erupt in the worst violence yet seen in the county. The terrors to come would harden hearts on both sides. Men were set on a journey into the worst parts of themselves.

On the day Mee left Listowel, the country witnessed one of the biggest funerals in its history. The Sinn Féin Lord Mayor of Cork,

Terence MacSweeney, had died after seventy-four days on hunger strike in Brixton prison, London. His body was brought home to Cork where the crowds stretched far and deep in the city's streets.* The following day an eighteen-year-old medical student, Kevin Barry, was hanged in Dublin for his part in an IRA ambush which killed three British soldiers. Barry was a past pupil of the Jesuit Belvedere College (James Joyce's alma mater) and a son of the Catholic middle classes, who went to mass on his way to the ambush. He became the first Republican to be executed since the 1916 Rising and was immediately propelled into the pantheon of nationalist martyrs. The three soldiers killed in the ambush – Privates Harold Washington, Thomas Humphries and Marshall Whitehead – were scarcely a couple of years older than Barry, but they were forgotten victims in an unpopular war where the insurgents excelled at propaganda. 'Another martyr for old Ireland, another murder for the Crown,' went the popular ballad which summoned up images of Barry's grief-stricken mother but assured the listener that his death was part of the sacrifice necessary to secure the Republic.

The violence that followed into the first week of November 1921 was a racing fire. Strike and counter-strike, the well of bitterness full to overflowing. In north Kerry, and several other parts of the country, IRA units were sent out to avenge the deaths of MacSweeney and Barry. Two Black and Tans were kidnapped on the day of the MacSweeney funeral after being lured by local girls. The men were killed and their bodies 'disappeared' by the IRA. Believing their

---

* MacSweeney's predecessor as Lord Mayor, Tomás MacCurtain, was shot by off-duty RIC men the previous March, as revenge for the IRA shooting of a policeman. To avenge MacCurtain, Michael Collins ordered the killing of RIC District Inspector Oswald Swanzy, whom an RIC informant had blamed for the assassination. Swanzy was shot dead in Lisburn, County Armagh, on 22 August 1920 by a gunman using MacCurtain's own pistol. Just as was the case with the killing of Lieutenant Colonel Ferguson Smyth, the Swanzy assassination was followed by days of anti-Catholic rioting and the expulsion of Catholics from their homes and workplaces. The charred body of a Catholic man was found in a burned factory.

comrades to be still alive, the Tans posted a chilling notice in Tralee, the largest town in north Kerry:

> Warning ! Unless the two Tralee police in Sinn Fein custody are returned by 10 a.m. on the 2nd inst., reprisals of a nature not yet heard of in Ireland will take place in Tralee.[10]

They rampaged through Tralee, burning shops and shooting randomly. The nationalist *Weekly Freeman's Journal* reported how 'many people rushed panic-stricken to their homes, and others took refuge in neighbour's houses'.[11] For seven days the population was terrorised and subjected to curfew. The British journalist Hugh Martin found that he was on a Tan death list because of his earlier reporting of events near Listowel. His analysis of the Tralee terror was remarkably fair-minded given his situation:

> The police in Ireland are themselves the victims of a condition of terrorism which is only equalled by the condition of terrorism that they themselves endeavour to impose. They are, for the most part, quite young men who have gone through the experience, at once toughening and demoralizing, of fighting through a long and savage war. They are splendid soldiers and abominably bad policemen. They are unsuitably and inadequately officered, quite insufficiently trained for their special duties, and expected to keep sober in nerve-racking circumstances in a country where drink is far more plentiful and potent than in England.[12]

Two days later an IRA ambush at Ballyduff, about five miles from the Purtill homestead, led to the death of a Black and Tan and the wounding of several others. In retaliation the Tans descended on the village and stormed the house of James Houlihan, an IRA volunteer who had taken part in the ambush. He had decided not to stay at home but his younger brother John was not so fortunate, as James later described:

After surrounding the house, the Tans broke in the doors and windows, searched the house, and found my brother, John, in bed upstairs. They seized him, not giving him time to dress, pulled him downstairs and out the side of the road, placed him against a ditch and riddled him with bullets. As he was dying, he moaned, after which one of the Tans approached and drove a bayonet through his body. They had previously dragged my mother out onto the roadside to witness the shooting ...
Having shot my brother the Tans proceeded to the village where they looted several shops and set fire to a number of buildings.[13]

One of the mutinous Listowel constables, Michael Kelly, later told the American commission of inquiry that 'in command of the party that night was District Inspector Tobias O'Sullivan who was in charge of the RIC and Black and Tans stationed at Listowel'.[14] But he was not present himself and his dating of the incident is out by almost a month: Kelly said that the killing of John Houlihan had taken place 'around 5 October' when in fact it was on 1 November. Tobias O'Sullivan might have been there, but apart from Kelly's statement there is no other documented reference to his presence. His brother James's account of the reprisal refers to 'eight lorry loads of Tans' and does not place the District Inspector at the scene, although he does mention the later fate of Tobias O'Sullivan.[15]

On the same day as the Houlihan killing two more police were abducted after they had been accused of 'interfering with the congregation leaving church after devotions' in Ballylongford.[16] It appears the two had attempted to search people leaving evening prayers. Ballylongford already had a bad name with the Crown forces. At the very start of the Troubles the army was humiliated there when the IRA frustrated its attempts to stop a Gaelic League concert. There had been attacks on the police and raids for arms.

The two men, Constable William Muir, a Black and Tan, and James Coughlan, from the regular RIC, were unarmed, as were the IRA men who overpowered them. Among the IRA group was

Ballylongford local Brian O'Grady, who would become a comrade in arms of Con Brosnan and Mick Purtill through the years that followed. Con Brosnan also took part in the operation with a unit from his home village of Newtownsandes. Coughlan was brought to a house in the village where he suffered savage beatings and feared he was going to be executed. Muir was taken to a townland outside Ballylongford. It was a small stretch of country but, search as they might, the police could not find their men. It was only when the Tans threatened reprisals against the local population in Ballylongford that the IRA released the prisoners – Muir within twenty-four hours and Coughlan after three days. Coughlan was apparently so badly beaten, after having been dragged blindfolded for miles across country, that a local doctor said he had 'never seen a man in such a condition. He was black and blue from head to foot'.[17] But it was William Muir who suffered the greatest trauma. He committed suicide about five weeks after being released. The army court of inquiry heard that Muir 'was, on his return, in a nervous and shaky condition, he became silent and would only speak when spoken to'.[18] He cut his throat with a razor in Ballylongford RIC barracks on 27 December 1920. Was the dead man an already traumatised ex-soldier, driven to the brink by his abduction, or broken by physical or psychological torture at the hands of the IRA? Nobody told.* But the abductions added to the picture of Ballylongford as bandit country and the brutality meted out to Muir and Coughlan would have enraged the police. The word from RIC headquarters in Listowel was that a crackdown was imminent. A spy warned of shooting and burning to come.

---

* Con Brosnan told the Bureau of Military History that he had helped guard the prisoner at Newtownsandes and that he was released after the intervention of the local parish priest. Brian OGrady went to Newtownsandes to secure Coughlan's release but told the BMH that 'the local company captain [Brosnan's commanding officer] would not release him without a note from the Brigade O/C'. See Witness Statement 1,390, BMH.

II

The first mention of Tobias O'Sullivan in local IRA accounts describes him leading a raid on Ballylongford at the end of November 1920, soon after his arrival in Listowel. That night, 22 November, there was a hard frost on the ground and a full moon, the kind of weather where sound travels far and moving targets are easier to spot. The only witness accounts come from surviving IRA members, but they are consistent. One man remembered how 'several lorries of RIC and Tans arrived and began a house-to-house search in Ballylongford, adjourning from time to time to visit public houses which they looted, eventually becoming almost mad from drink. In the streets they assaulted everyone they met and fired several thousand rounds of ammunition.'[19] Houses were burned, a creamery, sawmills and shops. The local IRA was caught without weapons to defend the village as they had been dumped outside the village a week earlier to avoid searches.

While one IRA party went to recover weapons several men hid behind a wall about quarter of a mile from Ballylongford. Footsteps approached, which they took to be those of other IRA men. One of them, Eddie Carmody, called out: 'They are the lads.' But stepping into the road he saw a party of Black and Tans. 'He turned and ran,' recalled a comrade, '[but] the Tans opened fire, shooting him in the back. He managed to throw himself across a low wall in front of the doctor's house. The Tans immediately raided the doctor's house but found nothing there. As they were leaving they found Carmody behind the wall, pulled him out on the road and shot him dead on the spot.'[20]

Brian O'Grady was also present in Ballylongford and had to jump into the bitterly cold waters of a tidal river to swim to safety. 'I was fired on by a party of Tans from the behind the creamery,' he remembered. 'During all this, the people, especially the women, were terrified. They went through a terrible ordeal.'[21]

The terror in Kerry was overshadowed by an extraordinary spasm of violence in Dublin. On the day after the Ballylongford raid, the IRA launched dawn missions against men Michael Collins had identified as British intelligence agents living outside military barracks. Fourteen were shot dead and another died of his wounds.[22] Two civilians were also killed. Later that day, in reprisal, the police opened fire on spectators at a Gaelic football match in Dublin. Fourteen people, including women and children, were killed in what became known as 'Bloody Sunday'. The IRA killers were led by the so-called 'Squad', a group of assassins who worked directly for Collins and offered him their total loyalty. They established a reputation for ruthlessness which set the example for many IRA gunmen around the country. Several of the Squad would later achieve notoriety under very different conditions in north Kerry.

What happened in Ballylongford would have been enough to make District Inspector O'Sullivan a priority target. But threatening talk had been mounting from the moment he arrived in north Kerry. To the IRA he was the O'Sullivan who killed Liam Scully at Kilmallock; O'Sullivan sent in by the Castle to take control after the mutiny. There was another possible reason for his becoming a priority target in the eyes of the IRA leadership in Dublin.

The death of Liam Scully was only one legacy of Kilmallock. But Scully was gone; nothing could be done but to avenge him in due course. There were the living IRA men to worry about. The man who led the raid on Kilmallock barracks, Seán Forde, was alive but had been arrested in Cork. Just before Christmas 1920, two weeks after the burning of Cork city centre by the Auxies, Forde was caught by the Tans. By now he was one of the IRA's most senior and aggressive operatives in Munster and his face was probably known to police in the Kilmallock area. He had been in Cork to collect weapons and ammunition. But the Tans stopped him on the street and found bullets in his pocket. He tried to make a run for it but was on unfamiliar ground. Another party of Tans cornered him in an alleyway and beat and tortured him. He was asked about Seán Forde. 'They questioned me. I gave all sorts of names – the usual thing ... I told them I had heard about him but that I heard his health had broken down and that he had gone to America. He [the policeman] said, "It must have been very recently. He was in some ambush – I think it was Glenacurrane – only a week ago.'"[23]

The prisoner was charged with attempted murder and possession of ammunition. The attempted murder charge would be difficult to sustain. Forde represented himself at the court martial and argued that he prevented a Tan from murdering him. The two fought hand to hand, with the Tan firing the only shots, before the fight was broken up and Forde arrested. In his cell in Cork he was sure he would escape murder charges as long as nobody could positively identify him as the leader of the raid on Kilmallock barracks, plus several other attacks in County Limerick. To the arresting Tans he was just another IRA man. Forde was sent on remand to prison on Spike Island, a military base in the middle of Cork harbour.

But HQ in Dublin feared that Forde might be identified. According to his own account, captured British dispatches revealed that 'a man answering the description of Seán Forde was a prisoner in Spike Island and that DI Sullivan of Listowel, who was made a DI after his defence of Kilmallock barracks and transferred to Listowel would be able to identify him'.[24] There were concerns over other prisoners as well. There was a precedent. RIC men from Limerick had been brought to Dublin to identify a prominent Republican, not in custody, the previous September. They misidentified and a police death squad executed the wrong man. Forde later testified that an order was sent from one of the most senior IRA commanders in Dublin for Tobias O'Sullivan to be killed. The decision to set a plan in motion was taken at an IRA battalion council meeting in December 1920.

It was a potentially suicidal mission: to attack the most senior police officer in Listowel, in daylight, near a barracks crowded with RIC, Tans, army and Auxiliaries. There was also the strong likelihood of reprisals as the brutal days of late October and early November had shown in north Kerry. The IRA knew precisely what could be wrought upon the civilian population by such an audacious attack.

After an RIC District Inspector was shot in County Clare in September 1920 there had been counter-attacks on several local towns. Twenty-six buildings were razed and four people killed.

Yet the IRA also knew that as well as alienating the public, reprisals were creating growing unease in Britain itself. In October 1920, the same month that O'Sullivan was leading the police raid on Ballylongford, Sir Oswald Mosley asked Prime Minister Lloyd George whether the 'promiscuous reprisals'[25] in Ireland enjoyed government support. He also called for a sworn public inquiry. A few days later Mosley stressed that he supported the army's work in Ireland. Indeed, he had a close relative serving there. His implied targets were the Black and Tans and Auxiliaries. 'Famous regiments, that for generations past have performed most magnificent services to this country, are to-day labouring under certain imputations – imputations which I have every reason to believe are unjust,' Mosley charged. 'They are shouldering the guilt of others. It is only fair to the troops actually engaged in Ireland that the matter should be sifted and that we should know who are guilty of the outrages.'[26] Mosley went further, adding the incendiary claim that reprisals were worse than German behaviour in Belgium at the start of the First World War and more reminiscent of 'the pogrom of the more barbarous Slav'.[27] The latter reference is tainted with historic irony. Mosley would later become leader of the British fascists, who tried to terrorise the streets of London's Jewish East End.

III

Volunteers were sought for Tobias O'Sullivan's assassination. The call was heard by all the men of the north Kerry IRA, including my great-uncle Mick Purtill and his friend Con Brosnan. There was no rush to respond. As Brosnan later drily recalled: 'Some time elapsed before anyone volunteered.'

It was a month, according to another witness, before anybody came forward. Eventually Con Brosnan and three other men from his parish – Dan O'Grady, Jack Sheehan and First Lieutenant Jack Ahern – volunteered to shoot the District Inspector. Con had never killed before. His comrades likewise. His family was devout and respectable. Nor did he have any real experience of the heat of battle. He would be woefully unprepared if the police and army arrived on the scene. His teachers and priests had taught that killing was a mortal sin. At school he learned that Irishmen had fought for their King across the empire. The curriculum was still set by civil servants trained and paid by Dublin Castle. Except that Con also learned, at meetings of the IRB, in the ranks of the Volunteers, that Irishmen had fought the English for centuries. His consciousness had been shaped by inherited narratives of oppression, famine and dispossession; of the Fenian rising and the Land War; and by the immediate circumstances of that Christmas of 1920, when men he knew had already been killed and tortured by the Black and Tans. The great national cause had become local and personal. Brosnan was told by the IRA battalion commander that O'Sullivan had killed Liam Scully at Kilmallock. Con Brosnan's son, Gerry, was in no doubt that the killing of Scully had made O'Sullivan a target. 'He was after shooting a Kerryman … the Moyvane men decided they would do it.'[28]

Closer still was the death of Eddie Carmody near Ballylongford in November. In Con Brosnan's telling, and that of his fellow assassins, the killing of Tobias O'Sullivan was a settling of several scores. Jack Ahern, a twenty-two-year-old farmer's son, remembers that the shooting of Eddie Carmody 'put new life into the company here and the men … were very anxious to avenge his death'.[29] Motives abounded and the moral restrictions that prevented ordinary men from killing had been swept away in the terrible atmosphere of late 1921 when the pitch of attack and fierce reprisal had permeated life across north Kerry. Men had crossed over to where violence was normalised, a crowded, claustrophobic hellish island. The orders had come from above, the motivation from within. Now it was left to the assassins to make their plan.

Hats off to Brosnan, our midfield wonder
He's par excellence in feet and hands
Oh where's the Gael can pull down the number
Of Kerry's idol from Newtownsandes.
(Kerry ballad, 1924)[30]

When I was growing up Con Brosnan was a legendary name in Kerry, not for anything related to the wars but for his Gaelic footballing prowess, the most important talent a man could possess in any part of the county. It was said by my father that Con Brosnan helped to heal the wounds of the Civil War through bringing men from opposing factions onto the same team. Brosnan captained Kerry and won six All-Ireland medals. He was a welcome figure in my uncle John B's public house on William Street and in the home of his old comrade Mick Purtill. They shared the experience of a war about which the town did not usually speak. Along with everybody else in the area they observed the rituals of 1916 remembrance at Easter, but beyond that their memories of war remained private.

There is an expression in Ireland that says somebody looks 'shook'. It is both literal and highly evocative. A man is shaken, made frail and older-looking by the travails of life. As Con Brosnan aged there came dark periods when the smile receded and melancholy took hold. Nobody knew it in the Listowel of my childhood, but Con Brosnan did tell some of his story of the war to the interviewers from the Bureau of Military History. Like all of the other veterans who participated he knew that his words would only be read by the public long after he was dead. Distance might help the Irish people better understand the terrible things that had happened.

The first attempt on the life of Tobias O'Sullivan was made in late December 1920 under cover of darkness. Con Brosnan and Dan O'Grady joined several others and prepared to ambush the District Inspector on his way home at teatime. But a scout came and told them O'Sullivan had 'ceased to go home to his tea and [is] probably having it in the barracks'.[31] The plan was deferred.

Then towards the turn of the year something happened in Listowel which deepened hostility towards the police.

John Lawlor was a seventeen-year-old trainee priest home on holidays from the seminary in Dublin. The local parish priest, Father Dennis O'Connor, had known him for two years as a 'quiet and law abiding youth'.[32] The records give different dates. On the afternoon of 31 December, or 1 January, John Lawlor was walking in Listowel when he was stopped by a Tan patrol. He had troublesome family connections. Lawlor's father was the parish clerk and a prominent Sinn Féin supporter. His age also made him a likely candidate for police harassment. The civilian witnesses who later testified to the army court of inquiry all told a similar story: Lawlor was stopped by the Tans, surrounded and then beaten with the butt of a rifle.

> The police surrounded him. I saw him struck on the head with the butt end of a rifle. He fell, afterwards he got up and ran away ...
>
> I saw a policeman strike him in the face with his hand and another hit him on the back of the head with the butt end of his rifle. He fell – A policeman told us to move on and we saw no more ...
>
> He put his hands up and the next thing I saw him falling down. I did not actually see the blow struck as I was too far away ...
>
> He said: 'Oh! My head, Oh! My back.' He was bleeding from the mouth.[33]

Five witnesses testified to the beating of John Lawlor. The parish priest said he had found him on Market Street 'and he told me he was sore all over his body, especially his head because of a beating'.[34] The next Father O'Connor saw of the youth was when he was called to give him the last rites that evening. 'I found him drowsy and not inclined to speak much.' A local doctor, Timothy Buckley, testified that he found a cut with bruising on the right side of Lawlor's head and cuts inside the mouth. He agreed with the army doctor that Lawlor died from a brain haemorrhage caused by 'an external injury to the right side of the head'.[35]

However, Tobias O'Sullivan stood by his men and denied that Lawlor had been struck. 'I can find no evidence that any of the men under my command were in collision with civilians on the 1st Jan. 1921,' he declared. 'I examined the men on patrol duty that night and found no persons to support the truth of that rumour. I reported the matter and asked for an inquiry into it.'[36]

Two more policemen repeated the denial. Unlike Tobias O'Sullivan they had been present. A Sergeant William Watson said that after being searched, Lawlor 'was ordered to go home, and he proceeded in the direction of his home. There were six other constables and myself present. I saw no blow struck.'[37] The court of inquiry found that Lawlor died as a result of a blow from 'person or persons unknown' but that 'no blame attaches in the matter to the Military authorities or to any member thereof'.[38] The local army commander, Captain John Bidwell Watson of the Loyal North Lancashire Regiment, the veteran of the Great War in East Africa, commanded the court of inquiry. After the miseries of German East Africa he would have seen Listowel as a comparatively benign place when the troops first arrived the previous year. He was respected in the town, having put at least one of his soldiers on a charge for stealing ciga-rettes. But by now Watson knew where real power lay. Not with the army or with politicians in distant Westminster, but with the RIC and the local command of the Auxiliaries. He declared the witness evidence unreliable 'as the wound is on the right side of the head and not the back where the blow is said to have been struck'.

The police were not officially blamed but a note scribbled on the official file says responsibility for the death lay 'probably with the RIC'. The police had killed young Lawlor and everyone knew it. That was the nature of the war in Ireland in 1920–1. In the spirit of rampant viciousness of that winter, the Tans later shot Lawlor's father's cow as he brought it to pasture.

Three weeks later the IRA decided to try again to kill Tobias O'Sullivan.

In the days before, Con Brosnan and the rest of the killing squad were each given a revolver and seven or eight rounds of ammunition. None of the men tasked with killing the District Inspector had fired at a living target before. They took a single practice shot each to test the weapons and ammunition. For such inexperienced men to be sure of killing they needed to be close to O'Sullivan. The chances of getting killed, wounded, or caught and subsequently executed were high. The District Inspector was known to have bodyguards who accompanied him to and from the barracks every day. Con Brosnan recalled that they 'had been informed of his movements by a number of scouts in Listowel who had been put on his trail as soon as the order was received'.[39]

Two brothers, Robert and Patrick McElligott, ran the intelligence operation. Read nearly ninety years afterwards, Paddy McElligott's account of the planning of the killing is chillingly spare. 'I supplied a detailed account of O'Sullivan's movements to my brother who planned the execution,'[40] he said. He did not reveal who supplied the detailed timings of Tobias O'Sullivan's walks to and from his home near the barracks. But whoever was keeping the daily watch sealed his fate as surely as the gunmen.

The IRA was by now confident that the majority of locals could be depended on to stay silent. Rising resentment of the Crown forces and the fear of being labelled a spy deterred all but the bravest, most financially desperate, or foolhardy, from passing on intelligence. As in every war there were many who privately wished the killing and the disruption of their lives would end. But such words could easily be interpreted as disloyal and cast suspicion. There were loyalists in and around Listowel. Most were Protestants or landed gentry, but not exclusively. An IRA volunteer derisively remarked of Charles Street that it was 'well known for the pro-British type of people living in it'. By this he meant ex-servicemen, and police and military families. James Kane, a former RIC sergeant who lived on the town square, was viewed with suspicion. He was a fisheries inspector and his job was to catch poachers, an occupation that linked him with the courts system and which required him to patrol stretches of the River Feale. Who knew what he saw and reported on his patrols? Then there was Paul Sweetnam, the agent for Lord Listowel, who mixed freely with the military and traversed the countryside with a watchful eye. And Sir Arthur Vicars, who hosted fishing parties for young officers of the Crown.

On the night of 19 January, Jack Ahern stayed at Con Brosnan's house in Newtownsandes. The two other north Kerry IRA men, Dan O'Grady and Jack Sheehan, were at their own homes. Brosnan and Ahern made their way into Listowel separately the following morning at about ten o'clock, Brosnan by bicycle. It was one of the mildest Januaries on record. There was no ice or frost. Con would have felt the wind on his face as he pedalled down the road, the fields stretching before him towards the mountains and the sea.

In Listowel it was market day. There would already have been crowds of farmers and travelling salesmen on the streets. Around noon the four IRA men met at Stack's, a public house about a hundred yards from the barracks and directly beside O'Sullivan's home. According to Ahern it was known as 'a friendly place for the boys'. They knew that O'Sullivan usually walked home for his lunch between half past twelve and one o'clock. Jack Sheehan was posted outside to watch and wait. When O'Sullivan appeared at the barracks gate, the scout would shadow him, walking ahead of the approaching policeman on the opposite side of the street. The men in the pub would see the scout and then rush outside to shoot O'Sullivan. The woman who ran the pub gave them drinks. On the threshold of killing, Ahern spoke to the others. 'We all felt somewhat nervous … I said to Con Brosnan and Dan O'Grady: "We have a duty to perform and must do it."'[41]

Just up the street, a couple of minutes' walk, O'Sullivan's wife, May, mother of his three young children, was at home waiting for her husband to return for his lunch.

9

Between Gutter and Cart

Come into the tossing dust
Scattering the peace of old deaths,
Wind rising out of the alleys
Carrying stuff of flame.

Lola Ridge, 'Wind in the Alleys', 1918[1]

I

Vincent Carmody walked me over the ground. They say locally 'he is a fair man to talk'. But that can be said of many men in the town. It is a place that encourages loquaciousness. Storytellers are valued. It is why Vincent loved my father, who spun stories to everyone he met on Church Street when he was a boy and when he returned from Dublin in his later years, weakened by illness, to find comfort among old friends. But where my father mythologised the past in colourful tumbling sentences, Vincent Carmody is Listowel's historian of the real.

Every town and village in Ireland has people like Vincent who deepen our collective memory by foraging in the smaller fields of history. I came to him because of what he knew about the Tan days in Listowel. We started outside my grandparents' home, 45 Church

Street. These days it is a solicitor's office. The old wooden entrance is gone, and so too are the door jambs where my father used to point out the bullet hole left by the Tans one night they went firing down the street. The Keanes no longer live on Church Street but our presence is remembered here on a mural displaying a poem by John B. It is one of his earliest:

> I love the flags that pave the walk
> I love the mud between
> The funny figures drawn in chalk
> I love to hear the sound
> Of drays upon their round
> Of horses and their clocklike walk
> I love to watch the corner people gawk
> And hear what underlies their idle talk.[2]

He wrote the poem when he was a schoolboy. Twenty years later I would come here on my school holidays, Christmas and summer, to stay with Hannah. In my memory Church Street was a place of open doors and talking women, of donkeys and carts plodding back and forth from the creamery; a place of somnambulant men sitting at the bar amid the smell of porter and cigarettes in the numerous pubs.

In parts of the rural hinterland electric light had only arrived a decade before my first memories begin in the 1960s. There was a relentless parade through my grandmother's front door of country relatives and neighbours, like Alla Sheehy, the publican who always brought her tips for the races, and whose wife Nora Mai could 'strip paint off a wall with her tongue' if her temper was sour; and Toddy Connor who sold hairy bacon and cabbage with the furtive air of a gold smuggler; and Roger 'True Blue' who worshipped Michael Collins with a reverence that surpassed that of my grandmother. All of these people came in to impart or receive bits of local news. The life of Church Street flowed into the house and out again; it carried the stories of each family – those they would give up – so that they

Church Street in the early nineteenth century

became a shared store of communal knowledge. All the boasting about children who had passed exams or entered the civil service was done here; the scandals of girls who had got in the family way or husbands who had strayed, were whispered and sighed over, and, unfailingly, the recital of sicknesses and terminal declines and upcoming funerals. In the intimate landscape of Church Street there was more generosity than malice and whatever happened here happened, in some way, to everybody. I wondered how my people reacted to the District Inspector and his young wife. Up and down the country RIC families were frequently boycotted in the manner of the Land War of the previous century. They would have avoided the policeman, although he was their neighbour. With Hannah active in the IRA, it would not have been prudent for her husband to be or his relatives to be on anything other than nodding terms with the most senior police officer in the town. But his wife, May O'Sullivan, went to the same shops as the Keanes on Church Street and went to mass in the same church. She may have felt the hostility of Republicans towards her husband and, perhaps, the cold shoulder of others uninvolved in politics but unwilling to break the communal compact of exclusion often imposed on police families. Did they acknowledge her and pass the time of day when she came up and down Church Street with her three children, the two boys and the toddler girl?

On the day Con Brosnan and his comrades came looking for Tobias O'Sullivan, my grandfather, Bill Keane, would have been teaching a few miles outside Listowel at Clounmacon national school. Hannah was likely either at work in the draper's or on IRA business further out in the countryside. But my great-grandparents and their children Dan and Julianne, my grandfather's siblings, would probably have been at home at No 45.

From our old front doorstep on Church Street, I looked up at the barracks, on the opposite side of the road to the left. It took me less than a minute to walk there with Vincent Carmody. The Gardaí have been in the building ever since the Free State days, doing much the same job as the RIC did before they became militarised during the Revolution. Nowadays, in addition to the routine work of rural policemen, there are drug dealers to chase, hard young men who care nothing for the law and have no ideology but greed.

We called in at the barracks, a squat, three-storey mid-Victorian building. I spotted a bronze plaque in the outer hallway erected to the memory of Constable Jeremiah Mee and the mutineers of 1920. A young Garda answered the door and politely informed us that as he didn't have the keys he couldn't admit us to the upstairs room where Tobias O'Sullivan had his office. 'Can we come back maybe on Friday?' Vincent asked. The policeman explained that the guards might be on strike then, the first such police strike in the history of the state. I thought about telling him that it would not be the first police strike in the history of Listowel, but I could see his mind was on the present. These days in Listowel only the local historians such as Vincent are bothered with the complexities of the distant past.

We walked out and at the gate I stopped and turned around to look at the upstairs windows with the view across the street and right, down towards my grandparents' house. 'Let's go across here,' said Vincent, leading the way out of the barracks' garden and beckoning me to follow him left and up the street to the place where Tobias O'Sullivan met his destiny.

II

Inside the pub, time was dragging on. Half twelve passed with no sign of the District Inspector. I can imagine the newly promoted officer busy with work before heading home to his lunch, or 'dinner' as it is known in the country, the main meal of the day. There would have been meetings with his sergeants, the army officers and Auxiliary commanders. They had raids to plan, intelligence files to analyse, and liaison to manage with the RIC commands in Tralee and Dublin Castle. The building was well protected with sandbags, barbed wire and sentries, and the danger from within posed by the mutiny appeared to have passed. O'Sullivan was unaware that there was a spy in the barracks, one of Hannah's comrades in Cumann na mBan, who was feeding information to the IRA. He would have realised by now, however, that Republicans wanted him dead. But still he insisted on living at home and not being barricaded into the barracks.

The District Inspector looked at the clock and saw it was time to set off home: just a few minutes' walk, to the left out the gate and up Church Street towards where it becomes the road to Tarbert.

Around one o'clock a local man, Dan Farrell, decided to walk to the barracks to ask Tobias O'Sullivan about an award of money for his son. The young man, a former policeman, once defended the barracks from an attack but had since left the police force to live in America. On his way Farrell saw the District Inspector leaving the barracks and he crossed the road to walk towards him. We are talking of small distances, a matter of yards, of the moments between life and death waiting to spring. According to the historian priest Father Tony Gaughan, the two bodyguards who accompanied the District Inspector were sent back to the barracks at this point. He must have felt himself safe. O'Sullivan and Farrell stopped and chatted briefly just a few doors down from where the IRA unit was waiting. O'Sullivan told Farrell to come to the barracks later. Farrell walked away down Church Street, passing a slight bend in the road which took him out of view of the District Inspector. Their exchange was seen by the publican William Toomey and a local teacher, John Kirby, who were talking on the street outside the pub.

The scout, Jack Sheehan, saw O'Sullivan stop and talk to Farrell. This was a critical moment. He had already started walking ahead of O'Sullivan and now had to double back and loiter. Sheehan knew this could look suspicious. But if he was to alert the others to O'Sullivan's approach he needed to stay abreast of him. He waited for the conversation between O'Sullivan and Dan Farrell to finish and presumably saw the bodyguards being sent back to the barracks. O'Sullivan started to walk again. Sheehan moved ahead, every step bringing the District Inspector closer to the gunmen. When Sheehan appeared opposite the pub window the others knew their quarry was close behind him. As Tobias O'Sullivan came alongside the pub window Con Brosnan stood up and walked out, quickly followed by the others. They would initially have been behind him.

Dan Farrell was down the street when he heard a succession of shots. 'The first three shots were fired so closely together that I thought at the time they were one shot,' he recalled.[3] Another witness heard a shot and saw 'a man with his hands raised to his head staggering on the footpath. Immediately behind, about three feet away, was a man dressed in a grey suit ... and wearing a cap. His right arm was drawn up close to the body in such a position as might be adopted by a man firing a pistol. He was the only man I saw. I was very frightened and I went straight into my house where I remained.'[4]

The image of the wounded man with his hands to his head is haunting. The raised hands could not close the wound. They could not ward off further bullets. The strong man staggered his last yards before tumbling into death.

Con Brosnan remembered that he and Dan O'Grady fired four shots each. Jack Ahern said he fired six, 'making sure that the execution was complete'.[5] The post-mortem recorded that only four of these fourteen bullets hit their target. But even with inexperienced gunmen, at that range Tobias O'Sullivan had no chance of survival.

These are the physical facts of how death came to Tobias O'Sullivan.

The autopsy carried out by the army doctor on the day of the killing recorded that of the four bullets that hit the District Inspector two were fired from behind. One bullet struck the back of his head, the other entered between the spine and shoulder blade and passed into the chest. Another blasted into the side of his head between the ear and eye. Another bullet fractured his right arm. The report noted 'considerable bleeding from the right ear'.[6] There were lacerations where the bullets left the body. His jaw was fractured, his face and forehead were covered in bruises and cuts, possibly when he fell to the ground. Finally the report notes that the cause of death was due to 'shock and haemorrhage following the fracture of the skull and laceration of the brain and caused by the above bullet wound'.[7] Tobias O'Sullivan was possibly dead by time he hit the ground.

The killers ran a few yards, swerved to the right into a laneway which led towards a sports field and beyond that, the immediate safety of the woods of Gurtenard. They raced to put as much distance as possible between themselves and any pursuers. They wore no balaclavas, scarves or face paint to hide their identity. One might be tempted to believe that this was evidence of brash confidence, that nobody would dare inform on them. But the possibility of being seen and identified by the police was high. The same pattern held for many IRA operations in this period. Men did not hide their faces. This was hardly because of tradition. The Whiteboys and Moonlighters of earlier times often carefully disguised themselves even though they largely operated by night in the age before electric light. But the guerrillas of this new army felt, and knew they must act, like soldiers, not fugitives who should be hiding their faces.

They passed a gaggle of schoolchildren and through the lane, a shortcut between town and country used by locals for decades, and ran directly into trouble.

The land agent and staunch loyalist Paul Sweetnam was crossing the field and saw the fleeing men. 'Stand your ground and take your punishment,' he shouted. Sweetnam could not have known they had just killed a senior police officer, but would have suspected some form of IRA activity. They ignored him and kept running, escaping through the woods to safety.

There is a mystery here. Brosnan later told Irish army interviewers that they 'would have shot him on the spot only for the fact that our ammunition was very low'.[8] Sweetnam fitted the profile of a despised enemy. He hosted the British military at his home. He had a bad name as a landlord's agent during the Land War and had still been involved in evictions at the turn of the century. Now he had seen the faces of the men responsible for some sort of IRA attack. His evidence could have seen them hang. By their own account the gunmen had each been given between seven or eight rounds of ammunition. Fourteen of these had been used in the attack on O'Sullivan. There were still at least seven rounds left. Why did they not use these to kill a man who could possibly testify against them? Con Brosnan's son Gerry heard his father say 'they had only the authority to shoot one man'.[9] Or it may just have been panic of the moment that drove the men onwards across the field without stopping to inflict more violence.*

Back on Church Street Dan Farrell turned around and walked back to find O'Sullivan lying face down in the gutter, between the wheel of a donkey cart and the footpath. He saw some children standing near the corpse. A 'girl' was crying.

The publican, Toomey, heard the shots but assumed it was a vehicle backfiring. Then he heard his wife cry out: 'Oh My God, there is a man shot.' Toomey went outside and together with Farrell

---

* Sweetnam was called to give evidence at the subsequent court martial in Cork but failed to turn up. According to the historian Father Anthony Gaughan, the land agent apparently got off the train when it was stopped outside Listowel by the IRA searching for Tans, among them Darcy, who had threatened my grandmother and was high on the execution list. Fearing they were looking for him, Sweetnam ran away.

dragged the dead policeman's body out of the street. 'I told Mr Farrelly [Farrell] to run for the priest and the doctor.' Toomey and another man brought the stricken policeman into the public house. The limpness of the body told him that the doctor would be too late. 'Mr O'Sullivan was dead when I lifted him,' he said.[10] More children were appearing on the scene. It was lunchtime and they were flocking home from the two local schools.

Soon afterwards a military curfew was imposed. People were confined to their houses. That night the Tans drove around Listowel firing at random. But there were no killings. The violence was limited, probably through the influence of the Army captain John Watson, who was now the most important authority in the town. The police were reeling. On the same day that Tobias O'Sullivan was killed, across the River Shannon in County Clare, six policemen, including an inspector and a sergeant, were killed in an ambush. The Listowel police were under pressure to make arrests. Eight men were brought in for questioning, and four charged with the murder. One of the men, twenty-nine-year-old John 'Jaco' Lenihan, was already suspected – correctly – of hiding weapons and taking part in IRA patrols. After the shooting of Tobias O'Sullivan the RIC came to his home on Charles Street at teatime, around six o'clock, and took him to Listowel barracks, where his 'watch, pipe, tobacco, collar and tie' were removed.[11] Thereafter he was shuttled between police and military jails until finally being moved to Tralee barracks.

'Tralee county jail was manned by RIC and Tans. The first three days here I received no food,' he said in a statement. 'After I had kicked the door of my cell several times the Tans came in and beat and threatened to kill me.'[12] The identification parades dragged on for six weeks. Other potential witnesses were brought to the barracks and asked to look through a blind into an open yard where Lenihan and other prisoners were standing. He was eventually picked out and identified as one of the District Inspector's killers.

The most dangerous period for the prisoners at Tralee, Lenihan remembered, was in the aftermath of the IRA attack on a train at Headfort in south Kerry on 21 March. Ten soldiers, two IRA men, three civilians and an informer were killed as a result of the ambush. The bodies of the dead soldiers were brought into the barracks and that night 'the Tans and military went wild', said Lenihan. 'I with the other prisoners expected to be shot right away.'[13] A soldier came to his cell door, handed him a set of rosary beads and whispered: 'Say the rosary Paddy, I think you are for it.'[14] But discipline prevailed. There were no arbitrary executions that night or in the fervid days that followed, though Lenihan said that he and the other prisoners were deprived of food for a week after the Headfort deaths.

The only trial for the O'Sullivan shooting revealed that a handful of locals were willing to defy the threats of the IRA and give evidence. Their names were not given but in a small town like Listowel and with the barracks infiltrated, the IRA would have known who they were. In the case of Lenihan it was a near neighbour who wrongly identified him as one of the shooters. The woman, who lived one door up from him on Charles Street, placed her hand on his shoulder and declared: 'That is the man.' She was the daughter of an ex-serviceman, and had been born in Malta when her father was stationed there. Lenihan had previously warned his IRA commanders that certain people on Charles Street were passing information on to the police, and was angry that they hadn't moved to silence them.

When she was cross-examined in court the woman admitted that in a conversation with her mother later that day she claimed not to have seen the killing because she 'was afraid she [the mother] would tell other people'.[15] A policeman had also interviewed her on the day but she told him nothing 'because I was afraid that I might be shot myself'. She had changed her mind by the time a second interview took place on Saturday – two days after the assassination. Under cross-examination she was accused of delaying the search for the alleged killers: 'Do you know the result of your not giving evidence on Thursday was that no search was made for these men?'

'Yes.'[16]

The woman served in the Women's Auxiliary Corps during the Great War and had returned from England only seven months before. Then the defence moved to discredit her character, asking: 'When you returned from service, I think you had the misfortune to have an illegitimate child?' The prosecutor objected but the question was allowed and the witness 'admitted it was so'. In the deeply conservative Ireland of the times the defence knew that such an admission would cast her as a woman of low moral character and create suspicion of her testimony. The young woman is thought to have fled Ireland soon after she gave evidence.

In the newspapers it was reported that Tobias O'Sullivan was walking with his four-year-old son John when he was shot. It first appeared the day after the assassination, based on information released by the publicity department of Dublin Castle. It was the story given to Parliament several weeks later by the Chief Secretary for Ireland, Sir Hamar Greenwood, who described a visit by May O'Sullivan to the Viceregal lodge in Dublin. Greenwood told the House of Commons of how the District Inspector was killed as he held his son's hand. Greenwood also claimed that before O'Sullivan died he asked his wife to bring her sons to meet the Chief Secretary whom he, allegedly, called 'his champion'. However, no witness describes Mrs O'Sullivan listening to her dying husband speak and the idea that the Chief Secretary would have been foremost on his mind as he was dying, with a bullet having entered his brain, is, to put it mildly, improbable.

In having himself described as a 'champion' by a dying Irish policeman, Greenwood was well aware of the potential boost to his own reputation in the propaganda war with the IRA.

Two witnesses working in the barracks, looking out on Church Street from different windows, said they saw Tobias O'Sullivan holding the hand of his son at the barracks' gate as he left for lunch. One of the witnesses claimed there was a man watching the District Inspector from the other side of the road; the other said there were two men watching. However both of these witnesses later picked out innocent men at an identification parade to catch the killers. None of the other witnesses, including the former RIC man Dan Farrell, mention seeing Tobias O'Sullivan walking from the barracks with his son. The same holds for the testifying gunmen. This is perhaps not surprising. It is the kind of terrible detail the men involved in the shooting might be strongly minded to leave out. Two witnesses did refer to children at the scene, possibly the young boys and girls from the local school, but this may also have included young John O'Sullivan. There was also mention of a 'girl crying'. This could have been a schoolchild. But it might also have been the District Inspector's wife May or another woman who came quickly on the scene. The world 'girl' is often used in this part of the country to refer to adult women. The woman who took part in the identifi-cation parade at Tralee, and picked out Jaco Lenihan, said she was standing at the door of O'Sullivan's home, where she appears to have been working as a domestic servant, and was 'watching the District Inspector's son coming from school'.[17] This may have been the older child, Bernard. The school is in the opposite direction from where Tobias O'Sullivan would have been walking but it is perfectly conceivable that the child came upon the aftermath of his father's assassination. It is from Desiree Flynn, the policeman's granddaugh-ter, that I come closest to clarity about what happened. Her under-standing is based on what she was told by her uncle Bernard, the oldest child of Tobias. He was between six and seven years of age when his father was gunned down. 'It happened within sight of the family home. John ran out to see his father from the open door. He did not wander up Church Street to the police barracks as described in the witness testimony. He was four and would not have been roaming around, though he was big for his age. May saw Tobias being shot. Uncle Bernard saw him immediately afterwards and told me "they didn't shoot him clean".'[18] According to Desiree, May O'Sullivan was watching her husband come up the street when he was attacked. Because of this, she was brought to the identity parade in Tralee but could not recognise any of the men as her husband's killers and refused to be pressured by the police. I discuss all of this with Vincent Carmody. We agree it is impossible to know exactly what happened, not at this distance. But the O'Sullivan house was so close to the shooting, a question of yards, that the chances that his wife and children were confronted with a horrific scene are high. Con Brosnan's son, Gerry, heard talk over the years, not from his father, about there being a child who 'wasn't in his [the District Inspector's] arms but he was alongside him'. In this version Con told his comrades he was worried about what would happen to his own family after the killing of Tobias O'Sullivan. But from Con himself, Gerry heard nothing. He never questioned his father. Exact detail will probably never be established but there is no changing the essential truth of the event: May O'Sullivan had lost her husband, the children had lost their father, and would follow his coffin to Glasnevin cemetery, and live the rest of their lives without him. Of the eight men arrested two, Jaco Lenihan and Eddie Carmody, were sentenced to death for the murder of Tobias O'Sullivan. Con Brosnan and the others in the killing squad would surely have learned of the sentence. Two innocent men, men they knew, were sentenced to die for their actions.*

III

The news of the killing spread fast. The Associated Press circulated a short item after the killing saying Tobias O'Sullivan was 'one of the most popular officers in the constabulary'. To gun down a senior RIC officer in such times invited swift reprisal. Locals retreated indoors. Businesses were closed. Some townspeople headed for the homes of relatives outside Listowel. From my grandfather's front door, the Keanes could see the furious activity around the barracks all that afternoon and through the night. They lived a short distance away from a favourite drinking haunt of the RIC and the Tans. Lorryloads of Tans roared around the streets for hours. After the burning of Cork city centre and the rampage in Tralee at the end of the previous year, Listowel was at risk from severe retaliation. But

---

* They were spared by the signing of the Truce between Irish and British forces on 11 July 1921. Jaco Lenihan's grandson Donal would captain and manage successive British and Irish Lions rugby tours.

the presence of the army appears to have deterred immediate violence. In the crucial hours after the killing, command of Listowel seems to have been taken over by the military.

Three days later, on Sunday 23 January, Captain Watson from the Loyal North Lancashires summoned prominent locals to a meeting at the Carnegie Free Library in the town. The army officer was introduced by the parish priest, Canon Dennis O'Connor, the same man who had given the last rites to the student priest John Lawlor after he was beaten by the Tans at New Year. O'Connor was the acknowledged moral leader of the community and had already denounced the murder at mass that morning. But his words at the meeting were not recorded.

Captain Watson said the authorities were 'in possession of certain information regarding the identity of the perpetrators [and] it was up to the inhabitants of Listowel to supply further information'. Then came the warning. Watson said he had 'taken every precaution in his power to protect the inhabitants … but, of course, there would be some official reprisals'.[19]

A week after the killing the most senior policeman in Munster, District Commisioner Phillip Holmes, came to Listowel to gather evidence. He collected statements from several locals and, on 28 January, set out on his return journey to Cork. Holmes never reached the city. He was ambushed and killed on the Kerry/Cork border and his entire cache of documents fell into the hands of the IRA. Among them were the statements with the names of his Listowel informants.

I imagine my grandmother and her brother at this point. Mick Purtill was on the move with the IRA, taking part in ambushes and vanishing across bogs and mountains. There was little time for him or his friend Con Brosnan to dwell on what had happened in Listowel. Hannah was still visiting her husband-to-be Bill Keane on Church Street, still working in the draper's shop, still running messages and weapons, undeterred by the threats from the Tans.

There were brutal killings all over Ireland in those days. Children in other places had lost their parents. They had become victims themselves. But these things happened elsewhere. They did not provide context for this local trauma. The shooting of Tobias O'Sullivan happened outside the front doors of the people of Church Street. The District Inspector's wife and children were known to many in Listowel. May O'Sullivan was a young mother and an Irish country person like themselves. The pool of blood between the wheel of the cart and the footpath was drying on their street. This knowledge fostered questions. How could this killing be acknowledged and understood in the houses where people heard the shots, among those who walked past the blood, heard the cries of the dead man's wife and children? Schoolchildren had seen the gore. How would it be remembered in the years to come? This was the killing of an Irishman in the name of Ireland. Nobody celebrated this killing. But neither could I find any record of public mourning by locals. This was not out of malice but because the temper of the times dictated caution, a suppression of customary instincts. The memory of men killed by the Tans and Auxies would have hardened some hearts too. Tobias O'Sullivan would be carried away from Listowel in silence, and into silence he would vanish for decades, mediated by my own family into a ghost story, the green shape summoned by my father, moving night after night across the ceiling of 45 Church Street.

The war had come into the town. No policeman could feel safe walking the streets. A week after Tobias O'Sullivan was killed a group of four policemen were drinking in Hannan's bar on William Street. The stroll from the barracks to the bar is about ten minutes. They moved past people they knew, or people they thought they knew. But by then did they really know anybody? Who among the watchers, the cold faces, the fearful glancers, the occasional nodders, was noting the time and route, the number of men; how many were sizing them up for death? Three of the policemen were Irish, the other was an Auxiliary, a veteran of the trenches in France whose presence in Listowel at that time is a mystery since he had been officially discharged two weeks earlier.

Twenty-three-year-old Charles Ingledew was from Inverness and the son of a Seaforth Highlander, a regiment from the northern highlands of Scotland. Father and son fought in the Great War. When the war ended the younger Ingledew came home to Scotland to a world without work. The Irish war offered an escape. In November 1920, Charles joined the Auxiliaries and was posted to Listowel as a driver. By January he was in trouble. The police records show a punishment fine of £1, though the reason is not declared. Subsequent events suggest drinking might have been his problem.

The four policemen were the only customers in Hannan's bar that night. It may have been late, after closing time, because Susie Hannan, the wife of the owner, heard Ingledew tap on the door, the usual signal for admission after hours. He and the other policemen were admitted by her sister. Constable Denis Gallogly recalled how they were led into the snug, the small parlour often tucked away inside the front door of Irish pubs. There was another knock. At that point Gallogly heard Ingledew say there was someone outside and he 'didn't want to know I am here'.[20] The only light in the snug was a single candle. The policemen settled down. Pints were ordered. There was risk here. The IRA might have been tipped off. An ambush could be prepared at quick notice. The Hannans could possibly be targets simply for serving the police. Unless, of course, they were working for the IRA and passing on the gossip they heard from drinking constables.

'They were enjoying themselves,' recalled Susie Hannan. Then she saw Ingledew take out his revolver. He 'began playing with it. I was frightened and asked one of his friends to tell him to put it away ... the friend said it was "quite safe"'.[21] Ingledew was almost certainly drunk. As he played with the gun he asked the others: 'What would the old head say if he had seen this?' – a reference probably to O'Sullivan, his recently deceased boss. Ingledew blew out the candle. It was re-lit. He blew it out again. In that moment of darkness there was a shot.

'We four were all chatting in a friendly manner,' Constable Andrew Sheridan told the subsequent inquiry. 'At a moment when the room was in darkness, I heard a shot which at first I thought was from outside and I ducked.'[22] When the candle was lit again, Ingledew was lying dead on the floor with a bullet wound to his forehead. The coroner's court returned a verdict of accidental shooting. Inside his file an officer wrote: 'It is apparently a case of too much drink – no foul play.'[23]

But what really killed Charles Ingledew, veteran of the Western Front and the dirty war in north Kerry? He was a troubled and traumatised man. Why was he still in Listowel two weeks after his discharge? Perhaps war was the only home he knew. In this place and time, death could come in the swift dying of a candle. Blood covered floors, splashed upon walls, seeped under the frames of doors. It deadened country kitchens with silence. The war did not explain, or ask for explanations in return.

IV

At night they listened to the sounds of the barracks: shouts, the clatter of boots, engines growling. A town waiting. Denis Quille, IRA volunteer and neighbour of the Keanes, said Captain Watson encountered a party of Tans preparing to take revenge but he 'told them to go back to their barracks and stay in'.[24] The newspapers reported that markets and fairs were shut for months on end. At home in Church Street, Dan Keane would have cursed the bans that threatened his livelihood as a cattle jobber. The official newspaper of the Republican movement reported that before dawn on 3 February in 1921, thirty prominent residents were hauled out of bed by the Black and Tans and 'were placed in a big cage of barbed wire which had been erected for that purpose. They were "kept on view" for over an hour.'[25] In this way the Tans reminded everyone who was in charge.

Immediately after the shooting the killers of Tobias O'Sullivan went into hiding using the network of safe houses around the district.

Con Brosnan made an elementary mistake by sending a dispatch signed 'Con' to his IRA company commander. It did not implicate him in the killing but it revealed his status as a member of the IRA. The messenger was arrested by the RIC and the incriminating dispatch found. The Brosnan home and public house in Newtownsandes were burned to the ground. Con Brosnan's sisters were later sent to a convent, became nuns and eventually left for America. The rest of the family was dependent on the kindness of relatives and neighbours. The demolition of the homes of suspected insurgents would become commonplace in the counter-insurgency wars of the twentieth century.

The hunt for IRA volunteers was stepped up. The army, Auxiliaries, RIC, including the Black and Tans, swept the countryside. They hunted the IRA but could not pin them down in a single decisive battle. Unarmed men were shot down. Prisoners were beaten and executed. Young men playing cards were fired on and two badly wounded. There were unexpected gestures of mercy. Two British soldiers who were lured to a remote hillside were simply stripped of their uniforms and weapons and released. Had they been Tans or Auxiliaries the response might have been very different. The tempo of war varied day by day. The police killed the cousin of the Flying Column leader in reprisal for an attack on a train near my grandmother's farm. Robert McElligott, one of the brothers who planned the death of Tobias O'Sullivan just weeks before, was killed fighting Crown forces near Tralee in February. His brother could not attend the funeral but alleged later that 'people attending were rounded up, abused, searched and beaten. The wreaths numbering forty, which had been placed on the grave were taken out on the public road and broken up by the Tans.'[26]

They kept killing: the IRA, the RIC, the Tans, the army and the Auxies. One man's death could not alter the logic of the war. In the first six months of 1921, twenty-two of O'Sullivan's comrades were killed in north Kerry. The IRA lost twenty-seven in the same period.

The squad responsible for killing Tobias O'Sullivan had been immediately accepted into the ranks of the newly formed north Kerry Flying Column. Con Brosnan, Dan O'Grady, Jack Ahern and

IRA graves, Listowel

Jack Sheehan had proved themselves bold and ruthless and a tight bond had formed between the four. Towards the end of January 1921 they and other members of the Flying Column were moving west of Listowel, billeted in the Stack's Mountains that range beyond the town towards the Limerick border.

My uncle, John B, who spent his young summers here with his relatives, described the Stack's as 'too small to be called mountains, too big to be called hills'. The highest peak is just over eleven hundred feet. When the Elizabethans arrived here centuries earlier they found all the land forested, tough country in which to fight an elusive Irish enemy. The forests were gone by Con Brosnan's day, but the area was still a formidable redoubt, a mix of moorland and bog where a protective human cloak enveloped the fighters. They could rest and be fed at trusted local farms, where the tradition of silence in the face of official interrogation was absolute.

About thirty men of the Column zigzagged across the Stack's that January, marching 'through a continuous downpour of rain and lashing wind'.[27] Most would have been wearing labourer's boots, the belts of their trench coats pulled tight and peaked countryman's caps pulled down over their foreheads. The West Cork IRA leader,

Tom Barry, described his own men on a similar march: 'Their faces were unshaven, unwashed and greying with fatigue but their steps were still springy as they came in to pass where I stood, their shoulders jerked back so that no one would assume they were tiring ... they not only looked rough but they were tough. Yet I knew them as light-hearted youths who would normally have been happy working on their farms or in the towns or back at their schools, had they not volunteered to fight.'[28]

On the second night Brosnan and Dan O'Grady were on guard when they spotted lights in the distance. Despite the rainstorm it was still possible to tell that the lights were coming towards them. A scout was sent forward and came back within minutes. 'Holy ... they are on top of us!'[29] he cursed. Volunteers asleep in the farm buildings were swiftly woken. Soon the entire Column of nearly thirty men was on the move again, marching away from the lights of the advancing force. 'We retreated some distance ... it was one of the worst nights I can remember,' recalled Brian O'Grady. 'A biting north-westerly gale, with heavy rain and sleet, went through our clothing into the skin.'[30] The bad weather saved the Column. The enemy retreated. At dawn Brian O'Grady was scanning the main road with a pair of German field glasses when he saw six lorries heading away towards Listowel. Later that morning the Auxiliaries approached within a mile of the hideout but failed to spot the Column. The Auxiliaries were led by the notorious Major John McKinnon, who was hated by locals after burning the homes of those he suspected of IRA involvement. In another incident McKinnon tied a suspect by his feet to a horse and had him dragged along the country roads. By April, the major was dead, shot by the IRA as he played golf.

Over the next few months, with the weather growing milder, the Flying Column kept on the move, crossing open countryside; sleeping in farms, barns and dugouts, carefully concealed in woods or scrubland.

Towards the end of February Con Brosnan and his comrades attacked the RIC again in the bandit country of Ballylongford, and killed two Black and Tans. Brian O'Grady described the cost for civilians of this incident:

> In the early hours of the following morning several lorry loads
> of Black and Tans and RIC arrived in the village and burned
> down the local hall, the private house of Tom Carmody, his
> mother's private house and of Eugene O'Sullivan, Mrs
> McCabe's, Mrs Barrett's, Martin Collins's public house, Michael
> Morris's butcher shop and Mrs Enright's sweet shop. Two
> houses on the Well road were also burned. All shops were
> looted; barrels of stout and whiskey were machine-gunned.
> Shops looted included the drapery houses of Messrs. Lynch,
> Banbury and Finucane.[31]

The Column attacked a party of ten RIC in Tarbert village, close to the mouth of the River Shannon, wounding two. But they were caught unawares by a Royal Marine detachment which opened fire, forcing the men to retreat. A month later they were back in Tarbert, again attacking the RIC. The town had a name as a haunt of retired colonels and loyalists. Every raid was aimed at demonstrating that the guerrillas could strike where they wanted.

In March 1921, Mick Purtill and three others were sent to Ballybunion to kill three Tans who were '"out on their own" in doing the blackguard in the town'.[32] By this the IRA meant men with a reputation for harassing and ill-treating locals. What happened after may help to explain Mick's reluctance to speak later of those times. Notable police or soldiers were often quickly identified by name and targeted. All it took was a nod in a man's direction by a local who had suffered abuse, his name slipped by a friendly RIC man inside the barracks or overheard in a bar, then the usual watching of behaviour, routines and times. The role of public avenger was central to the IRA's claim to defend an oppressed community. Given the Tans' reputation for hard drinking, striking when they were inside or leaving a pub made tactical sense. The problem with the pub used by the Tans in Ballybunion was that it stood opposite the police barracks. The gunmen would need to enter, kill quickly and be gone up the main street and into the darkness of the countryside before the large force of RIC was alerted.

The seaside town of Ballybunion – 'Bally B' as we called it growing up – is just over three miles from the Purtill family farm. Then, and now, it was a favoured summer resort for people from across Munster. It faces onto the Atlantic with steep cliffs and golden sands. The cliffs are dominated by a castle ruined in the wars of the sixteenth century. On the March night in 1921 when Mick Purtill and his unit walked up the main street, Ballybunion would have had a desolate, out-of-season feel. Each man carried a rifle and a pistol. They were met by a waiting scout who nodded towards the pub to indicate the Tans were inside. It would take seconds to reach the door, a few seconds more to identify and shoot the Tans.

Halfway across the street the darkness erupted. From the window of the RIC barracks, machine-gun fire swept the street. 'We immediately ran for it,' said Volunteer Timothy Houlihan.

They made for the countryside and headed across the fields, walking until three in the morning when they reached the house of a friendly farmer named Walsh. They were given beds for the night but kept their weapons close by. The adrenalin of the attack had been spent and the men were washed by an immense weariness, their craving for rest trampling over the natural instinct of flight. At night here the only sounds were the barking of farm dogs and the occasional cry of curlews out on the bog.

The men had been asleep at Walsh's farm for two hours when potential disaster approached along the lane. On the edge of dawn, a lorryload of Tans appeared. I am trying to picture the man I knew as uncle Mick – solid and quiet, always with half a crown for you to buy an ice cream, the farmer and local politician – as he was then, a slender youth in his early twenties listening to the motor of the lorry getting louder as it came along the lane and then hearing the voices of the Tans outside. Mick would have clasped his rifle knowing that if they found him there would be no quarter in a fight against their superior numbers. Death stood in the yard outside.

Walsh was interrogated. As the questions went back and forth there was a growing feeling of relief: the Tans were lost and needed directions to Ballylongford. The farmer was press-ganged into showing them the way. The lorry moved off into the growing light towards Ballylongford. Twice on this mission Mick Purtill had come close to being killed. Later he found out why the machine gun in the barracks had suddenly opened up on them in Ballybunion. An informer had tipped off the police.

Fear of spies remained pervasive. Despite the threat of execution there were still people willing to give information. Michael Collins's claim to have paralysed the British intelligence-gathering capacity clearly did not hold entirely true for north Kerry. A Miss Carroll was abducted by the IRA solely because she had received a letter from the RIC apologising for having taken her bicycle. She was accused of being 'very friendly with a couple of the Tans' and put under house arrest until the end of the conflict.[33] Motives varied. Solid loyalists did not need persuasion to inform. But nationalists could be compromised if their personal circumstances made them vulnerable to cajoling or coercion. The IRA testimonies refer to a Mrs Wallace, who was lured into carrying letters for the RIC because they promised an early release from prison for her husband who was in the IRA. She was also accused of being 'friendly with the enemy garrison in Ballylongford' but doesn't appear to have been punished.[34]

In the official telling it was all one great struggle. The dashing men in their long coats swooping down on the Black and Tans, armed with rifles and boundless courage and led by wise, respected commanders, and all pressing inexorably to victory. That was not the true story of the war in north Kerry. It is not the true story of guerrilla war anywhere. There were brave men and women and there were less than brave men and women; there were commanders who were loved by their men and others regarded with disdain; at times victory seemed closer, at others very far away. As summer approached the IRA command moved to replace the leader of the north Kerry IRA, Paddy Cahill, who was seen as overly cautious.

Dublin wanted more action as a prelude to negotiations. The move was a failure and the newcomer, an outsider from Tipperary, could not sway the local loyalty of Cahill's supporters.

There were not the numbers or resources, to mount a large offensive. The war would not be nudged out of its predictable routine of harassment, ambush, reprisal, assassination. A small, nasty war but enough to keep the country off balance, and to kill the unwise, the suspect and the unprotected.

10

Executions

For there's blood on the field and blood on the foam
And blood on the body when Man goes home.
And a voice valedictory ... Who is for victory?
Who is for Liberty? Who goes home?

'Who Goes Home?' G. K. Chesterton, 1914[1]

I

Sir Arthur Vicars and the estate at Kilmorna were being closely watched. In May of the previous year Vicars had refused to open his strong room and was suspected by some IRA men of stockpiling weapons and spying. His continued association with British officers deepened the mistrust. On 7 April 1921, the IRA laid an ambush near his home at Kilmorna after hearing that Captain Watson, the army officer who had addressed local notables after the killing and was credited with helping to protect some locals from the ill-disciplined soldiers and Tans, was fishing there with a party of soldiers.

My great-uncle Mick Purtill was one of the attackers, along with Dan O'Grady, who had helped kill Tobias O'Sullivan. Captain Watson

St John's Protestant Church, Listowel

was well guarded. There were ten soldiers with him, all cycling along the narrow road. They had reached a stretch between two bends when the shooting started. Two soldiers went down wounded. Then Watson was hit on the forehead and dropped. One of Mick Purtill's closest comrades, a neighbour from Ballydonoghue, Michael Galvin, was sure the officer was dead. He stepped out of cover and was immediately shot dead by Watson. The captain had had only suffered a flesh wound. This was the closest death had come to my great-uncle since the war began and his third brush with danger in a matter of weeks. His friend lay bleeding to death in the roadway but in that moment there was no time to contemplate the loss.

They were almost trapped by a force of Tans and soldiers who had rushed to the scene from Listowel. The Volunteers escaped over the fields. That night the angry Tans shot dead a drunken ex-soldier who had strayed out after curfew. The army brought Galvin's body to Listowel but nobody would come to identify him. There was a brutally pragmatic calculation to be made. Reprisals were being taken against the homes and families of those involved in IRA violence. One account alleged that Michael Galvin's mother was taken to the mortuary but 'refused to make an identification lest there should be reprisals against the dead man's brother and comrades'.[2] The army buried Galvin in an unmarked plot in Teampallin Ban, the Famine graveyard on the edge of Listowel. A few weeks later his comrades returned in the middle of the night, disinterred the body and reburied it in Gale cemetery near Ballydonoghue.

Throughout this period Sir Arthur Vicars corresponded with a friend in Britain. 'So far we have not suffered, but are about the only people in north Kerry whose house has not been raided,' he had written at the outset of the Troubles, 'one never knows what may happen. We have all our arms, etc., in a strong room. I have heard privately that they won't raid us, but why I do not know, as I am a strong Unionist, and this they know. Last week they broke into a house 7 miles from here and stole blankets, boots, and clothes, etc. – how patriotic! – for the good of their cause!'[3]

The world around him was darkening and closing in. Big houses were being raided and some were burned. But this was not a campaign of religious cleansing in north Kerry. The local Protestant landowning community had not been targeted for sectarian attack by the IRA. The danger for individuals like Sir Arthur lay in being perceived as collaborators with the police and military. The level of animosity depended on individuals. Families with a history of benevolence towards their tenants or shrewd enough to cooperate with Sinn Féin could expect a safer passage. Arthur Vicars would be targeted because the temper of the times was paranoid, angry and vengeful; because he failed to see that hosting soldiers at Kilmorna invited dangerous suspicion; because he had refused to open his strong room; and because he was believed to be spying for the British.

When the house was first raided, in May the year before, Vicars told the IRA he did not have the keys to the strong room where any weapons might be kept. Nonetheless he sought to placate them by offering them money and producing two bottles of whiskey and some glasses, as if imagining the business might all be settled over a convivial drink. Both money and whiskey were refused. The IRA left but his refusal to cooperate was noted. Other landowners, including a former army officer, had taken a different approach, handing over weapons without protest. Denis Quille from Listowel later described Vicars as 'an old anti-Sinn Féin type ... giving information about our movements. We had information from a good source about him.'[4]

Arthur Vicars was targeted by the same man who had set up the killing of Tobias O'Sullivan. Patrick McElligott and his brother had prepared the intelligence report on the movements of the District Inspector. With Robert dead, Paddy now commanded the local battalion. The attack on Vicars was not sanctioned by local leaders. They were never asked, because, according to McElligott, there was no time. In a statement McElligott later gave to Irish army historians there is a sense of a man seeking to justify what happened. Vicars is described as a 'large landowner' (in fact he owned nothing) and is accused of asking the Kilmorna tenants about the movements of the Flying Column. McElligott links the killing to the shooting of Michael Galvin in the ambush a few days before. 'Vicars was a spy and this house ... was being taken over by the military'[5] as a blockhouse to dominate the district. Most tellingly, he asserts that 'our intention was to arrest Vicars and have him tried'.[6] This meant tried and judged without lawyers or independent judges, but an important legal nicety in the eyes of the IRA. McElligott's version is contradicted by his comrade James Costello, whose account feels closer to the actuality. He was to help 'arrest Sir Arthur Vicars and have him shot as he had been sentenced to death for being a spy and assisting the enemy generally'.[7]

Another IRA man said that Vicars had seen him and a large party of guerrillas crossing the River Feale the previous week. Soon afterwards the Black and Tans and army were set on their trail. 'We concluded that Sir Arthur Vicars had sent word to the Tans of our movements on the previous day after he had seen us.'[8] In several statements Vicars is described as a former British Army officer, though he never served with the army. His class, background and position as resident of the 'Big House' may have led his attackers to assume otherwise and hardened their suspicions.

Vicars might have had a chance to escape. According to IRA volunteer James Costello, when he and other members of the attacking party arrived at Kilmorna on 14 April 1921, they were told by Vicars's valet, Michael Murphy, that Sir Arthur was not at home. 'I said to Murphy "We have a job to do and we are going to do it."' (The words are an almost exact echo of the language used by one of the assassins of Tobias O'Sullivan.) Another IRA man recalled that they approached Kilmorna but did not attack because the signal did not come from the battalion command in a nearby village. The IRA decided to leave and return the following morning. If this is true, then Murphy would surely have told Vicars, who may have believed it was another raid for arms. He stayed at Kilmorna. Murphy was an ex-soldier, a local man who had served in France with the Irish Guards from 1914–18 and who found work at Kilmorna when he came home to north Kerry. He was clearly fond of Vicars and decades later struggled to understand why Sir Arthur had been targeted.

The next morning the attacking party broke in through a window at the front of the house, and the smallest man in the company was hoisted up and opened the front door from inside. Murphy described men bustling through the house sprinkling petrol and paraffin on the ground floor. Soon rooms were set ablaze immediately. Murphy raced upstairs to Vicars's room at the top of the house. 'I warned him to get up. He got up and dressed at once.'[9]

From here accounts of what happened next diverge dramatically. According to McElligott, who ordered the killing, Vicars was 'running from room to room, armed with a revolver … he rushed out through a side window … As he rushed out on to the lawn, he was shot dead by two of our men. He was not taken prisoner. There was no form of trial in the circumstance.'[10] This account is a fiction, a story that made the shooting seem more like an act of war than cold-blooded killing. McElligott gave his account in 1955, thirty-four years after the killing of Vicars. He does not appear to have been present at the time but would certainly have spoken to his men afterwards. Yet his version is at variance, not only with Murphy's account but with those of two IRA men who were present.

Murphy said he was following close behind his employer. 'He had gone about 150 yards from the door when he ran into a second party of IRA who held him up and shot him dead on the spot. I followed him close on his heels. He was not questioned in any way.'[11] A group went to the strong room and blew open the door but found 'only a few dumbbells and a couple of dummy guns instead of revolvers, rifles or shotguns which they anticipated'.[12]

James Costello said that Vicars was found in an underground passage that led out of the house. 'He refused to say anything except that he had no information. Eventually two of our men shot him dead on the lawn where he stood.'[13] The obligatory sign was placed around his neck warning 'Spies beware'. Petrol was splashed through the house and it was set ablaze. The household staff ran out onto the lawn and huddled together. Lady Vicars escaped the inferno by running out through the rear of the house. Michael Murphy remembered that 'my life's savings and personal belongings, including medals and discharge papers, were destroyed in the blaze which enveloped the house so quickly that everything within was burned to ashes'.[14] When he was later interviewed by Irish army historians, Murphy brought with him his only memento, a photograph of Kilmorna – in case 'it had any value for historical reasons'.

Later on the night of 14 April, Murphy was arrested by the Black and Tans. He was held for three weeks but failed to identify anybody who had taken part in the killing. He said he 'knew nothing of the men' involved. This may or may not be true. Once again the past freezes over. At the end of his statement to the army historians there is an unexpected declaration. 'From the time of my discharge from the Irish Guards I was associated with the IRA, and had a brother who was an active member of that body.'[15] It is hard to know what 'associated' means in this context, but Murphy stressing his

Republican credentials to add force to his opinions on the Vicars shooting. He was angry over what had happened to the man he had served. 'The news of the burning of the great house: and the shooting of Vicars was received with dismay throughout north Kerry. I do not believe he was a spy or got the benefit of a fair trial.'[16]

After the burning, local people came 'to gaze at the great black ruin. Their children played with the dismembered pieces of suits of armour they found lying on the terrace. Some wandered among the tiny headstones of Lady Vicars's canine cemetery, but mostly they stood looking silently at the desolation before them.'[17]

II

In the eyes of the police the dead District Inspector would soon be avenged. Jack Sheehan, the scout who walked ahead of O'Sullivan as he strode to his death, was killed by the Tans near his parents' home towards the end of May. An RIC man would leak the name of the constable responsible to the IRA, and the policeman named Farnlow was added to the death list. Meanwhile, two men, Jaco Lenihan and Eddie Carmody – both wrongly identified in the police line-ups at Tralee – were in prison waiting to walk to the gallows. The IRA hunt for informers went on unabated. The woman who testified against Lenihan, had already fled the country. But others were now under suspicion.

In early June, Con Brosnan was told about IRA plans to kill a man accused of informing in the aftermath of the O'Sullivan killing. James Kane, the fisheries inspector and former RIC man, lived on Listowel Square, across from the Church of Ireland church of St John's. What caught the attention of the IRA was that Kane's house was 'quite adjacent to a house occupied by the Auxiliaries'.[18] Kane originally came from County Leitrim in the west. His brother was the famous Chief Inspector John Kane of Scotland Yard who investigated the theft of the Irish crown jewels from Sir Arthur Vicars's safe. The connections of act and place weaved and tangled. Kane and his family were long-time residents in Listowel and were popular on the square. They had known tragedy already. Father Gaughan, the Listowel historian, wrote that Kane's 'crippled son was robbed and thrown into the river from the parapet of the Big Bridge in 1919. It is generally accepted that the crime was not politically inspired – no member of the local IRA was involved. The person responsible, whose name was and is known to a number of local people, was never brought to justice because of the unsettled conditions of the time.'[19] The casual cruelty of the killing speaks much about the 'unsettled conditions' of the revolutionary period.

From the upstairs windows of his house Kane might have gazed at the River Feale as it curved around Listowel racecourse and disappeared into the thick foliage of early summer. The river remained central to his life. He walked it every day and night, up past Gurtenard Wood where the trees come down to the banks, up through the high grasses to the salmon pools.

I know this river. I fished here with my father who was never more at peace than walking its banks. In James Kane's time the fishing rights were still owned by the aristocracy. They had been since the reign of Henry IV, who granted 'all the fishings and fishing places of the rivers of Cassan and Feale ... from the sea to Listowel'[20] to John Fitzmaurice, Baron of Kerry. Kane tracked poachers. When he vanished the police noted that he had numerous poaching cases due for prosecution.

According to Brian O'Grady, who left behind a haunting account of Kane's killing, 'we received a despatch from HQ in Dublin to have an ex-RIC man named Kane arrested and executed immediately'.[21] Years later Denis Quille said that Kane was killed because papers captured from the British military during an ambush proved he had given 'information about the District Inspector O'Sullivan ... a list of many names'.[22] These were the papers found on the body of the RIC commander Holmes who was killed back in January returning from investigating the killing of Tobias O'Sullivan. The IRA leader who led the ambush recalled:

The papers I got were illuminating. As a result of the shooting of Inspector Sullivan, a number of Kerry men were prisoners in Cork Barracks. General Holmes' chief mission to Kerry was to collect the evidence that would condemn these men. He got it, but it never reached the official files, and the lives of those around whose necks might have [been] tied a noose were saved. Those who gave the information were unfortunately unable to repeat their story. They met the fate intended for the prisoners.[23]

The IRA knew that Kane walked the banks of the Feale 'practically every evening'. For three or four evenings – O'Grady was not sure – a party of men waited for Kane but he did not appear. They got news that he was sick. This was reported to Dublin who did not let the matter rest. 'A period of about two weeks elapsed and again the Order came,' says O'Grady. The killers went back to waiting on the river bank.

Eventually Kane reappeared, alone and unarmed. 'He was arrested by four members of the Listowel company,' recalled IRA man Thomas Pellican. Kane was abducted on 13 June 1921. First he was taken across country to the house of a man named Broderick, near Knockanure. The execution would be carried out by Brian O'Grady, the three men who shot Tobias O'Sullivan – Con Brosnan, Jack Ahern and Dan O'Grady – and two other prominent IRA men, Dan Enright and Denis Quille. The names will come again in this story. Another war. Other executions. The connections of place and acquaintance that weave constantly on a small island. Brian O'Grady asked that a priest be sent for to hear Kane's last confession and to ensure he made a will for his family. The killing squad 'had to have a good sleep because of the fact that we had travelled long distances the two previous nights, most of which was cross country'.[24]

They rested for several hours. It was a beautiful summer's evening when they set out in the direction of Knockanure to carry out the killing. O'Grady met the priest called to give the dead man the last rites. 'He asked me for what reason was the prisoner being sentenced to death. I replied: "I don't know, Father, the order has come from

GHQ and that is all we know of the matter." He then asked if the man's life could be spared. I informed him that we had no option but to obey the order and, I added, "we would rather be surrounded by the enemy fighting for our lives than to have to give effect to the Order, but we had implicit confidence in our intelligence officers, that there was no mistake being made and that this was our consolation."'[25] O'Grady remembered the priest saying: 'Very good, Brian, God bless ye,' before he left. The man who was guarding Kane came to O'Grady and asked him to read the condemned man's will. He could not do it himself as he was too well known to the prisoner and 'under the circumstances it was right that a stranger should read it'.[26] Every line of O'Grady's testimony feels haunted though he describes the prisoner as 'quite normal' when they meet.

After O'Grady read the will, Kane asked if he was sure it would be delivered to his family. 'I replied: Yes, I give you my word of honour it will be delivered.' Kane had a last request of his killers. Would they kill him and leave him as near to his home town of Listowel as they could? 'I told him we would do everything possible to comply with his request,' O'Grady recalled.[27]

At midnight they all left and travelled towards the main road. A scout was sent ahead. Con Brosnan pointed out a shortcut through the fields. The imagery of the night sat with O'Grady long after the event: 'It was a glorious night in early June – like one stolen from the tropics. The larks were singing all night and the northern sky was aglow with light from the Aurora Borealis.' Again O'Grady uses the word 'normal' to describe the mood of James Kane. But how normal can he feel, marching across summer fields to his death? He told stories to the men nearest him. What were they about? Old times on the river perhaps, or people they knew in common? The singing of the larks, the low murmuring of men, the sound of men's feet swishing across the dewy meadows. The glow from the Northern Lights disappeared. Darkness came again and they 'knew the dawn was near'.

Kane was allowed to dictate a last letter to his children:

My dear children,

I am condemned to die. I had the priest, today, thank God.

I give you all my blessing and pray God may protect you all. Pray for me and get some masses said for me ... Don't go to much expense of funeral, and have no drink or public wake. I am told my body will be got near home. I got the greatest kindness from the men who were in charge of me.

Go-bye now, and God Bless you and God Bless Ireland. Pray for me constantly, and give my love to all my friends and neighbours, and thank them for all their kindness to me,

Good-bye,

From loving father

James Kane

All my dear children

Bury me near my loving wife if possible.

Give my gold watch to Eddie, and watch in desk to Frank.[28]

They reached the road and Con Brosnan pointed to a cottage, a landmark on the main route into Listowel. They were alert now. Police and military patrols passed frequently along this route. The guerrillas all wore rubber-soled shoes and boots to avoid making noise. They checked the road for any sign of tracks left by a patrol. But it was clear. The light was coming up over the fields. Soon it was daylight. Brian O'Grady told the prisoner that they would go no further. He asked Kane if he would like to say a prayer. The man who was about to die said yes. O'Grady gave him his personal rosary. Then the killers and their victim knelt together by the roadside and said a decade of the rosary. Brian O'Grady, Con Brosnan and the others stood up, but Kane remained on his knees still praying, eking out the last minutes of life on that brilliant June morning.

O'Grady waited a few moments and then tapped Kane on the shoulder.

'I asked him if he would like to be blindfolded and he said "Yes, it would be better." I then asked the prisoner if he had anything to say before he was executed, and he said, "All I have to say is this, Ye are the finest young men I have ever met, and the only thing I am sorry for is that I am not dying for Ireland."[29]

This is Brian O'Grady's remembrance. There was silence. Then the simultaneous drawing of revolvers from their holsters 'with a speed that should be seen to believed'. Then the 'sound of gunfire reverberated from the hills and valleys'. In O'Grady's description the 'prisoner swayed back against the ditch and slid gently to the ground'. The usual notice warning 'Spies beware' was fastened to his coat.

James Kane's body was left where he had fallen. The killers walked back through the fields. Nobody seems to have spoken until they reached a safe distance from the road, when O'Grady remarked to Denis Quille that a 'brave man died tonight'. 'I thoroughly agree with you,' Quille replied. Then they rested, smoked and 'blessed the man who discovered tobacco'. A small sum of money found in the dead man's pocket, along with his will, was posted to James Kane's family a few days after his killing.

11

The Republic Bold

You may sing and speak about Easter Week or the heroes of
Ninety-Eight, Of the Fenian men who roamed the glen in
victory or defeat, Their names are placed on history's page,
their memory will endure, Not a song is sung for our
darling sons in the Valley of Knockanure.

Bryan McMahon, 'The Valley of Knockanure', 1946

I

By the spring of 1921 the forces of the Crown were lashing out
across the north Kerry countryside. After the killing of Arthur
Vicars, they hunted the IRA but struggled to find them. The home
of one of my grandfather's friends, the bookseller Dan Flavin, was
burned down. Flavin was a leading Sinn Féiner but he had nothing
to do with the killing. Most of what happened went unreported in
the national newspapers; it was part of an accumulating local
viciousness. But one incident in Con Brosnan's country became
notorious. Knockanure lay between Listowel and Newtownsandes,
close to Kilmorna where Arthur Vicars had been shot in April.

The men of the Flying Column were weary and beleaguered by
infection. They were suffering from the 'IRA itch', a nuisance plague

visited on men living in the dirt of dugouts and hay sheds. Scabies is the medical term for it. I suffered from it when travelling in the gorges of the Panshir valley with the Afghan Mujahidin as they advanced on Kabul during a long-forgotten spring offensive. The mites burrow under the skin, blossoming into angry red blisters. The urge to scratch is irresistible. The skin breaks and weeps. Scabs form.

An outbreak of the condition among members of the north Kerry Flying Column forced a break for recuperation in early May. It was while resting that the men heard of somebody in Listowel inform-ing. A barmaid overheard a woman telling police how they might capture the men of an IRA Column just across the border in Limerick. There was to be a religious retreat in Athea run by the Redemptorist fathers, the most famous of the travelling missions that passed through rural Ireland in these days. The missioners were hellfire men, denouncing sins of the flesh with such vigour that – in the words of the poet Paddy Kavanagh – 'the crooked old Men sat up and took notice ... they began to dream themselves violent young stallions who needed fasting and prayer to keep them on the narrow path'.[1] These Redemptorists were also sympathetic to IRA men on the run. The woman in the bar told the police she was sure the men of the West Limerick Column would be in Athea to attend to their spiritual needs. She promised to get more information from a friend who was selling religious goods at the retreat. Con Dee and another man decided they would warn the Limerick volunteers of the looming danger. The mission passed without incident and Dee and two of his comrades were on their way back to Knockanure when they met other members of the Flying Column.

Some of them wore puttees – wraparound leggings – a standard accoutrement of men on Column duty. That alone could have justi-fied summary execution in the minds of some Tans. Around half past nine on 12 May 1921, Dee and three others were sitting on the bridge at Gortaglanna, about five miles from Listowel, when they heard a Tan patrol approaching. By this stage every IRA man in Ireland could recognise the growl of a Crossley Tender engine. There were two lorries and an open-top car. Dee, his cousin Patrick Walsh, Patrick Dalton and Jerry Lyons scattered into a field. But they were too late. The Tans were on them quickly. They were beaten with fists and rifles, pistol-whipped around their heads. 'Murderers' and 'Bastards' the Tans yelled. Paddy Dalton said to one of the others: 'We are done.'

Another young man, also an IRA member, was dragged from a nearby house but his mother begged the Tan commander, a Scotsman, telling him that she had taken care of wounded Scots soldiers as a nurse in London during the Great War. Her son was released.

The others were marched to the lorries and driven for half a mile. At this stage they were probably wondering if they might somehow survive, having not been shot at the bridge. Then the lorries turned around and drove back for about a mile. The road runs along the top of the valley, with fertile farmland below and marshy open ground above. They passed the spot where they had been sitting and chatting a few minutes beforehand. The Tans stopped and ordered them out. Con Dee gave his version soon after the killings: 'I looked at my companions; I saw blood on Jerry Lyons's face and on Paddy Walsh's mouth. Paddy Dalton was bleeding from the nose. We were then asked to run but we refused. We were again beaten with the rifles

A Flying Column in County Tipperary

and ordered into a field by the roadside. We refused but were forced into the field. We asked for a trial but the Black and Tans laughed and jeered and called us murderers.'[2]

For the last two years these young men had evaded the Crown forces. They had lived in dread of being caught by the Tans. And now they were captured here, without weapons, on this lonely road with no witnesses but the Tans. Con Dee was with Mick Purtill once when they were surrounded by Tans near Ballydonoghue. They hid in the local church and eventually escaped across the fields. Now Con was trapped.

The four men were lined up in front of the Tan firing party. Dee reckoned they were no more than five yards away. Shots blasted out of the rifles. Jerry Lyons threw up his arms and fell, moaning as he hit the ground. Dee noticed a bloody patch appear on Lyons's waistcoat. He also suddenly understood that the Tan opposite him hadn't fired yet. Dee took to his heels. It cannot have been more than a fraction of a second between realisation and flight. 'I was gone about twelve yards when I got wounded in the right thigh. My leg bent under me, but I held on running although I had to limp. I felt that I was being chased and I heard the bullets whizzing past me.'[3]

I walked where Con Dee had run. It was hard going, uphill across uneven ground. The adrenalin must have driven him on, up to the top of the hill with the Tans in pursuit. He ran until weariness and blood loss brought him crashing into a drain where he hid for forty-eight hours until he was eventually rescued by locals. Vincent Carmody's great-uncle was one of those who helped Dee, and for years afterwards would receive a Christmas letter with a gift of money in gratitude for his help. Two days later the British released a statement announcing that a force of a hundred IRA men had ambushed the RIC, wounding two constables and leading to the deaths of 'three unknown rebels'.[4] Big lies and small lies. They were the currency of the times.

In the hills a doctor was summoned to attend to Con Dee. He was passed from one safe house to another as he recuperated in the months that followed. The bodies of his three comrades were tied to the back of the Tan lorries and reportedly dragged along the road towards Listowel. At the men's funerals, attended by thousands, the forces of the Crown baton-charged mourners, the customary civilities having long been obliterated.

Mick Purtill and the rest of the Flying Column were lucky to escape capture as summer wore on. In late June the army and the RIC launched a sweep through the Stack's Mountains and several nearby villages, part of a new saturation search policy intended to pursue the guerrillas to the point of exhaustion. They kept moving despite their exhaustion, and escaped the dragnet 'by about ten minutes'.[5]

II

To say that we were jubilant would be untrue. It was more
bewilderment. Through the years of struggle, the hangings and
executions and sufferings had generated in us something
unchristian. Our lust to kill had not been satisfied.

IRA volunteer, County Monaghan, 1921[6]

There had been serious talk of peace since the previous December, 1920, the same month that the IRA was planning the assassination of Tobias O'Sullivan. Michael Collins never believed that an outright military victory was possible. War was the continuation of the political struggle by other means. When news leaked of secret talks between emissaries of both sides Collins declared: 'We were not asking a truce ... if one were offered we would not reject it, but we did not ask for it. That is the position.'[7] He was already balancing the hopes of competing constituencies: a people worn down by terror and a substantial group within the IRA who feared peace might mean a compromise on the principle of a republic.

The mere act of sitting down with the British in London induced deep suspicion on the part of some Republicans, the old fear that the respectable classes would hijack the Revolution. While hiding in the mountains along the Cork/Kerry border, Sean O'Hegarty, commander of the Cork No. 1 Brigade, half-joked to a colleague: 'What will happen is we'll wake up some morning to find ourselves members of the civil population, with peace made and our occupation and our power gone. Then I'll go back to the poorhouse and I suppose you'll start selling collars again.'[8] Michael Collins knew that the Truce represented a gamble. He also feared that after nearly three years of war the army of the Republic was exhausted and depleted.

The shrewder political minds on the British side accepted that political negotiation was the only workable solution. King George V was horrified by the behaviour of the Black and Tans and backed the peacemakers. But the military leadership was reluctant to enter negotiations. Not for the last time in twentieth-century colonial history a rigid military believed the defeat of the enemy was close at hand. To achieve it there was a plan for martial law across the twenty-six southern counties accompanied by a dramatic escalation of the military campaign. Forewarned by his spies and British peacemakers, Michael Collins rightly feared the impact of this on the IRA's fighting ability and the people's morale. His plan to counter state terror was to target any government official that the IRA could find – from Lord Lieutenant to the humblest civil servants. 'Not to single out an particular institution but to get at them all.'[9]

An Australian–Irish archbishop, Dr Clune of Perth, was brought in as mediator. On board ship travelling from Ireland to Britain, his grace encountered the principal British negotiator, Sir Alfred Cope, Assistant Secretary for Ireland, who had become convinced the policy of state terror was counterproductive. Recognising each other, the clergyman and the civil servant stood chatting about the prospects for peace.

Cope was a civil service meritocrat. Born into a large working-class family in south London, he went to work at the age of fourteen. Within ten years he was employed by the Inland Revenue as a detective. This was followed by a stint in the Department of Pensions and after that a steady rise through the civil service. His great strengths were extraordinary stamina, a forensic intelligence and the capacity to see matters as they really were, never an historical strong point of British administrators in Ireland. He would later say that it was 'impossible to govern an enlightened country without the consent of the governed' and that governments should not 'always be suspicious of the hand which declares friendship'.[10] Cope was, unsurprisingly, a highly suspect figure for the British security establishment, but he provided a model for the figure of civil service negotiator – shrewd, patient, energetic, flexible – who would occasionally appear in Anglo-Irish history throughout the next seventy years.

Standing near the archbishop and the civil servant on the ferry was a party of senior British military officers. Seeing them Cope remarked: 'I do not like to see these fellows crossing in such strong numbers. They have convinced themselves that they have the boys in the hills beaten, and they want no talk of a truce to interfere with them now. But the Prime Minister may not listen.'[11]

Lloyd George was listening. Dependent on the Conservatives to maintain his coalition government, he initially moved warily, backing the military's insistence that the IRA surrender its weapons before agreeing to any truce. There were increasingly dire warnings from the military leaders. The RIC director of intelligence, Colonel Ormonde Winter (described by a colleague as looking like 'a little white snake ... clever as paint, probably entirely non-moral ... a super sleuth, and a most amazing original'[12]), predicted that a truce 'will only afford them more breathing space, and more time to negotiate the purchase of arms ... there will be no peace. And that is all there is to it.'[13] The British military was correct in one key aspect. The Truce provided a critical respite for the IRA, not beaten but certainly under immense strain with thousands of men arrested and a shortage of war materiel. A Crown offensive under martial law conditions could have seriously compromised the guerrillas' ability to wage war. By the late spring of 1921 the crucial condition for peace-making existed. Enough people on both sides believed peace offered more than war.

The IRA was allowed to carry on recruiting and training but committed to ceasing attacks on Crown forces and civilians and any 'provocative displays of forces, armed and unarmed'.[14] Attacks on government and private property were also forbidden. The IRA appeared to have gained more, as Colonel Winter feared. There would be 'no incoming troops ... No movements for military purposes of troops and munitions ... No pursuit of Irish officers or men or material or military stores ... No secret agents ... No attempts to discover the haunts and habits of Irish officers and men ... No pursuit of lines of communication or connection'.[15]

On the night in July 1921 that the Truce was agreed, a Kerry IRA man was in Dublin to meet with Michael Collins. Tadhg Kennedy, a brigade intelligence officer from the village of Ardfert, had once entertained hopes of becoming a naval civil servant. His uncle was a Royal Navy officer and nominated him for a clerkship. Kennedy's was a story of loyalties that, but for circumstance, might easily have swung the other way. He was also typical of a cultural Irishness that found its own niche in the imperial structure. 'I often saw my uncle and other Irish officers Collins, Aherne, Payne, etc. play cards in the Officers' Mess at Chatham Dockyard and they never spoke a word except in Irish, and they were all native Irish speakers!' he recalled.[16] But Kennedy's Fenian father threw his civil service nomination in the fire and Tadhg devoted himself to hunting enemies of the Republic.

Tadhg Kennedy had news for Collins about a detective in Dublin Castle who wanted to supply information. There was also another matter that needed Collins's adjudication. A Listowel man had attempted to frame a neighbour as an informer because he wanted his land. 'Mr Maher then told me,' Kennedy recalled, 'that a man named Relihan who was employed as a Roller driver by the Kerry County Council had made some kind of a claim to his land, that his people had owned it about one hundred years previously.'[17] Under the cover of war, old grudges and claims were given new momentum. It was land, always land, that mobilised the malice in men's hearts. Not only had Relihan tried to frame the other man, but he had been discovered supplying intelligence to the police. Now Kennedy wanted Collins's decision on what to do about him. With much subterfuge a meeting was arranged with Collins at Vaughan's Hotel, a haunt of Republican leaders in the centre of the city. The Kerry man was surprised to find the usually reliable night porter drunk. Collins appeared behind him.

'When we got inside the door in the hall he told me the war was over,' Kennedy remembered. He also told him that Sir Alfred Cope, Under Secretary of State for Ireland, was in the 'room to which he was taking me'.[18] Kennedy was to be polite but not disclose any information.

The astonished Kennedy was duly introduced to Cope and his two RIC bodyguards, one of whom recognised him immediately. He was a fellow Kerryman. 'Mick again announced about the Truce and we were both supplied with champagne and brandy and we drank quite a quantity of it. Cope and I got talking and we discussed the troubled times and I was regretting it was over and said I enjoyed it.'[19]

The two architects of the peace and the Kerry intelligence officer drank glass after glass, or so Kennedy thought. Later he found out that Collins, ever wary, was drinking some non-alcoholic drink with the colour of brandy. 'Both Cope and myself passed out completely,' he remembered. Kennedy's testament is a fascinating coda to nearly three years of savage warfare, although it is difficult to imagine Collins being invited to spend a similar evening with a senior British police or Army officer. The spy Relihan was saved by the Truce.

The last official day of the war found Mick Purtill and his comrades laying mines on the main road from Lixnaw, preparing to ambush military lorries expected along the route. The lorries never came. In this part of the country the war between rebels and the Crown was almost over. The men were lying up in safe houses when word of the Truce arrived. A message from IRA headquarters in Dublin was carried by hand to commanders around the country: 'In view of the conversations now being entered into by our government with the government of Great Britain, and in pursuance of mutual conversations, active operations by our forces will be suspended as from noon, Monday, 11 July.'[20]

The killers of Tobias O'Sullivan had one last mission. This needed no orders from the Kerry IRA commanders. It was a personal matter. They set out in a group for Tarbert with nine others. When they reached the outskirts of the town, Jack Ahern, Dan O'Grady and Con Brosnan went forward to carry out a reconnaissance. It had been six weeks since Jack Sheehan had been killed, shot dead by the Tan marksman Farnlow as he tried to escape across the fields by his parents' house. Sheehan's former comrades had come to avenge him. Their time was limited, the official Truce between the IRA and the British was less than a day away. They approached Mulcahy's pub where they'd been tipped off that Farnlow and other Tans were drinking. Ahern sent Brosnan and O'Grady back to the outskirts of Tarbert to bring on the rest of the unit. Almost immediately the Tans began exiting the pub. 'I was in the open street near the pub on the opposite corner and had to think quickly what to do. There were four of them so I opened fire with the revolver,'[21] Ahern said. There was no return fire until the Tans reached the barracks. But by then Ahern was away. Farnlow was wounded but survived and returned to England.

My grandmother was still living at home in Ballydonoghue when news of the Truce came through. At the age of twenty-two Hannah was a veteran of the guerrilla war, and still a devoted supporter of Michael Collins. If the peace was good enough for Collins it was good enough for her. Besides she was to be married soon. Her parents had paid the dowry of £150 – a solid sum in those times – and she was making ready for the move into Listowel, to the house on Church Street, to live with her husband Bill, his parents, his eccentric brother Dan and sister Juleanne. She had survived the Tan war. The conflict had not ended with clarity with the British driven out and a Republican government ruling the whole island from Dublin, but the killing had stopped. The relief for my grandmother must have been immense. Not only had the threat been removed from herself, but from her beloved brother Mick, and from her comrades in Cumann na mBan. The first months of the year had been filled with savage violence around Listowel. To live with the possibility of violent death every day and night, to feel the fear of raids in the darkness and informers hiding in your midst hurts the human personality. Fear is the most distorting of all emotions. Now Hannah could hope. While Collins prepared to sit down with Lloyd George and Churchill, she got on with the plans for her wedding.

There were a few last fatal spasms left in the war in Kerry. In Castleisland four IRA men and five soldiers were killed; in Killarney, the Royal Fusiliers were ambushed and two soldiers killed, and a hotel chambermaid, Hannah Carey, was fatally wounded by a stray bullet, the last casualty before the Truce. But on the day of the Truce, my great-uncle Mick came into Listowel and walked without fear of arrest for the first time in two years. He bought drinks for his comrades.

In the early days of the peace Con Brosnan came into Listowel with his brother and a neighbour from Moyvane. The three were going to Ballybunion to the beach; after two years on the run it was Con's first taste of a normal existence. The three were walking down the street past the RIC barracks, back over the ground where he had stalked and killed Tobias O'Sullivan, when Con saw a group of Black and Tans. They were standing in front of the barracks. The neighbour from Moyvane, eighteen-year-old Michael Finucane, recalled what happened:

> As soon as he saw them . . . Con Brosnan said to me, 'We'll go over direct here.' They had taken no notice but the minute they saw him they all became electric. They stood up, and each one was riveted to the ground. Each one knew about him . . . they saw his picture every day. They were looking for him. They were looking for two years for him . . . They couldn't touch him, or they didn't want to touch him. I saw the expression of every man in this crowd . . . stupefied . . . they were stunned to see him there.[22]

Con walked across to the Tans, Finucane believed, to show that he 'could fight any man alive'. Afterwards they took the train to Ballybunion and the three men swam into a strong Atlantic tide. Michael Finucane recalled Con being knocked over by the waves, standing up, being knocked over again, until he was exhausted and the other two intervened and helped him from the water.

Across the county there were celebrations. In Tralee, a brass band played rebel airs and rockets were fired. The locals jeered the Black and Tans, but there was no violence. Some of Mick Purtill's close comrades did not join in the celebrations. Those who had spent three years fighting in the hills could not believe the Truce would last. They knew that the British had not been defeated. The Truce only bought time. What if the British refused the Republic? The Flying Columns were warned to remain alert and keep training. There was a flood of new members, scornfully called 'Trucileers' because they joined after July 1921 when there was no immediate chance of capture or death. In Listowel the new recruits headed for Davie Carrol's drapery store to purchase puttees. A local wit dubbed them 'Davey Carrol's Fusiliers'. The Cork IRA leader, Seán Moylan, was caustic about many of those who joined the IRA during the Truce:

> The Truce gave these fellows an opportunity for posing as
> war-hardened soldiers. In public houses, at dance halls, on the
> road in 'commandeered' motor cars, they pushed ordinary
> decent civilians aside and earned for the IRA a reputation for
> bullying, insobriety and dishonesty that sapped public
> confidence. More than this they were an evil influence on
> young, generous, adventurous boys who, knowing of IRA
> achievements, sought, too, an opportunity of proving
> themselves.[23]

Scores of men made their way home from the prisons to north Kerry. But the man wrongly accused of the killing of Tobias O'Sullivan was not among them. People accused of capital offences were not immediately released. Jaco Lenihan was due to have been hanged at eight in the morning on the Saturday before the Truce came into effect. To try and force their immediate release Lenihan and a few others began a hunger strike which lasted for five days until a priest persuaded them to stop. By the time he was freed, on 14 January 1922, the struggles against British power in the south of Ireland had ended.

Newly released prisoner Éamon Broy, who had acted as one of Michael Collins's spies inside the RIC, remembered a spirit of hope. The day he came out of jail he was brought to meet Collins at a Dublin pub. 'We sat together at a table and he was full of optimism,' Broy remembered.[24] Collins spoke of forming an Irish government and encouraging Irishmen who had gone abroad to work, in the empire and America, to come home: he would bring back the 'trained minds to help us'.[25] But the IRA leader was worried about 'too much rejoicing going on all over the country, and too much relaxation'.[26]

That summer, the livestock markets opened again. The curfews ended. Young men and woman could once more gather at country crossroads in the long evenings. In Ballydonoghue, Mick Purtill went back to help his father and siblings with the work of the farm. Hannah joined them when she was not working at the draper's. There was no danger of a Tan patrol firing at them as they worked the fields. The forces of the Crown stayed in their barracks. But Listowel was unsettled. You can say a war is over. It can be declared finished between the two armies. But you cannot legislate for local grudges, not when your army is made up of so many small armies, and of men who have become accustomed to having the power of life and death at the end of a finger. Bad blood does not easily wash away. There were many in the IRA who felt the war should never have ended, and many on the other side who agreed.

For a policeman like Thomas Enright, war had been a constant since 1915. In some respects he represented a choice Mick Purtill might have made, had his father not been slightly more prosperous or had a larger family to support. Enright had grown up on a small farm near the Purtills. He was the eldest of ten children. His descendant, Donal McMahon, wrote that all ten emigrated to North America in the early part of the century. Thomas made his way to Vancouver and worked on the Canadian Pacific Railway. When the Great War broke out he enlisted and fought with the Canadians at the Somme and was badly wounded. While convalescing back in Vancouver he met a nurse who was a Listowel woman. For reasons that are not explained – homesickness, the urge to return to action perhaps – the two left Vancouver for Ireland in July 1919. The war with the IRA had been under way for nearly seven months. Thomas Enright enlisted in the RIC in April 1920. Four months later he was made a sergeant with the Auxiliaries. His military service had helped him gain the promotion.

When the Truce was declared, Enright was in charge of barracks defence in Thurles, County Tipperary. By mid-December 1921, with the Truce five months old and holding, Thomas was sure he had survived. He no longer needed to worry about an IRA assault with bombs and massed numbers. He was living a normal life.

Like many men from this part of Ireland Enright was a big fan of hare coursing. His dogs were well known on the tracks of Munster. One of his best, Bedford Lass, was named after his home place in Listowel. In the third week of December, Enright decided to take Bedford Lass to race in Thurles. But for Maurice Meade, another coursing fan, and still an active member of the IRA, Enright's appearance at the meet was an opportunity to settle a score. Meade was a veteran of the 1920 attack on Kilmallock where he faced Tobias O'Sullivan and his beseiged constables. He and other IRA men claimed later that Enright had been in charge of a police death squad. One account claimed that he had led a masked group to raid the house of a publican who was thrown downstairs, breaking his neck in the fall. 'Sergeant Enright, who was in charge of the raiders, shot him dead to put an end to his agony ... a detailed account of his shooting was given to me during the Truce period by Sergeant Enright himself.'[27]

But Thomas Enright's fate was decided because of a more recent incident. On 10 December 1921, a train carrying IRA prisoners home from internment was attacked at Thurles station. A bomb was thrown and an IRA man killed. *The Times* of London reported that 'the bombs were thrown under cover of the fog signals which were being exploded as a greeting to the returning men'.[28] The British authorities and the IRA were perplexed. There seemed to be no obvious motive. The IRA sent an investigator, John Sharkey, to find out what had happened. 'Our information was that a bomb had been thrown by a Sergeant Enright of the RIC ... The townspeople of Thurles appeared to be in a state of terror that night.'[29]

Maurice Meade assembled a team to kill Enright. The retaliation would have to be swift, while the memory of the original atrocity was still fresh in people's minds. Meade later told the army historians: 'this man ... was particularly active and bitter against our men, on one occasion bombing some of our captured men. For this we decided he should pay the death penalty. No opportunity to carry this out had arisen until the Truce occurred, but when we saw him at the coursing meeting, even though the Truce was then in operation, we agreed to shoot him and we did so that night.'[30]

A newspaper report noted that Enright was shot from behind. Afterwards the IRA headquarters condemned the killing, saying: 'such deeds are not the acts of members of the IRA, but are the acts of cowardly individuals who endeavour to cloak their misdeeds in such a manner that they may be interpreted as the actions of soldiers of the Republican Army'.[31] Already definitions had shifted. What was acceptable a few months earlier had now become 'cowardly'. Thomas Enright's body was taken home to Listowel for burial. The funeral was held just before Christmas. It was a quiet affair.

The first and last men to die in Ireland's guerrilla war against Britain were Irishmen and both from north Kerry. Three years and nine months had passed between the shooting of IRA men John Browne and Richard Laide in the attack on Gortatlea police station on 13 April 1918 and the death of Thomas Enright. A recent study estimated that 2,141 people died in the War of Independence:

514 police, 262 British Army, 514 IRA and almost 900 civilians.*
But the past was swiftly closing over Browne and Thomas Enright,
and James Kane and Arthur Vicars, over John Houlihan bayoneted in
front of his mother, and Dalton, Lyons and Walsh shot at Knockanure,
and over Tobias O'Sullivan and the Royal Irish Constabulary and all
the centuries of British rule in Ireland. The old story of rebels and
the Crown was over in the south. The Truce confronted Republicans
with the challenge of compromise and it would tear their movement apart.

In the beginning there was eager anticipation. Just after the Truce
was agreed, Éamon de Valera, as president of the Dáil, wrote to
Collins about his meeting with Lloyd George in London. Dev
sounded positive:

> I am sure you are anxious to hear whether any important
> developments have taken place. The position is simply this –
> that L.G. is developing a proposal which he wishes me to bring
> in my pocket as a proposal to the Irish Nation for its
> consideration. The meetings have been between us two alone as
> principals. The idea on which we the Ministry started out
> remains unchanged. You will be glad to know that I am not
> dissatisfied with the general situation.[32]

But Dev's emollient tone vanished over the next six months. It
became obvious that an all-Ireland republic was not going to mate-
rialise. The Government of Ireland Act of 1920 had partitioned the
country and given Unionists an effective veto over unity.[†] In the

---

* For a fuller breakdown of casualties see Eunan O'Halpin, *Counting Terror: Bloody
Sunday and the Dead of the Irish Revolution*, in David Fitzpatrick (ed.), *Terror in Ireland,
1916–1923*, Dublin, 2012, pp. 141–152.

† In June 1921, the Northern Ireland parliament met for the first time in Belfast,
beginning an epoch of Unionist rule that would last until the 1970s. By the time the
Boundary Commission came to deliberate in the mid-1920s, events had occurred that
turned southern minds away from questions of national re-unification.

north the Truce did not bring an end to violence. Sectarian tensions, never far from the surface, frequently erupted into violence. In February 1922, six Catholic children were killed when a bomb was thrown while they were playing outside their homes on Weaver Street in Belfast. The following April four Protestant workers were shot dead after being lined up inside a garage and asked their religion. A fifth man, who was Catholic, was allowed to leave. In May 1922 the IRA in the new state of Northern Ireland began an offensive. In Belfast the Truce was disregarded.

Between July 1920 and July 1922 more than five hundred people were killed in Belfast, fifty-eight per cent of them Catholics, a city where they formed just a quarter of the population. Thousands of Catholic workers were driven from their places of employment. Collins eventually intervened, making common cause in this with the men who became his enemies as the Republican movement was rent apart by divisions over negotiations with the British. It did not change the military outcome or improve the lot of the Catholics: the IRA campaign in the north was defeated.

To my family in Listowel the north was too far distant to be a concern worth dying for. In 1921 they were preoccupied with recovering from the strain of war. A month after the Truce came into effect the Dáil met openly for the first time with a huge and happy crowd surrounding Dublin's Mansion House. Seán Moylan remembered 'an atmosphere of confidence and victory'.[33] As he wandered around the corridors he saw the legends of the struggle. There was Michael Collins, 'big, handsome, in high spirits, a centre of attraction', and Liam Mellows, revolutionary and intellectual, who told Moylan that 'many more of us will die before an Irish Republic is recognised'.[34] His words were prophetic. Mellows and Collins would be dead within the year, fighting on opposing sides.

The British were not about to allow the Irish to depart the empire. Such a precedent would inspire other nationalist movements. The government would demand an oath of allegiance to the King. For so many of the fighting men in north Kerry the oath was more than a rhetorical abstraction. It struck at the heart of the separatist ideal. Had they killed and died only to end up paying obeisance to the British Crown? As a volunteer in County Monaghan put it, with the eternal weariness of the soldier confronted with compromise and backroom deal-making: 'During the period of the Truce, the politicians and respectables took over. It was they who interpreted our dream, the dream we fought for. It was they who decided the terms to which we must agree. In the mind of every [IRA] soldier was a little Republic in which he was the hero. But his dream was shattered.'[35]

The time of heroes had passed. Nothing would ever seem as simple again. To a majority of the IRA in Kerry the oath of allegiance became a symbol of humiliation. The bitter arguments among the national leadership would be replicated in the north Kerry Flying Column. Men prepared for a new war.

Denis Quille was with Con Brosnan on the night the fisheries inspector James Kane was killed. They had been solid comrades for several years. But for Quille it would be a republic or nothing. Up and down Church Street and out in Ballydonoghue families and neighbours divided: the Purtills and the Keanes were with Collins and compromise. Jack Ahern, who led the squad that killed Tobias O'Sullivan, also took the Free State side. Hannah immediately felt the effects of the schism on Cumann na mBan. The leadership was taken over by committed separatists and a letter was sent from headquarters ordering the women to 'support the existing Republic by every possible means'. More ominously it sought the names of those who were 'on the side which seeks to subvert the Republic'.[36] Hannah was one such subversive, as was her brother Mick and Con Brosnan. But in the split that was coming their mutual friend Con Dee, who survived the Tan death squad at Knockanure, went to the side of those who would become known in the pejorative description of the Free Staters as the 'Irregulars', or in de Valera's description, 'the Legion of the Rearguard'.

In London, Michael Collins, Arthur Griffiths and three other colleagues signed the Treaty with Britain at twenty past two in the morning on 6 December 1921, breaking a promise to de Valera and the rest of the cabinet that they would sign nothing until it had been brought back to Dublin for approval. Collins and the others signed conscious of the threat of 'terrible and immediate war', as Lloyd George put it to the delegates.

The Treaty negotiations became the bedrock of competing national myths. My father said Dev knew that the Treaty would be the best deal on offer and wanted Collins to take the blame for the compromise. But I need to remember that my father and all my kin saw only the worst in all that Dev did or said. It is equally possible that Dev was playing for time with the British and, in standard negotiating practice, holding back the assent of his cabinet to the last minute in the hope of more concessions. If so Dev misunderstood the British and he misunderstood Collins. The Republican version is that Collins and Griffith, who was never a Republican anyway, were outwitted and browbeaten, even seduced by the glamour and temptations of London, until they succumbed to the wily Lloyd George. Collins argued with justice that the Treaty needed to be ratified by the Dáil. He had not signed away the Republic but achieved a stepping stone to freedom. There are elements of truth and myth in each accounting, thankfully long picked apart by Irish and British historians, so that looking back I do not see heroes and villains but men and women caught in the grip of events, confronted by pressures for which nothing in their life experience could have prepared them, their passionate idealism mixing with human frailty, and propelling them towards a great rendering. It was all inestimably sad.

12

The War of the Brothers

When you have sweated, toiled, had mad dreams, hopeless
nightmares, you find yourself in London's streets, cold and
dank in the night air. Think — what have I got for Ireland?
Something which she has wanted these past 700 years. Will
anyone be satisfied with the bargain? Will anyone? I tell you
this — early this morning I signed my own death warrant. I
thought at the time how odd, how ridiculous — a bullet might
just as well have done the job 5 years ago.

Michael Collins to his friend John O'Kane, after signing
the Anglo-Irish Treaty, December 1921

I

As you leave the kitchen for the yard there is a flight of stairs that
leads to the living quarters above my uncle John B's pub on William
Street. During their lifetimes, John B. and his wife, my auntie Mary,
regarded this as the family sanctuary, out of bounds to the well-
wishers and occasional cranks who descended on the pub to see the
famous writer. It was also the place where John B wrote his plays,
short stories and poems and thousands of words of newspaper
columns, in the small room that overlooked the road that led to
Ballydonoghue and Ballybunion.

I climbed those stairs hundreds of times. Every time I did so I passed the black-and-white photograph of General Michael Collins, in full military uniform, smiling out from a day in the last months of his life. I doubt any photograph in the house mattered as much. He towered over the usual icons of the Irish kitchen – John F. Kennedy, the Pope, even the Sacred Heart and His flickering candle. Collins was the reason Mick Purtill joined the new army of the Free State and took up arms against his former comrades in the north Kerry Flying Column. Collins was 'the Big Fellow'. They didn't know him personally so might never have called him plain 'Mick' as his friends did. But they knew what he represented to them. He was the man who had run the British ragged and made his volunteers feel proud. He was their wartime leader, more than Dev could ever have hoped to be – though, at that point, they did not lack respect for Dev.

My grandmother's idol, Michael Collins

They would have seen Collins when he came to Listowel during the election campaign after the Treaty and Mick Purtill would certainly have seen him when the Big Fellow visited the troops just days before the Civil War broke out. My grandmother always said Collins was authentic. By this she meant you could trust what he promised. Their forefathers had been led by people like Daniel O'Connell, the son of Catholic gentry, and Charles Stewart Parnell, an Anglo-Irish landowner. But Collins was the child of a farmer. He was like them and he had risen to lead his people. In my family a wistful romanticism coexisted with flinty realism. Collins was handsome and dashing. He lent himself easily to myth-making. The Purtills did not love Collins the bureaucrat who ran the underground Ministry of Finance with forensic diligence. Rather they were seduced by the 'laughing boy' who summoned up an imagined heroic past. He was all flesh and blood. A man to drink a pint and sing a song with. A man to fight. For all his fabled intelligence and learning, de Valera could never match that glamour. He was more the boy you went to copy your homework from, than the one you called out to come and play.

Pragmatism also played a big part in my family's decision to accept a compromise. Like so many in the country, the Purtills were tired of conflict. They did not want an endless war against the British whose reprisals had hit the neighbouring towns and villages hard. The rural economy had ground to a halt, beyond the cultivation of food for subsistence. The Purtills had enough of a stake in the land to yearn for stability. Perhaps also, something of their older Home Rule, constitutionalist heritage was reasserting itself. For all the willingness to risk their lives, my grandmother and her brother must have been shaken by the escalation of the previous six months. I do not believe they were instinctual revolutionaries, rather that they felt enough of the job had been done for the guns to be put away.

I was never able to ask my grandmother or her brother Mick what they thought of the Civil War. Mick Purtill was part of that vicious struggle and my grandmother would have lost the friendship of old comrades in the bitterness that followed. There was a lot of talk when I was growing up of Civil War politics. My family was 'black' Fine Gael, and remain so to this day.* Mick Purtill became a Fine Gael councillor in the 1950s. His son, my cousin Liam, is now a local councillor for the party Collins founded. At every general and local election, family members have been part of the Fine Gael machine in north Kerry. I never questioned this as a child. It was how things were and as natural as supporting Kerry in Gaelic football, Cork in hurling and Munster in rugby.

Yet I know that John B felt conflicted by the tribal politics. He had too subtle a mind to believe either side owned the truth, and the cant and clientelism that grew out of the Civil War era of politics disgusted him. But that is in the future, after the madness that consumed his homeplace.

This is how it broke down in north Kerry. Figures compiled by the historian priest Father Anthony Gaughan show that of roughly forty-four men in the IRA Flying Column, twenty-four went against the Treaty, seventeen with the Free State, and five were uncommitted. Most of Mick Purtill's comrades in the 3rd Battalion either went Free State or decided to be neutral. Among those who were anti-Treaty was Timothy Houlihan, who had fled with Mick from the Tans after the abortive attack on Ballybunion police station just a few months before. Together they had hidden in a farmhouse while the Tans were outside. Now one was destined to become a hunter, the other the hunted.

Con Brosnan and the men who killed Tobias O'Sullivan, and some of those who shot James Kane after leading him across the summer fields at night, took the side of the Free State. Con had stature and whichever way he turned men would have followed him. As one of the men who was with him on the night of the Kane shooting put it: 'Connie Brosnan was a good influence to get the men to become

---

* To be described as 'black' in this context means 'ultra' or 'dyed-in-the-wool'.

Free State.'[1] Was it strange that men who had done some of the most ruthless close-quarter killing in the name of the Republic should now accept something less? I doubt they saw it like that. Collins was the most ruthless death-dealer of them all, and he got up in the Dáil debate on the Treaty to claim that it 'gives us freedom, not the ultimate freedom that all nations desire ... but the freedom to achieve it'.[2] The Treaty gave the Irish people an independent state within the British empire with their own army, police and control over taxation and foreign affairs. But there was an oath to the King and a Governor General to represent his interests; the six Ulster counties remained under Unionist rule and would not join the new state; and the British would have bases at key ports around the coast.

The Treaty debate got vicious quickly. The animosities previously kept in check by the exigencies of war convulsed the movement. Collins and the other negotiators were damned for signing the Treaty before they had referred it to Dublin as they were obliged to do. Collins said the Dail had the final say. The Treaty would not become law until it was ratified by a majority of deputies. Jealousies, remembered slights – real and imagined – resentments over status, tore away at the bonds of comradeship. The Tipperary IRA leader, Séamus Robinson, implied Collins was a coward and cast doubt on his war record. The official report of the Treaty debate is stippled with pained exchanges. 'Now, from my knowledge of character and psychology, which I'm conceited enough to think is not too bad, I'm forced to think that the reported Michael Collins cannot be the same Michael Collins who was so weak as to compromise the Republic.'[3] Collins's celebrity status in the movement made him enemies, not just people who could be derided as jealous, but those who mistrusted his secretiveness and the way in which so many around him observed a blind loyalty.

As so often before in the history of all nations, the glorious dead were summoned as witnesses to the spectacle, except that this time they were being asked to act as a ghostly chorus in a war of brother against brother. Fionán Lynch from Kerry, an ally of Collins, declared that 'the bones of the dead have been rattled indecently in this assembly'.[4] At the end of the debate, de Valera and the rest of the anti-Treatyites walked out.

'Deserters all!' Collins shouted after them. 'We will now call on the Irish people to rally to us. Deserters all.'[5]

Madame Markiewicz, the Anglo-Irish grandee turned revolutionary, sentenced to death for her role in 1916 but then reprieved, traded angry words with Collins during the debate, at one point accusing him of having a romantic dalliance with a British royal – a lurch onto the wilder shores of Anglophobia. 'Oath breakers and cowards,' she railed.

Collins's temper broke. He knew the worst insult he could hurl at de Valera, born in New York, and Markiewicz, the lady from the big house. The words were not worthy of a man who wanted to unite his nation, but the insults of past days, the strain of the debate, were showing. 'Foreigners,' he shouted, 'Americans, English.'

There was little discussion about the partition of the island. Years later when I read the debates for the first time I was living in Belfast. There were still people killing and being killed because of the decisions made in the early 1920s. But the division of the island did not loom large in the passionate exchanges of 1921/22. Patrick Pearse's mother was an exception. Her son would not have signed a treaty which left the country divided, she said.

II

So take it down from the mast, Irish traitors,
It's the flag we Republicans claim.
It can never belong to Free Staters,
For you've brought on it nothing but shame.

'Take it Down from the Mast', song by James Ryan, 1923

The flesh of the dead would be scattered on roads and in trees. Things came to pass in north Kerry that the Black and Tans and Auxies would never have been allowed to get away with by their commanders. Words preceded deeds. Before it even began, de Valera came to County Kerry and made a speech in Killarney on 18 March 1922, returning to a theme that had preoccupied him in the previous few days. With that intense look of his, the pedantic hammering home of his own absolute logic, he declared his prophecy: 'in future in order to achieve freedom, if our Volunteers continue – and I hope they will continue until the goal is reached – if we continue on that movement which was begun when the Volunteers were started, and we suppose this Treaty is ratified by your votes, then these men, in order to achieve freedom, would have to (as I … said yesterday) march over the dead bodies of their own brothers. They will have to wade through Irish blood.'[6]

Dev was making clear that the democratic process would not matter if it went against the Republicans. He knew the Bishop of Kerry had urged Catholics to support the Treaty two weeks before. It did not matter. The intensely pious Dev was on his own course and it did not matter to him that the bishops would excommunicate IRA men, and priests damn them from the pulpit. Later de Valera insisted he had been misrepresented. But he was speaking in a flame-soaked building and he knew it.

At the beginning of the same month, the Free State army set up its local headquarters in the Listowel Workhouse. Mick Purtill had been promoted to the rank of captain in the fledgling army and was part of a garrison of around 250 men. He is mentioned in the military archives as being an intelligence officer. This must have meant spying on the composition of enemy units, their armaments, sources of intelligence, who was helping them in the civilian population, where they hid from Free State patrols.

At this stage, however, there was still some collaboration between the two sides. Dublin was far away and old friendships still mattered. At least some of the men who had gone Free State might have been open to switching sides. The most prominent of the Listowel Republicans, Denis Quille, went for a drink with the Free State commander in Listowel, Tim Kennelly, a neighbour of the Purtills from near Ballydonoghue. Talk got around to guns. According to Quille, Kennelly offered to hand over weapons and control of the Workhouse to the Republicans. But when the moment came and the IRA arrived, Kennelly told them the deal was off. Somebody further up the line ensured there would be no handover. Quille remembered that Con Brosnan and Brian O'Grady, with whom he had shot James Kane, were among those who accompanied Kennelly to the meeting. A second attempt was made to talk the north Kerry Free State men into joining the Republicans, but that too failed.

In late April, Michael Collins came to Tralee and was confronted with a large armed Republican counter-demonstration. There was a bitter fistfight between pro- and anti-Treaty leaders which Collins himself had to break up. Later, as he addressed a crowd of several hundred, shots were fired around the perimeter, just as he was telling them the Treaty wasn't worth fighting a civil war over.

From his post at the Workhouse, Mick Purtill observed the situation in Listowel with growing apprehension. The Republicans were taking over key buildings around the square. They faced the Free State detachment in the Listowel Arms Hotel with interlocking fields of fire. There were also gunmen on all the approaches to other Free State positions in the town. By now Listowel was beginning to look increasingly isolated, one of two Free State islands in a Republican sea. The rest of Kerry was in Republican hands. The

Armoured car outside Listowel barracks during the Civil War
when the town was briefly held by Republicans

town sat forty-six miles behind what would become the Republican
front line at Limerick. At the end of the month the garrison was
buoyed by the delivery of 200 rifles, two Lewis guns and new
uniforms. But still there was no outbreak of fighting. Rival patrols
turned about and marched away when they met on the town's
streets. Hannah Purtill continued to travel regularly to Listowel to
visit her husband-to-be and organise their wedding. The curfews of
the Tan days, midnight raids and random shootings may have gone,
but the whole town felt the rising tensions.

My grandfather, Bill Keane, taught his class at Clounmacon
national school and walked past the rival armies every school day.
But when the summer holidays arrived he could retreat to his books
and the nightly consolations of porter. He would still drop in to chat
with his friend, the bookseller Dan Flavin, and I picture them speaking of poetry and prose, the divisions outside gathering with unstoppable and lethal intent but passed over in the quiet of the shop.

A love of literature kept friendship alive. It was Dan who supplied
the classics of English and American literature to my grandfather.
He believed in the purity of the Republican ideal, unsullied by an
oath of allegiance which under Irish leaders would promise to 'be
faithful to HM King George V, his heirs and successors by law in
virtue of the common citizenship of Ireland with Great Britain'. For

Dan Flavin it was about equality between all men, the dream of the French revolution and of Wolfe Tone and Robert Emmet. Dan Flavin could not support a settlement which he felt betrayed that ideal.

In the Dáil the Treaty was carried by a slim majority – sixty-four votes against fifty-seven.

The fighting started in Dublin. On 28 June 1922, Irishmen shelled other Irishmen in the capital city where they had risen together against the British at Easter six years before. They attacked the Republican headquarters at the Four Courts with artillery and some gun crews provided by the British. Two days later the tension in Listowel exploded. At half past eight on the morning of 30 June, Republicans opened fire on Free State troops who had taken over Walsh's drapery store. Bullets flew across the square and smashed into the stonework of the Listowel Arms Hotel. A correspondent in the town reported that 'the rifle and Lewis gun cross-street firing was terrific, and during the hours of operation the non-combatant inhabitants were kept confined to their houses'.[7] The first casualty of the Civil War in Kerry was twenty-year-old Private Edward Sheehy, the son of a local insurance broker, who was shot through the heart. By five o'clock in the afternoon the Free State garrison had surrendered. A joint statement from the Republican leader, Humphrey Murphy, and his Free State counterpart, Tim Kennelly, announced that as Kerrymen they did not want to fight each other in a civil war. 'We the officers of the opposing forces,' they stated, 'have declared that Ireland's interests cannot be served by war. When comrades who fought together have shot one another down neither the Republic nor the Free State will benefit ... unfortunately the dreaded spectre of civil war is now in our midst.'[8] Neither man, at that moment, could have imagined the bitterness and horror that was to come.

Fifty men immediately deserted to the Republicans, although the newspapers would claim that the entire Free State force had switched sides. Mick Purtill and Con Brosnan stayed loyal to Collins. They briefly became prisoners along with nearly two hundred other men. But the IRA released them, hoping some, at least, would give up the fight. It was a mobile army with scant resources to jail and feed large numbers of prisoners. The Free State men went home and waited. The Republicans left a small detachment in Listowel and headed for the front line in Limerick, where the Free State army was advancing.

Before they left there was a funeral service for young Edward Sheehy. The procession moved up Church Street, past the Keanes' front door, past the police barracks and the gutter where Tobias O'Sullivan bled to death. They reached the cemetery next to the football field and filed slowly towards the graveside. Directly ahead, at the end of the graveyard, a gate led into Gurtenard Wood and below that, invisible because of the trees, the River Feale. Looking back, after all that was to come, men on both sides might have marvelled at this moment when Free State and Republican soldiers stood to attention for the dead youth. The *Cork Examiner* noted that 'the most pathetic feature was when his comrades in uniform, but without equipment, formed a firing party, carrying rifles lent to them by Republicans'.[9] A local brass band played the funeral march. It was a last moment of brotherhood in north Kerry, the final shared gesture of the dying revolution. The following January, Sheehy's distraught father wrote to the Free State authorities asking that his son be given a headstone over his grave:

> His body lies in a nameless grave in the local public cemetery.
> Though he gave the last drop of his heart's blood for the Free
> State, yet over the grave there is nothing to show how he died
> or what he died for. I wish I had the means of rectifying this.
> Twenty-two years of age and six feet two in height and an
> athlete of the first order, it is not surprising that his mother's
> health should have suffered from the loss of such a son. It is a
> serious state of things for me that her present state of health is
> so impaired that at any moment I am liable to lose her also.[10]

Two weeks later the army replied regretting that 'owing to the present disordered state of the country it has not been possible to erect suitable tablets in memory of those who have given their lives for the Free State', and advising that it was 'the intention of the Government to erect suitable memorials at the earliest possible moment'.[11]

Up in Dublin the Republicans suffered swift defeat. Falling back, they established a front line which theoretically stretched from Waterford in the south-east to Limerick in the mid-west, the boundary of the so-called 'Munster Republic'. But they lacked the numbers and the artillery to hold a fixed front line of more than eighty miles. Most of the troops were guerrilla fighters with no experience of conventional warfare in which territory was seized and held. On 21 July, less than a month after the outbreak of the Civil War, the Free State captured Limerick city, about forty-six miles across the Shannon estuary from Listowel. One of the Purtills' neighbours from Ballydonoghue, Patrick Foran, was killed in the fighting, the first Kerry Republican to die in the Civil War. Suddenly men were retreating back down the roads from Limerick. In Kilmallock, where District Inspector Tobias O'Sullivan had defended the barracks against the IRA, the IRA was now under siege by the Free State army. The town stood in the way of the advance deeper into Munster. A *New York Times* correspondent observed Free State troops moving south: 'As I sat watching on a gray stone wall they marched past singing cheerful songs,' and called out to him: 'Praise be to God, the Guards are coming.' The 'faith of the countryside in the Dublin Guards is almost legendary,' he noted.[12] The faith of some country people in the Guards may have been legendary, but it was by no means unanimous. The Dubliners were outsiders down here in Munster and in Kerry they would become notorious.* *The New York Times* reported that all eyes were 'directed towards Kilmallock,

---

* The nucleus of the Dublin Guards Regiment was formed out of men from the IRA's Dublin Brigade and members of Michael Collins's 'Squad'. They took over the first British garrisons to be handed over to the Free State on 31 January 1921. As Civil War approached the ranks were swelled by men from the pro-Treaty IRA in southern border counties and unemployed youth in Dublin.

where the fighting has been stubborn and the casualties numerous'.[13] The town fell to the Free State on 5 August 1922. More than forty men from both sides were killed.

Soon after the fall of Limerick city the main IRA leader in north Kerry, Humphrey Murphy, went to a meeting of concerned locals in Tralee. The farmers had called the gathering but businessmen and trade unionists came too. They were all worried about the state of the country, with mounting reports of crime and social breakdown. 'Irregulars continue to harass the people,' noted *The New York Times*. 'Shopkeepers and farmers are pillaged without mercy and cattle and sheep slaughtered in the fields.'[14] With no proper police force and the IRA focused on the fighting, any thug with a gun could rob and intimidate with little fear of prosecution. The fundamental conservatism of Irish rural life was attempting to assert itself. The IRA leader had a very different message for them. A schoolteacher of vehement separatist principles, his words must have inspired a mood of foreboding in the audience. Murphy promised endless war: 'I am certain they are going to fail as the Black and Tans failed, because the war did not come properly until it came to Cork and Kerry. We will defend every town to the last. You will have towns in ruins and famine finishing those who have escaped the bullet. We will stop at nothing, and we are going to win even if it takes years.'[15]

The very idea that an IRA leader could summon up famine as a weapon is indicative of the furious temper of the times. Did he consciously echo the history of sword and hunger in his words? He was certainly well enough educated to be aware of the historical context. Murphy was deliberately putting the wind up his audience, knowing his words would be reported back to the Free State authorities. The respectable citizens of the district might wish for an easy life. The IRA had no intention of obliging them.

III

When Redmond was about two yards from me I fired and he
fell mortally wounded, shot through the head.

Paddy O'Daly, leader, 'The Squad'[16]

Nobody told me to bring kid gloves to Kerry. So, I didn't bring
them.[17]

General Paddy O'Daly, National Army

With IRA attention focused on the Free State advance, after
Kilmallock the National Army sought an alternative to a potentially
long bloody march through Munster. There was an easily realisable
alternative. At the end of July 1922, a coastal steamer, the *Lady
Wicklow*, set off from Dublin with over five hundred men, soldiers
of the Dublin Guard, an armoured car and an eighteen-pound field
gun. The ship also carried the man whose methods would stain the
reputation of army and government and leave a trail of
bitterness.

General Paddy O'Daly, commander of the Dublin Guard, was a
former leader of Michael Collins's 'Squad', the close-kit unit which
had carried out the campaign of assassination against British intelligence officials, RIC officers and informers in Dublin. Like the rest
of the Squad his bond of loyalty to Collins was absolute. O'Daly had
shot men up close in the name of the Republic. He knew what it was
to see the terror in the eyes of a man about to be killed and what it
meant to deny him mercy. There were some who said later that he
took too easily to the business of killing. He told of how Collins once
chastised him 'in a towering rage' after hearing rumours that O'Daly
planned to kill a policeman who had knocked over one of O'Daly's
children, a disabled girl:

Michael Collins then gave me a lecture on revenge and
said that the man who had revenge in his heart was not fit
to be a Volunteer. I had to convince him that I had no
thought of shooting Winters, but I passed the remark
that if Winters was on our list I would like to carry out
the job.[18]

Revenge would come all to easily to Paddy O'Daly in the war ahead.
A comrade from the close-knit Squad, Tom Keogh, and six of his
men had been blown up and killed by an IRA landmine the previous
September. The Black and Tans and the Auxies had their share of
men traumatised or hardened by their experiences of the Western
Front. On both sides in Kerry were Irishmen brutalised, accus-
tomed to killing in the War of Independence. Now into Kerry came
men like O'Daly and the Free State army head of intelligence, David
Neligan, a Limerickman, who had spent the years of the War of
Independence as an IRA mole inside both the RIC Special Branch
and MI5. O'Daly and Neligan were determined to end the war in
Kerry quickly and by whatever means they could get away with.

The rank and file of the Free State army was a mix of ex-IRA
men, new recruits with no fighting background, and former
members of the Irish regiments of the British Army. When the
National Army appeared offshore at Fenit in north Kerry on 2
August, the IRA was taken by surprise. A landmine hastily placed on
the pier failed to explode because locals disarmed it, fearing the
damage to their livelihoods if the pier blew up. This was a strong
indicator of local feeling. The IRA fought a rearguard action towards
Tralee, about eight miles away. At one point they fired on medics
clearly marked with the Red Cross insignia. O'Daly took this as
proof of the IRA's refusal to abide by the laws of war.

Further up the coast there was another landing at Tarbert and the
relief force for Listowel reached the town within three hours. The
IRA melted away. Marching into town, the Free Staters found the
Workhouse and police barracks burned out. A communiqué on the

invasion of north Kerry asserted that 'the progress of the troops was greeted everywhere by enthusiastic welcomes from the civilian population who had been treated disgracefully by the Irregulars'.[19] But this was an exaggeration. There had been thieving and bullying by individual volunteers but – unusually for civil war – no campaign of killing directed against civilians.

Normal life had, however, become impossible after the Republican takeover of Listowel. Restrictions on movement returned and there was an attempt to shut down the mail service. Notices appeared close to the town warning postmen that they would be shot. A letter from a Listowel resident to the *Cork Examiner* from the times contains a litany of complaints against the IRA:

> Many happenings have taken place in Listowel and district
> during the last month due to the stoppage of trains services ...
> as well as the dislocation of telegraph wires and telephone
> apparatus, no means of communication was to be had with the
> outside world. To complete our misery, roads leading to the
> town were destroyed by trenches, making it impossible for
> farmers to carry on their usual avocations to the town, as a
> result no fairs or markets took place, traders have to all intent
> and purposes closed down. The strike on the wage question ...
> and disruption of rail added to our distress ... e.g. numerous
> bridges were destroyed.[20]

The reference to the wage strike reveals another troubling aspect for the local establishment. Farm labourers, the perennially downtrodden caste of rural society, had gone on strike for better pay. For the bigger farmers this radicalism was the consequence of the IRA takeover. Food supplies were disrupted by an IRA campaign against the rail system.

These are matters which taken as singular events would aggravate but eventually drift out of the public consciousness. But when events multiply a collective view starts to take root and every event that conforms to that view is seized on and added to the weight of evidence, and this evidence becomes the justification for all that is to follow. In this way the Free State commanders can construct a story for the nation, but most importantly for themselves: 'We did what had to be done to save Ireland from anarchy.'

On 12 August, Collins visited Tralee to thank the troops for recapturing the town from the Irregulars. On the same day a Free State army patrol was ambushed two miles outside Listowel: a soldier was killed and another wounded. This was followed by the blowing up of bridges and a train line. Five days later two young Free State army medics, one of them only sixteen, were shot dead at a beauty spot near Killarney. They were unarmed and wearing Red Cross insignia. These were still early days, but on both sides any reticence about shedding the blood of fellow Irishmen was vanishing.

In the third week of August 1922, the frail hopes of any compromise disappeared. Everybody on Collins's side and most of his enemies would remember where they were when the news came in. Mick Purtill was on duty at Free State headquarters in Listowel. My grandmother would have been at home in Ballydonoghue. At first people did not know whether to believe it. In their minds he was beyond the reach of mortal men. But the news did not change. That night Hannah Purtill wept for her lost leader and for the Revolution that had descended into fratricide.

Collins was killed by the IRA on 22 August at Béal na mBláth (the Mouth of the Flowers) in his native West Cork, shot dead in an ambush by veteran Cork guerrilla fighters. Before leaving for Cork he had been warned by a senior officer that he was taking an unnecessary risk, to which he is said to have replied: 'Surely they won't kill me in my own county?'[21]

When his convoy was ambushed on a country road he chose to fight rather than flee his attackers. His killer was reputed to be a former RIC man and British soldier, Denis 'Sonny' O'Neill, who shot Collins as the Commander-in-Chief stood firing back at the ambushers from the middle of a country road.* Collins abandoned the basic principle of defence when he strode out from the cover of his armoured car as the enemy retreated and was gunned down with a single shot to the head by a man who had once fought on the same side as him. The slain leader died in the arms of his comrade General Emmet Dalton, a veteran of the Tan war and also of the Somme and several other bloody encounters. Facing roadblocks and downed bridges, Dalton and the rest of Collins's escort had to carry the commander's body across the fields with 'blood and brain matter dripping down on top us'.[22]

The alleged killer of Collins, Dennis 'Sonny' O'Neill, had later claimed, when applying for an army pension, that he only 'accidentally ran into the Ballinablath [*sic*] thing'.[23] The officers of the army pensions board described him as 'having a downcast appearance, hardly ever smiles, never looks a person in the face when speaking … a first class shot and a strict disciplinarian'.[24] It took ninety-two years for the files on O'Neill to be released, though his name had been locally mentioned for decades in relation to the killing of Collins. But, in the way of the country, they kept the information to themselves. The man who may have carried out the most notorious political killing of the Revolution was granted a military pension in 1939 but took his story to the grave.

There were conspiracy theories. My father blamed de Valera and said Dev's own wife never forgave him for what happened to Collins. De Valera had been in the area and knew that Collins was also in West Cork, lending credence to the theory. But whatever responsibility Dev bore for his fiery words at the start of the conflict, it was wrong to blame him for Collins's death. By August 1922, de Valera

---

* This has never been conclusively proved and it is unlikely that it ever will be. As an ex-soldier, O'Neill was believed to have been the best shot, lending credence to the claim that he fired the fatal bullet. The University College Cork historian, Dr John Borgonovo, believes it likely Collins was hit by a ricochet from the armoured car. 'I have never seen any documentation of his pulling the trigger, and I know another IRA veteran from West Cork also claimed to have fired the shot.' (Correspondence with author, 20 Jun 17.)

had little influence on the military leadership of the IRA and was in the area trying to convince IRA leaders to lay down their arms. The war had found its own savage momentum without any help from Dev.

To the end Collins was true to his nature: he never fought without contemplating how the end of fighting might be brought about, and he was not yet ready for a war of extirpation against the Republicans. The month before his death he had warned that abusing them publicly was 'not the best way to tackle them. The men who are prepared to go to the extreme limit are misguided, but practically *all* of them are sincere.'[25] At least some of his Republican enemies would have felt the same about him.

Collins's comrade and army chief of staff, General Richard Mulcahy, urged that 'no cruel act of reprisal blemish your bright honour ...The Army serves — strengthened by its sorrow.'[26] But the viciousness would come. The death of Collins dismantled the last hopes on the Free State side of a compromise, and the words of new political chief of the Free State, W. T. Cosgrave, president of the Dáil, cast the war as an existential struggle and set the tone for what would follow. 'I am not going to hesitate and if the country is to live and we have to exterminate 10,000 Republicans, the three millions of people are bigger than this 10,000.'[27] This was August, less than a month into the Civil War, and the most senior constitutional politician in the land was talking about extermination. This was not a nod and a wink from the political elite but plain words that could be used to justify extreme measures. Paddy O'Daly and David Neligan had the backing they needed for a campaign without kid gloves.

The first death-squad actions took place before the end of August in Tralee. Men were abducted under cover of darkness, taken to a remote place and shot. The war settled into localised butchery. The IRA lacked the strength to engage the National Army in big battles. Even if it could take territory there were not enough men to hold it. But it did not act like an organisation preparing to attend its own funeral. In September, the IRA cut telegraph wires and blew up a railway bridge near the ruins of Arthur Vicars's house at Kilmorna. Then they attacked the village of Tarbert and, after pumping gallons of petrol into the building and firing incendiary bullets, seized the Free State headquarters. They might have incinerated their old comrades but the bullets failed to ignite the fuel. The countryside was in a state of perpetual apprehension. Armed men appeared at remote farmhouses in the middle of the night seeking food and shelter. Nobody dared refuse, though some did pass on information to the Free State.

Throughout the autumn months, tip-offs flowed to the army. Captain Mick Purtill used local knowledge to track the movements of the IRA units around the district and had filed into his memory the safe houses and bunkers from his own time with the Flying Column. There were sweeps through the countryside, much like the British in the latter stages of the Tan war, and more than two hundred Republicans were captured. Because this was Irish army, with the support of a significant number of locals, their intelligence officers could obtain information undreamt of by the Crown forces in the War of Independence. Still the IRA was able to keep up sufficient momentum to kill an estimated thirty-five National Army soldiers and wound a hundred in September and October, compared to nine deaths in their own ranks. Four of those were reprisal killings. An IRA prisoner John Galvin was shot after his arm was broken under torture and he confessed to the killing of a soldier. Seventeen-year-old Bertie Murphy was also shot, after being tortured. In September the government brought in an Emergency Powers Bill allowing the state to execute those caught in possession of arms and explosives. It was carried by forty-eight votes to eighteen. A two-week amnesty was offered to IRA men. If they came in and pledged not to take up arms again the war would be over. The Catholic bishops issued a pastoral letter calling on Republicans to lay down their arms and accept the amnesty, and threatened to refuse sacraments to IRA men who ignored the bishops' commands.

But Humphrey Murphy and the other defenders of the Republic ignored the overture from the government and regarded the

Church hierarchy as the religious wing of the Free State. The chief of staff, General Liam Lynch, was one of the small group who had tried to bridge the divide between the two factions of the IRA and prevent civil war. But when war came he proved every bit as ruthless as his Free State adversaries. Lynch was twenty-nine years old at the time and wrote of how sad 'it was to risk having to clash with our old comrades but we cannot count the cost'.[28] Four months later Lynch's tone towards his old friends had changed dramatically. He told a comrade that the IRA 'have now been hopelessly let down by their former comrades & leaders ... they have stooped to lower methods than the British, including murder gangs & vile propaganda ... Who could have dreamt that all our hopes could have been so blighted'.[29]

The IRA moved deeper into the mountains. IRA men had already staged walkouts from churches where there had been clerical criticism from the altar. And the men knew that not all the clergy opposed them. A friendly priest would always be found to whisper an act of contrition into the ear of a dying man or hear his last confession. They kept up the ambushes, hitting a general's convoy five miles from Listowel and killing one of his escort. The Free State responded by using a tactic pioneered by the British. IRA prisoners were placed on vehicles as human shields. As winter came on, the Free State was still unable to defeat the IRA. From mid-November to early December the war took on the intimately merciless character which would define it in the nation's collective memory. The first judicial executions of IRA prisoners under the emergency legislation took place at Kilmainham jail in Dublin. Republicans were being shot in the same jail and in the same manner as the heroes of 1916. This new rule of Ireland by Irishmen largely disavowed sentimental attachments.

On 30 November, General Lynch responded with his so-called 'orders of frightfulness' which targeted TDs (Teachta Dála – members of the Dáil) supportive of the executions, some judges and newspaper editors who were hostile to the Republican cause. On 7 December the IRA assassinated one TD and wounded another in an attack in Dublin. The following day the four most prominent IRA prisoners in Dublin were executed. All had been old comrades of members of the Free State government and army leaders. One, Rory O'Connor, had acted as best man at the wedding of the minister who signed his death warrant, Kevin O'Higgins. Liam Lynch responded by expanding the category of 'traitor' to all who supported the Free State and advocated the burning of their homes.

On 10 December, the seven-year-old son of a member of the Dáil was killed when the IRA burned down the family home. This prompted a newspaper to ask: 'Since when has the burning of innocent children become part of the tactics of clean fighting?'[30] Notices appeared in villages near Listowel warning that 'for every Republican shot, two Staters will fall'.[31] The father of the Justice Minister, Kevin O'Higgins, was shot in February 1923 after the IRA destroyed the family home. The army's chief legal advisor wrote to General Mulcahy, the former IRA chief of staff and new Minister of Defence, that the execution of prisoners could be justified because the 'circumstances of the nation at present justify almost anything that would serve to end the present [Irregular] campaign of murder and arson … [and] the execution of persons tried and convicted in pursuance of a resolution of the Dáil as a reprisal, is preferable to the execution of persons untried and unconvicted'.[32] The Free State forces killed men after court-martial, and without any trial at all. A trial usually meant a hastily convened meeting of senior officers. Any man caught with a gun could expect to be shot on sight.

Around Listowel the peace that initially accompanied the return of the Free State troops vanished. Jittery soldiers shot one of their own men in the dark outside a dancehall. In the early New Year of 1923, the Republicans intensified their campaign against the railways, a vital source of provisions for civilians and military alike. On 19 January the IRA wrecked the tracks on the Listowel–Tralee line, causing the train to crash. The driver and his fireman died agonising deaths, scalded by boiling water and crushed by the locomotive.

Four Republican prisoners were sentenced to death in reprisal. Four days after the derailment two railway workers were shot dead outside Tralee station. The National Army officer Niall Harrington claimed the killings had been carried out by men on his own side to further discredit the IRA. Near the Purtills' farm at Ballydonoghue the IRA attacked and destroyed the station building. The Civil War divided the family of Hannah's childhood friend, May Ahern. Her brother, for whom May had scouted during ambushes against the police, joined the Free State army with Mick Purtill. May went to the Republican side and turned her skills as a scout and weapons smuggler against the Free State. Years later, when applying for a military pension, she wrote of the conflict of personal and political loyalties of that time. Writing of her home she says: 'I got my brother ... to leave'[33] – and this so that she could hide IRA men on the run. Her brother would have known why she wanted him to go. People made accommodations or they did not. They found ways of looking the other way or they hunted old comrades to death.

By January 1923, the National Army had promoted Paddy O'Daly to the rank of major-general in command of Kerry. He pressed Mulcahy in Dublin to confirm his orders for the execution of the four prisoners after the train derailment. The men had nothing to do with the derailment but were considered by O'Daly to be 'exceptionally bad cases'.[34]

In a sign of where broader public sympathy stood, a deputation of railwaymen who had received death threats went to O'Daly to pledge that 'neither murder nor assassination would prevent them from carrying out their duties'.[35] Two days later the IRA held up the mail train between Ballybunion and Listowel, stole the mail and wrecked the engine and carriages, forcing the passengers to walk the rest of the journey.

A Free State soldier who witnessed the executions described how the men were lined up beside their coffins to be shot. According to Private Bill Bailey the condemned were kept waiting by the coffins because the commander of the firing squad was still in bed. 'The men were looking into [the] coffins and they could see their

Mick Purtill on his wedding day
with Madge, after the war

names and then [they] got into coffins to see were they the right size, then they exchanged coffins and their names on [the] coffins.'[36] According to the witness the firing squad was made up of young men, most of whom were crying.

O'Daly surrounded himself with old associates from the Squad. Most of his troops were either from Dublin or the west of Ireland – men without ties to the locality. Once the war was over they could leave and never have to face the relatives of those they had killed. For Con Brosnan and Mick Purtill it was different. Beyond the bare few lines in a military file in Dublin there is nothing to suggest how Mick dealt with any conflict of loyalties, except for something my cousin Liam Purtill said when he was remembering a story he heard from the family of an old comrade in the Flying Column. According to this source, Captain Mick Purtill was based at Tarbert when a patrol brought in an old friend – Con Dee – who was already a legend among local Republicans. Mick and Con had been on their very first IRA mission together at Ballybunion RIC barracks, and had hidden in the church at Ballydonoghue to escape a Tan round-up. Hannah Purtill had guided Con to safety across the fields. Con had later cheated death at the hands of the Tan firing squad at Knockanure by running until he collapsed from his wounds.

But the Civil War had placed Con Dee and Mick Purtill on opposite sides. Con had been captured in arms and the punishment was death by firing squad. By Liam Purtill's account, Mick made a quick intervention. 'He just shouted "My prisoner", and took Con Dee away.' Mick could not see his old comrade face a second firing squad. So he took him to Tarbert harbour and put him on a boat across the Shannon to County Clare. This is the story that has been handed down in our family. It invites so many questions. How did Mick explain the loss of the prisoner to his superiors, and what was his role at Tarbert? But he is gone and my cousin only remembers the short account the Dee family gave him. All we know is that it was a harsh time when neither side was given to the habit of mercy and that Mick Purtill took a risk to free his old friend. Con Dee was eventually recaptured and went on hunger strike before he was released and left permanently for the United States. Like so many of the defeated Republicans he found the new Ireland of the Free State a cold place. He died in Chicago in 1967 at the age of seventy-one, exiled from the country for which he had been willing to sacrifice his life.

It was local bad blood that set in chain the worst of the atrocities. Up to the present day there are Republicans who will shout 'Ballyseedy' to remind the descendants of the Free State government of their perfidy. Paddy O'Daly was the one who gave the orders but the source of the viciousness lay in the hill country of Knocknagoshel, about twelve miles to the east of Listowel, among men who had known each other all of their lives. Pat O'Connor was a farmer who yearned for an end to the war. When he saw IRA Columns moving across his land he passed on the information to the Free State army. The IRA got wind of this, fined him £100 and warned against any further association with the soldiers. But O'Connor and his son Paddy 'Pats' were proud men. They would not be told what to do by a bunch of young bucks with guns. When the farmer refused to pay the IRA fine his home was raided and smashed up and his cattle and life savings seized. It meant financial ruin and a very public blow to the pride of the O'Connors.

At this point the story spirals towards a blood feud. The younger Paddy 'Pats' O'Connor's response was to join the Free State army, where he would be accused of taking part in violent interrogations of Republican prisoners.

A decision was taken by the IRA to kill Paddy 'Pats' and he was lured by a tip-off to a dugout where arms were supposedly hidden. The dugout had been booby-trapped with a mine. O'Connor and four other soldiers – including three Dublin Guards known personally to O'Daly – were blown up, ripped to pieces by high explosive in the middle of the night. A survivor was hideously maimed. IRA man Seamus O'Connor, a native of Knocknagoshel, was lying in a dugout several miles away when he was woken by the blast. 'Somebody lit a match and noted the time on his watch ... "It's the mine," he said. "Lord have mercy on their souls."'[37] An IRA message reported 'that a trigger mine was laid in Knocknagoshel for a member of the F. S. Army Lt. O'Connor who had made a hobby out of torturing Republican prisoners in Castleisland'.[38]

O'Daly responded by ordering a group of nine Republican prisoners to be brought before him in Tralee. At first the men were forced to look at the mutilated remains of the dead soldiers. One account, published within a year of the massacre, alleged that the men were beaten with hammers, had shots fired around their heads and were then shown their own coffins. This was written from a staunchly Republican standpoint but it rings true. The commander and his chief of intelligence, David Neligan, would become hate figures for a generation of Republicans.*

---

* David Neligan had been a spy for Michael Collins inside the police in Dublin Castle. A native of west Limerick, he would have known the geography of north Kerry and some of the IRA personnel. The IRA commander Ernie O'Malley, who chronicled the period in several acclaimed books, believed there was no conclusive evidence linking Neligan to killings.

Early on 7 March 1923 and on Paddy O'Daly's command, the nine men were loaded into a lorry and brought to Ballyseedy Cross, a known Republican ambush point. The men were taken out and made to sit on the ground among tree branches and other debris, under which had been hidden a landmine. The executioners were all men of the Dublin Guard. The blast blew eight men to pieces and sent Stephen Fuller flying through the air. The National Army issued a statement saying the prisoners were victims of an IRA landmine which had also injured several soldiers. A young Free State lieutenant, Niall Harrington, one of those men of conscience who appears on occasion in war, a man whose belief in truth overpowers atavism, a rare man in that place and time, suspected that the men had been summarily executed. Despite denials by his superiors Harrington carried out his own investigation and reached a damning conclusion: 'Reprisals for the mine [Knocknagoshel] were deliberately planned by a clique of influential Dublin guards officers ... the facts are that the mines used in the slaughter of the prisoners were constructed in Tralee under the supervision of two senior Dublin Guards officers.'[39]

An IRA account described how 'the road was covered with blood, pieces of flesh, bones, boots, and clothing were scattered about'.[40] When the army brought the coffins with the dead prisoners to Tralee, the victims' families were asked to collect them for burial. But they refused to accept the military coffins. The bodies, or what was left of them, were taken out in front of the barracks. Looking at the mangled remains the relatives turned on the soldiers and 'stoned every member of the Free State army they saw ... [the bodies] were removed to other coffins and those provided by the Free State army were kicked through the Barrack gate'.[41]

Private Bill Bailey, a native of Tralee and more likely to be sympathetic to Kerry prisoners than the Dublin Guards, was on duty that day and recalled that around four in the afternoon relatives arrived with donkeys and carts to collect the dead. Seeing the rough coffins, and then opening them to identify their kin, the people became enraged, hurling abuse and stones at the soldiers. They smashed the coffins and transferred the bodies to others they had brought with them. Bailey claimed that the army band had been marched to the gate to greet the relatives. 'Just before coffins were given out, the band lined up and played ragtime [jazz] inside [the] gate – "I'm the Sheikh of Araby" etc. on either side of the main gate. Completely shocked and dazed the people.'[42] General O'Daly and his subordinates had carried out atrocities which they justified in the name of terrorising the IRA into submission. But they had also revelled in their ruthlessness.

O'Daly led the official investigation of the Ballyseedy incident and, unsurprisingly, exonerated himself and the Dublin Guard. He lied and the Minister of Defence, Richard Mulcahy, backed him up, preferring to protect the honour of the National Army than investigate atrocities on his own side. The Catholic Church, meanwhile, said nothing that would upset the Free State. As the IRA commander Ernie O'Malley bitterly remarked: 'The thundering pulpits were strangely silent about what the crows ate in Kerry.'[43] Only the Free State Lieutenant, Niall Harrington, displayed a moral compass, travelling to Dublin to make a report to the authorities. He was thanked and sent on his way back to Kerry. The north Kerry men seem to have been kept away from the worst violence. Perhaps they were not trusted to torture and kill old friends? Mick Purtill was based at Tarbert, twenty-seven miles from Ballyseedy, with his friend Con Brosnan. The dirty work around Tralee and south Kerry was left, largely, to the Dublin Guard.

There were further massacres of prisoners after Ballyseedy. In south Kerry the same tactic of tying men to mines was used to kill eight men in two separate blasts. Spring came and the IRA were being hunted down with relentless ferocity. Information continued to flow to the army. A detachment of the new national police force, the Garda Síochána, arrived in Listowel to take up the work once done by the RIC. But they were not armed and left the fighting to the army. The bitter end was approaching.

In the last fortnight of April 1923 there was a spasm of killing around north Kerry as O'Daly's men fought the Republican diehards.

After an ambush on a Free State patrol, Timothy 'Aero' Lyons and his group took refuge in the caves at Clashmealcon, about nine miles up the coast from Ballybunion. Lyons's nickname came from his apparent ability to appear out of nowhere in attacks. But on this occasion a captured guerrilla told the army where he was hiding. The caves were surrounded and fires set outside to try and smoke Lyons and his comrades into the open. Two men tried to escape by night but were washed away by the sea. There was firing from the caves and two soldiers were killed. After two days Lyons came out and surrendered, but as he was being hauled up the rope snapped and he fell to the rocks below. The Free State soldiers fired on his body. His comrades gave themselves up and were subsequently executed. My grandfather's friend, Dan Flavin, was in custody with the condemned men. At one point the other IRA prisoners were told they could save their lives if they would sign a document calling for an IRA surrender. They refused and were beaten. They lived in constant fear of being executed. 'They took out seven men that night and ours was a corridor room through which they would have to pass. We got a terrible fright as the men passed out for you didn't know who would be next,' said Flavin. 'Next morning four of them were carried to hospital. Their shirts were stuck to them with their own blood.'[44]

Another of our Church Street neighbours, Denis Quille, was among IRA prisoners who set fire to their jail near Dublin. 'The prison was blazing. The Staters shouted at us to get in. In reply, we shouted, "Up Kerry!" "Up the Republic".'[45] The Free State guards opened fire with machine guns and killed a prisoner before a priest was summoned and stopped the shooting.

Seventy-seven Republican prisoners were officially executed during the eleven months of the Civil War, triple the number executed by the British during the Tan war. For years Richard Mulcahy would endure the nickname 'Dirty Dick' and hear shouts of 'Remember the 77'. Talk to many Fine Gael people of the older generation and they will agree that the executions were brutal but argue that nothing else would have saved the state. Except that there was no forgetting and no forgiving. In time some of the men who fought on the Republican side would help form the most successful political party in the history of the Irish state, and they would sit in parliament opposite the men who had sanctioned the executions and covered up the atrocities. Political power, decades of power, was their reward. In the wider public realm, in schools especially, there was silence about the brutal facts of what happened in north Kerry. But this was a different thing to forgetting.

13

A New Ireland

And as he travels back he thinks of history, sees something
old, tarnished and achingly human rising out of the
chaos of the present ...

Niall Jordan, *The Past*, 1980[1]

I

The end was preceded by horror and delusion. Although pursued
across mountains, the IRA commander General Lynch believed that
mountain artillery, imported from Germany or America, could
change the course of the war for them. 'You realise that even one
piece of artillery would do this. One such piece could be moved
round amongst our strong forces and this would completely
demoralise the enemy and end the war,'[2] he announced to his
exhausted staff. How the miracle weapons would reach Ireland or
be transported into the mountains of the south, past the Free State
army, was never clear. Even de Valera, who had been looking for a
ceasefire since July, enabled this blind faith, telling a supporter in
early February 1923 that 'one big effort from our friends everywhere
and I think we would finally smash the Free State'.[3] Having spent the
Civil War sidelined by the militarists, the master politician was

reasserting himself, sounding tough but knowing privately that victory was no longer possible. Dev could feel the end coming. By late February even the redoubtable Humphrey Murphy was warning that the 'steamrollering of the South would soon finish us'.[4]

The fear of execution by the Free State, legal and summary, was pervasive. On 14 March 1923, Listowel man Dan Enright was shot by firing squad in County Donegal. He had gone north with a team of Cork and Kerry guerrilla veterans to help the struggling IRA forces along the border. Enright was an old comrade of Con Brosnan and Mick Purtill. He was with Brosnan the night they killed James Kane, an executioner who now faced his own violent death. On the eve of his execution Enright wrote that the 'sentence of death is just after being passed upon me, but I am taking it like a soldier should'.[5] The following morning Dan Enright and three others, including another Listowel man, Timothy O'Sullivan, were taken into nearby woods by National Army troops and shot. For a few years now, men had been walked into woods, down lanes, across bogs, a gun pressed to their backs, maybe a blindfold to help propel them unseeing into the forever darkness, men walking to the end of their lives. Seamus O'Connor, on the run in north Kerry, remembered of the Free State army: 'there was no yardstick now by which their actions could be measured: they had started to kill indiscriminately'.[6]

IRA ambushes were swiftly followed by Free State counter-attacks. By late spring the Free State confidently predicted the impending collapse of the IRA campaign. Mick Purtill had another narrow escape. A bullet went through the shoulder pads of his tunic. Survival rather than resistance became the focus of hard-pressed IRA fugitives. Liam Lynch was killed in the first week of April 1923, shot by a sniper as he scrambled his way across a mountainside in County Tipperary. At Lynch's urging, his comrades left the dying leader to be captured by Free State troops. Frank Aiken, who succeeded Lynch as IRA chief of staff, wrote to Lynch's brother that the fight had taken place 'on a mountain as bare as a billiard table':

Sean Hyde had him by the hand helping him along when he was hit ... To leave him was the hardest thing any of us ever had to do. I was last leaving, having been carrying his feet. I was afraid to even say 'Good-bye Liam' least it would dishearten him ... Liam's death was a great blow to our chances of success, coming at the time it did. But they ... [the press] ... are quite wrong if they think they have heard the last of the IRA & the Irish Republic.[7]

But the last hopeless dreams of Republican victory had died with Lynch. 'Events of the last few days point to the beginning of the end so far as the irregular campaign is concerned,' an army report said. 'The general feeling of the people seems to be that the Irregular Organisation ... is doomed.'[8] IRA commander Frank Aiken, later to become a celebrated foreign minister under de Valera, ordered the Irregulars to dump their weapons.

The Civil War allowed all kinds of grudges to float free to the surface. Men took the opportunity to thieve from neighbours or avenge old slights. Much harm was done in the name of the Republic and the Free State. The lawlessness touched Ballydonoghue. It can be traced in the financial compensation claims lodged by the victims. Johanna Sheahan of Moybella was told to clear out the tenants on her farm before her house was burned down. She had offended some group of armed men but the claim for compensation does not indicate who they are. Margaret Brown, who ran a shop at Lisselton Cross, was robbed on several occasions. 'Tobacco and provisions taken ... by armed men on various dates.'[9] IRA man Seamus O'Connor entered a shop near Knocknagoshel and found two armed men in the process of stealing all they could carry. A terrifying stand-off followed with one of the men pressing his cocked revolver into O'Connor's stomach. It ended when the thieves backed down, faced with the levelled weapons of O'Connor's comrades; the robbers might have killed O'Connor but they would never have left the shop alive.

The home of the steward for Eyre Massey Stack, a local landlord, was attacked. The steward, Daniel Sweeney, was also a farmer and the claim records that a 'dwelling house, gates and land [were] damaged at Ballyconry on various dates in 1922'.[10] Over in Con Brosnan's home parish of Newtownsandes the local priest submitted a claim for the destruction of the national school at Knockanure, which was burned down in January 1923. This is close to where the Tans executed three men and badly wounded Con Dee. Why would the IRA – if it was them – burn down the school? Was it revenge for the church damning them from the pulpit, or was it the action of louts taking advantage of the febrile times?

In the same parish in April, Keating's Creamery was bombed and a train carrying cream was destroyed. This was the kind of thing the Tans had done to inflict misery on local communities. The Minister for Justice, Kevin O'Higgins, declared that the Free State had to vindicate law and order 'as against anarchy'.[11] But O'Higgins would not live to become an old warrior looking back on the terrible battles of his youth. Four years after the war's end, at the age of thirty-five, he was shot dead by the IRA as he walked to mass in Dublin. One of Kevin O'Higgins's killers said that they had spotted him by chance and were 'taken over and incensed with hatred ... with the memory of the executions'.[12] The story loops back to Listowel. O'Higgins's bodyguard on the day he was assassinated was Brian O'Grady, comrade of Con Brosnan and Mick Purtill, and the man who left the haunting account of the killing of the alleged informer James Kane.

The war of the brothers lasted barely a year, beginning with the occupation of Dublin's Four Courts building and ending soon after Lynch's death in the mountains. Historians have not yet agreed on a reliable figure for Civil War fatalities, with the best estimates ranging from between 1,000 and 2,000 combined deaths by the ceasefire of 24 May 1923. The years of war, from the first ambushes in 1919 to the agony of Ballyseedy and the final executions, had deeply destabilised society. Around Listowel attempts were being made to restore a normal order. A week after the ceasefire, policemen were on the beat, seizing a boat and poachers' nets on the River Feale; in this new state the police carried no guns and, because they were not regarded as political, they could walk without fear of ambush. By the end of August the local council was threatening to send the Army in to collect rates, such had been the collapse in revenue collection in recent years; a homeless man named Brown broke into the Listowel Workhouse with his wife and family and took over the male tramp's ward; a landowner from Limerick was claiming compensation for the loss of forty-five acres near Ballybunion where landless people had taken up squatters' rights. This was near the Purtills at Ballydonoghue and would have reinforced their determination to see a stable order return after the wartime chaos. A judge hearing compensation claims for war losses in the town remarked caustically that 'the Kerry people were not going to lose much from the war, judging by the claims they are putting in'.[13] He was a tough mark. His judgements were five hundred per cent below the amounts sought.

Paddy O'Daly was the malign master of all he surveyed. In a notorious incident he and two other officers assaulted the daughters of a Kenmare doctor, dragging them out in their night clothes, flogging them and rubbing oil in their hair. He again escaped censure.

The great survivor of the Revolution was de Valera. He escaped execution in 1916 because of the late timing of his court-martial and survived the Tan war by virtue of a growing political status that would have made killing him a catastrophic option for the British. The Civil War destroyed some of his best friends and greatest rivals. By the time it ended the majority of Republicans opposed to the Free State were ready to take the political road, leaving an IRA hard core that would struggle on until a Dev government rounded on them, at one point importing the English hangman Albert Pierrepoint to execute the IRA chief of staff. De Valera had broken away from Sinn Féin in 1926 and formed his own party, Fianna Fáil (the Soldiers of Destiny). The following year he led his elected comrades into the Dáil after swallowing his objections to the oath of allegiance. Five years later, in March 1932, he formed the first Fianna Fáil-led government and would remain in power for sixteen years, dominating Irish life in a manner nobody has ever, or is ever likely, to rival. One of his first acts was to abolish the oath of allegiance. There was little London could do or was minded to do.

Within two years of coming to power, and with the IRA firmly in Dev's sights, the Special Branch were harassing Republicans in Listowel, raiding meeting rooms and ripping up floorboards. Men who had followed Dev in the Tan war and the Civil War watched him set out to dismantle the IRA without a backward glance.

Hannah Purtill stayed loyal to the memory of Michael Collins, and when some of his former comrades formed a movement known as the Army Comrades Association in 1932 she joined up. The ACA adopted a uniform of blue shirts and black berets and were quickly known as the Blueshirts. Con Brosnan joined too. The context is important. The Blueshirts were different things to different people. There were those, especially in the leadership, who admired Hitler's Blackshirts and Mussolini's Brownshirts. They saw Franco's Spanish nationalists as saviours of Christianity in the face of a godless communist onslaught and sent a brigade to fight in Spain against the

My grandmother's comrades in the Blueblouses, the women's wing of the Blueshirts

Republicans. There were fascists among the Blueshirts but my grandmother was not one of them.

Around Listowel, and certainly for Hannah, the Blueshirts were primarily the defenders of Collins's political legacy, and the physical response of his followers to Republican intimidation. They had formed a new political party, Fine Gael – the party of the Gael – but with de Valera's Fianna Fáil in government and escalating harassment from the rump of the IRA, they looked to the Blueshirts to protect political meetings and crack the skulls of their more militant opponents. The low-level violence that spluttered from 1934 through the following year was a coda to the Civil War. A former IRA guerrilla and Free State soldier, Paddy Joe McElligott, led the Listowel Blueshirts. In the War of Independence he planned the killing of Tobias O'Sullivan, helped shoot the fisheries inspector James Keane, and grieved a brother killed by the British. A party of Blueshirts from Listowel, including ten women, was shot at on their way to a Fine Gael meeting in Ballybunion, close to the Purtill farm. The IRA raided the homes of Fine Gael supporters and a parish priest told his congregants that 'the spirit of bitterness and hatred which springs up from political differences in Ireland [is] diabolical and inspired by hell itself'.[14]

On the night in May that the Blueshirt leader, General Eoin O'Duffy, came to town Hannah had a fateful choice to make.* There were six hundred policemen backed up by soldiers in armoured cars and a general expectation of serious trouble. Several hundred Republicans had already massed in the square, boiling for a fight. My grandmother had been warned by Republican acquaintances that if she marched down to welcome O'Duffy, she would have the 'blue shirt torn off of her back'.[15] It was a threat to humiliate her in front

---

* General Eoin O'Duffy, 1892–1944, was a former IRA commander, general in the National Army and founder of the Gardai, as well as being the first leader of Fine Gael. His erratic political behaviour saw him finish his public life in obscurity. During the Second World War he offered to send an Irish legion to fight with the Nazis on the Eastern Front. His offer was disregarded

of the entire street. Hannah ignored the threat and went. A contemporary account described how O'Duffy 'passed through a guard of honour of about a hundred blue-shirted young men and women' and mounted an ass and cart, the workers at the local timber factory having refused to give wood for a stage.[16]

There is a photograph of O'Duffy standing on the a cart outside the Protestant church of St John's. He is stocky and bald and the Blueshirt uniform gives him the look of an Irish Mussolini. Republicans remembered that O'Duffy was one of the leaders of the military campaign against them here in the Civil War, a comrade of Paddy O'Daly and the other outsiders who had tortured and executed their comrades. The blood could not have been any badder. The general announced that armed Republicans had already tried to attack the Blueshirts but a large party had 'been driven off by a man over sixty years of age armed only with a sweeping brush, with which he injured many of the Republicans besides capturing one of

The Blueshirt leader, General Eoin O'Duffy,
speaking in Listowel

their rifles'.[17] It sounded like a tall tale. But I am sure my grandmother loved it. After the speech four hundred young men armed with sticks attempted to attack O'Duffy's supporters and 'repeated baton charges were necessary before order was restored'.[18]

De Valera saw the danger of private armies swarming the countryside. First he banned the Blueshirts, who duly disappeared back to their farms and businesses. The IRA was next up for proscription and was not so obliging. During ensuing decades it split, surged, shrank and split again. It has claimed the right to kill its enemies in the name of the Republic to this day.

The hatred festered in north Kerry for years afterwards.

Mick Purtill was attacked by Republicans while cycling home from a football match. 'He was very badly beaten,' my cousin Liam recalled. Revenge was not long coming. 'I know for a fact that two or three of them paid the price. He was a fearless man.'[19] On another occasion Con Brosnan cycled out to visit Mick at the farm. On the way he stopped to chat to a neighbour and Con asked about the man and his family. 'We are fine but there is a man down there, Mick Purtill, if we could only get rid of him,' the man said. To 'get rid of' meant a bullet in the head. Con replied: 'If I had my revolver, it isn't Mick we would be getting rid of but you.'[20]

Years later Mick Purtill's wife, my great-aunt Madge, was out canvassing for votes in the county council elections when she was verbally abused by a woman who pointed to a hole in her living room wall and shouted: 'That's the shot he [Mick] fired to kill my father.'[21] The man had not been killed but the anger had endured.

The man Mick and Hannah had worshipped faded out in the larger public memory. Michael Collins became, among his followers, the object of an idealised counter-factualism that endures to this day. 'What if he had lived? What kind of Ireland would we have had?' … 'Would he have united the nation? Yes. Of course, yes.' … 'If only. If only.' To Hannah he became in death the lost leader who might have saved us from the suffocating rule of lesser men. This was dreaming of a man that never was. A man who died too young, and in such a fractured country, to be able to show what kind of a peacetime leader he would have made. The story of Collins and de Valera was reduced to a contest of virility, an argument about 'who would you want with you in a fight', which only the tall handsome Mick, the laughing boy, whistling bravely from beyond the grave, could ever win.

De Valera lived to enjoy the worship of his supporters and to mould modern Ireland in the image of his dreams. I don't think Hannah ever forgave him.

What's the news, what's the news?
De Valera's pawned his shoes
To buy ammunition for his men.
They were eating currant buns
When they heard the Free State guns
And all the dirty cowards ran away.
(Street Ballad, Civil War period)

Éamon de Valera – the leader who more than any other
shaped the Ireland in which I grew up

I learned the ballad in my grandmother's kitchen. I grew up with the mantra of Dev the crooked, Dev the true killer of Collins. I came to believe that he was responsible for all the ills of the nation. Economic stagnation, mass emigration, censorship, the power-hungry bishops, the way we were forced to learn Irish at school, the absence of sex or even pictures of sex ... all this and much more was the fault of that 'long miserable hoor', as my father called him. A family anecdote illustrates the depth of the loathing. A relative of Dev's was courting my auntie Peg. She had met him in Dublin where she was training to be an air hostess for Aer Lingus, the new national airline. My grandmother was an hospitable woman and would not have held the young man's lineage against him. Others in the house felt differently. When the young suitor was brought home to Church Street he was shown into the kitchen for the obligatory tea and small talk. In the middle of the pleasantries the door opened and in walked my eccentric uncle Danny, occasional cattle dealer and denizen of the high attic, bearing his chamber pot. Danny stood to attention, held out the pot and then marched outside to dispose of the contents. The love affair ended soon afterwards.

Dev was no monster. Nor was he solely responsible for the gloomy state of the nation in which my grandparents raised their children. There is no evidence, apart from youthful anti-clericalism, to suggest that had Collins lived they would have grown up in a paradise of full employment and liberal social mores. The nineteenth-century struggles of faith and land had bequeathed a legacy of conservatism in rural Ireland which moulded the world view of Dev and Collins. The greatest of all myths was that the Irish were a nation of natural rebels. Far from it. The conservatism of the mid- to late nineteenth century came out of the long sacrifices and struggles of centuries. The Irish yearned for a stable order. Social and economic radicalism was confined to small pockets in the countryside and a slightly larger space in the cities.

The claustrophobic Catholicism and bitter politics did not stifle cultural expression in north Kerry. With the English gone there were the new targets for the pens of angry young men, and the poets and playwrights flourished. As in the days of the Gaelic bards, satire became a potent weapon. During the bitter election campaign of 1951, my uncle, John B, and several friends decided to challenge the prevailing Civil War politics. Sick of the old bitterness they put up a mock candidate, Tom Doodle, with the campaign message 'Vote the Noodle and Give the Whole Kaboodle to Doodle'. On the night before the Taoiseach was due to appear at a rally in Listowel, the Doodle campaign arranged for their candidate to arrive by train where he was met by a brass band and a crowd of several thousand. To cheers he outlined his promises, chief among them that 'every man would have more than the next'.* Inevitably, created as it was by young men of high spirits, the hour of Doodle passed and the old politics continued undisturbed well into my adulthood.

I look back on my grandparents' generation and see a people exhausted and traumatised by conflict. Their horizons were narrowed by the desire for stability, above all else, in a country that was beggared and a wider world staggering between mass confla-grations. I cannot blame them for the inherited narrow ground on which I took my first steps. They wanted to hold what they had and add a few acres, a few more head of cattle, send their children to college, or get them into the civil service. In 'Strong Beams' the poet Máirtín Ó Direáin wrote tellingly of that rural mind for whom the memory of dispossession was just a generation away:

Stand your ground, soul:
Hold fast to everything that's rooted ...[22]

---

* It is likely John B. found the name in Dicken's *Bleak House*, where 'Lord Coodle would go out, Sir Thomas Doodle wouldn't come in'. Estimates of the crowd vary but around three thousand are thought to have attended the rally. Among Doodle's other promises were to open a factory for shaving the hair from gooseberries and to plough the Rocks of Bawn which, being both mythical and rocks, were unploughable.

Dev was driven by the desire to establish beyond all question or threat the sovereignty of Ireland. His Ireland would be economically self-sufficient and culturally independent. Instead it was blighted by unemployment and mass migration. Because of this it is tempting to regard de Valera as a failed leader. I held to that view for much of my life. But wider reading, the influence of more dispassionate historians, has given me a more rounded view of the man and his times. Now I think of him, at least in his larger vision, as a romantic hobbled by a failure of imagination when it came to economic and social progress. His lyrical imagining was of an Ireland as 'the home of a people':

> who valued material wealth only as a basis for right living, of a
> people who, satisfied with frugal comfort, devoted their
> leisure to the things of the spirit – a land whose countryside
> would be bright with cosy homesteads, whose fields and
> villages would be joyous with the sounds of industry, with the
> romping of sturdy children, the contest of athletic youths and
> the laughter of happy maidens, whose firesides would be
> forums for the wisdom of serene old age. The home, in short,
> of a people living the life that God desires that men should
> live.[23]

This speech is regularly held up as an example of Dev the obscurantist. But the context is all-important. He was speaking on the radio on St Patrick's Day, 1943, while war raged in Europe and totalitarianism preached a doctrine of invincible might, where humanity was reduced in Hitler's words to mere 'biological plasticine'. Set against the inhumanity of fascism and Stalinism, de Valera's bucolic Ireland offered a consoling idea. In a time of fear Dev was offering a tempting vision whose symbols – land, family, secure homes – would have resonated deeply across the nation. It was a vision of its time, not unlike the promised land of Steinbeck's *Grapes of Wrath* (1939) with its celebration of the 'way kids laugh when they're hungry and they know supper's ready, and when the people are eatin' the stuff they raise and livin' in the houses they build', although rooted in devout religiosity that would have appalled the American writer. Dev was neutral in the sense of not joining the war as a combatant, but carefully balanced his neutrality in the direction of the Allies; he interned captured Germans but allowed Allied airmen to reach Northern Ireland. Had Ireland entered battle as Churchill wished, the prospect of a renewed civil war was real. The IRA had not vanished and the prospect of Irishmen being sent to war as allies of England was too close to the memory of Redmond and the Volunteers of 1914. Dev knew well that if he entered that war he could have no guarantees about the kind of Ireland that would emerge.

De Valera stepped down as Taoiseach in 1959, two years before I was born. Yet the Ireland in which I spent my early years was smothered in his essence. Fragments of memory: an old man getting out of a car accompanied by an army officer. I think it is at my Irish-speaking school, perhaps the fiftieth anniversary of the Rising, and in my mind children are singing for him an old ballad fashioned anew by Pearse as the marching song of the Revolution.

Oró, sé do bheatha 'bhaile,
Oró, sé do bheatha 'bhaile,
Oró, sé do bheatha 'bhaile,
Anois are theacht an tsamhraidh.

(Oh-ro, you're welcome home,
Oh-ro, you're welcome home,
Oh-ro, you're welcome home,
Now that summer's coming.)

The song was about routing the foreigners. The great sixteenth-century pirate queen Grace O'Malley and a thousand warriors would return home from over the seas to drive the English out.

Dev still talked about the unity of the island. Officially it was his party's most important priority. But the Catholics living under

Unionist rule in the six counties hardly merited a debate in the Dáil. The north was marooned in the zone of forgetting by the governments in Dublin and London. When conflict exploded in 1969 national passions briefly surged. Then came the long attrition with its thousands of dead. When the violence did cross the border – the bombings of Dublin and Monaghan in 1974, for example – the effect was to reinforce our desire to be left alone. Thirty-three people were killed and we briefly experienced the terror that haunted the lives of our fellow islanders to the north. It was part of the same story that had overtaken my grandmother and her brother in their youth. Yet its virulent quarrel over faith and identity made it ineffably different. For my people, the north was always too far away, the conflict with the Unionists too complex, and the memory of the Civil War too haunting for them to do anything but mind their own business. Partition did not begin for them with the Government of Ireland Act in 1920. It had been part of the psychological atmosphere of the family into which I was born and reared since at least the late nineteenth century. Ulster was the troublesome country of the Home Rule riots, sectarian murder gangs, burning houses; it was also the industrial north with its linen mills and shipyards, and it was the home of a flinty Protestantism whose adherents believed they were the elect of God. It was the place that the great nationalist leaders, Daniel O'Connell and Charles Stewart Parnell, had taken trouble to avoid setting foot in for most of their political careers.

The Purtills and Con Brosnan did not go to war to capture Belfast and impose Gaelic Catholic supremacy on the entire island of Ireland, but to be masters in their own place, believing they might build a more prosperous happy country outside the British Empire. Their own freedom of religion had been secured a century before. There were no loyalist ghettos in Listowel or Tralee and the local Protestants had long ceased to represent any kind of overlordship. In his later years when he spoke of the Protestants of Listowel, my father became wistful. He compared them frequently and favourably to the Catholic clerics of the district. His Protestants were the local rector and his family, and a daughter of the manse for whom he harboured a secret longing. In those days romantic visions swam eternally before him.

II

In my own barony of Iveragh in the County of Kerry ... there are no Protestants in the world, less apprehensive of Roman Catholics, or Papists, than they are. We live in perfect harmony.

Daniel O'Connell, House of Commons Select Committee on Ireland, 1825

If I seem preoccupied with the fate of the Protestant minority it is because I have witnessed, so often, the trampling underfoot of religious and ethnic minorities around the world. We are to be judged, rightly so, on the way we treat those outside our inherited tribal identity. The Civil War was won by the side they had favoured but the world they knew was gone. The Protestants began to leave. In north Kerry they were few to begin with and they faded out rather than vanished. By the start of the twenty-first century the Protestants of Listowel and its hinterland had all but vanished. This was not like Smyrna in September 1922 when massacre and fire drove the Greeks and other Christian minorities out of Asia Minor. Nor was it like Bosnia decades later when the mosques were blown up and everybody of the wrong religion was taken out and killed. There were no speeches from politicians denigrating the minority, much less declarations ordering their expulsion, or lists of victims to be slaughtered – all of which typify my own experience of ethnic cleansing and genocide. Yet Protestants left the south in large numbers in the period of the Revolution and in the decade that followed.

Between 1911 and 1926 the Protestant population fell by thirty-three per cent. Take an even longer timeframe and the Protestant decline reflects the immense shift in social, economic and political power in the south. Between 1861 and 1936 the population dropped by sixty-one per cent. Some of this was down to the departure of Protestants in the British administration. Declining birth and marriage rates further eroded the numbers. Some, especially in the border counties, preferred to take their chances in the Protestant state up north.* The burning of the big houses, the targeting of those who were known or suspected to be sympathetic to Crown forces, the retreat of the order which had guaranteed their security, all combined to create a pervasive unease. One leading Presbyterian wrote that the 'break up of the big estates ... and the transfer of the army, police and government officials as well as businesses of various kinds to the North, or across the water to Great Britain, have diminished our numbers and depleted the strength of our congregations. To those who knew the Ireland of the last century ... the contrast is at once startling and depressing.'[24] These were not colonial settlers in the modern sense of the term, with a century or less of the earth beneath their feet. Some pre-dated the Dutch who landed in South Africa in 1652 by nearly a century and the Pieds-Noirs of Algeria by 300 years.

In the spring of 1922, during the Truce and on the eve of the Civil War, there was an outburst of violence against Protestants in West Cork. Thirteen men were killed in the last week of April. All of the dead had survived the War of Independence and might have had cause to believe the worst was over. Motives for the massacre in the Bandon Valley were probably mixed: score-settling for the killing of a local IRA leader during a raid on a Protestant house, the suspicion that some of the victims had provided intelligence to the British and would do so again if the war restarted, and the murky territory of buried resentments that only neighbours of long stand-

---

* In the years of the Revolution, between 1919 and 1923, somewhere between 2,000 and 16,000 Protestants left for what University College Cork historian Dr Andy Bielenberg calls 'non-voluntary' motives. In other words, they were scared or could no longer survive economically.

ing would comprehend.* Did raw sectarianism play a part for some of the assailants? The young Irish historian John Dorney puts it well, I think: 'Republican guerrillas were not in the main motivated by sectarianism [but] sectarianism was a fact of Irish life and where people's loyalties were called into question, such divisions could be lethal.' I can only write from the perspective of my own experience of civil war in other places. When members of a minority are targeted in a wave of violence they immediately feel their isolation. Bonds of neighbourly trust established over centuries can fray in an instant. 'Are we next?' ... 'Are they going to kill us all?'

If you were a Protestant in the Bandon Valley in that dark April of 1922 such a massacre might easily have seemed the signal for the start of a pogrom. Whatever their motives, could the killers have been unaware of this fact? In the north of Ireland, Catholics were being terrorised by Protestant gangs, a campaign that was overtly sectarian. It would have been logical for the Protestants of West Cork to see the violence inflicted on them as sectarian revenge.

The killings were not officially sanctioned by the IRA; commanders, like the legendary Tom Barry, condemned the slaughter and rushed to the area to prevent further outbreaks of violence. A Republican irredentist in the Civil War, Barry wrote years later that Protestants were not required to support the rebellion against Britain. His words are probably a fair summation of the official nationalist outlook:

> What we did demand was that they in common with Catholics
> should not commit any hostile act against us and that they
> should not actively aid the British troops or administration. The
> majority of Protestants accepted this position, and let it be said

---

* The episode is one of the most contentious in the history of the period. See Andy Bielenberg and John Borgonovo with James S. Donnelly Jr., '"Something in the Nature of a Massacre": The Bandon Valley Killings Revisited', Éire-Ireland, Vol. 49, 2014, pp. 7–59.

that we found them men of honour whose word was their bond. Aloof from the National struggle, they did not stand with our enemy and they lived their days at peace with their neighbours in spite of all British propaganda, and the bigotry and intolerance of the very small section of bigoted Catholics. Alas, religious bigotry was not confined to the Protestants for the ignorant and petty-minded Catholics, too, had their fair share of this ancient curse.[25]

On the other side the leading pro-Treatyite politician Kevin O'Higgins also spoke out in the Protestants' defence. 'These people are part and parcel of the country,' he wrote, 'and we being the majority and strength of the country ... it comes well from us to make a generous adjustment to show that these people are regarded, not as alien enemies, not as planters, but that we regard them as part and parcel of the nation, and that we wish them to take their share of its responsibilities.'[26] The IRA plan in the War of Independence and Civil War had not been ethnic cleansing. The men of the Flying Column in north Kerry did not set out to eliminate Protestants. But they killed Arthur Vicars because they saw him as a loyalist and a friend of the British Army, and his death would have reinforced the sense of minority vulnerability.

On the eve of the Second World War the Church of Ireland newspaper the *Christian Irishman* offered a gloomy assessment of Protestants' position in the new state: 'Protestants enjoy toleration at the moment but that is very largely because they no longer possess anything, either power or property, which others want. It is the toleration we accord to the dead.'[27] This was not entirely true. Political power had certainly vanished. The Catholic middle classes dominated the world of agriculture and commerce. But the majority of Protestants were not reduced to penury by dispossession. The Protestants who stayed largely kept their heads down and got on with farming or business. They maintained a healthy representation in the business sphere. As more and more intermarried with Catholics their numbers dwindled further, the Catholic decree Ne

Temere insisting that children of a mixed marriage be raised in the faith of Rome.[28] By the twenty-first century, the Protestant population stood at only thirty per cent of its pre-revolution figure.

The new state of the 1920s and '30s was very far from the Republic which would 'cherish equally the aspirations of all its children' proclaimed by Pearse on the steps of the General Post Office in 1916, or the all-Ireland utopia of Wolfe Tone where Catholic, Protestant and dissenter and all would go by 'the common name of Irishman'.[29] Observing the Catholicisation of the new state, W. B. Yeats, appointed a senator by the Free State government, waded into the debate over the ban on divorce in 1926. To Yeats the bill represented the marginalisation of Protestants and he denounced the clericalist drift in one of the finest political speeches in Irish history. '[We] are no petty people. We are one of the great stocks of Burke; we are the people of Swift, the people of Emmet, the people of Parnell. We have created the most modern literature of this country. We have created the best of its political intelligence.'[30] It was high Protestant exceptionalism and its tone might have aggravated the likes of James Joyce, whose fiction was already the most modern in the English-speaking world. But the nation at large was preoccupied with economic survival and ill-disposed to listen to Yeats's anguished polemic. In 1957, the Anglo-Irish writer Brian Inglis captured the illusions and uncertainties of life as experienced by the people of the big house:

> For those of us who grew up in post-Treaty Ireland, the
> problem was of assimilation. The Free State was at first in the
> Commonwealth; we sang 'God Save the King'; Irish politicians
> we regarded as silly or sinister; and we thought that the Irish,
> the real Irish, were happy-go-lucky peasants out of Castle
> Rackrent, anxious to keep on your-honouring us, but afraid to
> do so, the way irresponsible agitators like Dev might get them
> shot in the back. To realise that the agitators were our masters;
> that the national anthem – What a laugh! – was 'The Soldier's
> Song'; that we might need Irish to get a job, was a shock. We

could get out of the country; or lapse into the social coma of the Punchestown circuit; or adapt. And adapting was not easy.[31]

The majority who stayed on after independence did adapt, however. The contribution made by Protestants to the Republic spanned business, politics, the arts and academia. They did exist not as representatives of some exalted caste. The teenage Protestants I met as an adolescent in Cork were very different to the marooned gentlefolk described by Brian Inglis. My friends belonged to another Protestant Ireland. They came from farms in County Cork or had parents who worked as craftsmen or businesspeople in the city. They were part of the social mainstream. I knew them through my mother who taught in a Protestant school in Cork. When she arrived back in her home city from Dublin, jobless and exhausted after the break-up of her marriage, it was the kindness of a Protestant neighbour that saved the hour. Johnny Hornibrook bore the same family name as one of those killed in the Bandon Valley massacre back in 1922. Yet he was a close friend of my maternal grandfather, Paddy Hassett, an IRA veteran. It was another reminder of the essential lesson: the past cannot be understood as a story of simple tribal allegiances. Human relationships complicate every historical narrative and get in the way of absolute conclusions. Johnny Hornibrook interceded on my mother's behalf with the Church of Ireland Bishop of Cork, who put his considerable influence behind her job application. She was highly qualified and an inspirational teacher. The children of Cork Grammar School were lucky to have her. So it came about that I danced at school hops with girls who had names like Pritchard, Brookes, Newenham, Wolfe and Payne. They were the descendants of Elizabethan and Cromwellian settlers but as Irish in their being, outlook and belonging as any Catholic child. We lived in an Ireland in which all kinds of social barriers were collapsing. The Cork of my mother's childhood where Catholic and Protestant children might shout 'Catty Watty' or 'Proddy Woddy' at each other – the most notorious sectarianism she can remember – was gone.

Around Listowel there had been fewer Protestants to begin with and the majority belonged to the remnants of the old landowning class. By the time I was in my adolescence the vanishing of the Protestant community around the town was unstoppable. The story of St John's church in Listowel Square is emblematic. Throughout the nineteenth century it had been the spiritual heart of the Church of Ireland community. Kitchener worshipped there. When Sir Arthur Vicars was killed his body was brought to St John's under military guard. There were renovation works on St John's in the early 1960s but these could not forestall the demographic reality. One Church Street neighbour of the Keanes', Eamonn Dillon, remembered how the last Archdeacon, Reverend Wallace, a much-loved local character, pursued a congregant into his [Dillon's] family shop in order to collect the parish dues 'and hung around our shop for over an hour while she hid in the kitchen ... I suppose that the congregation was so small at that stage that every contribution was valuable and necessary'.[32] As the congregation faded away, the empty church became vulnerable to vandals. In 1975 St John's windows were smashed, leading a judge to remark 'we are living in unenlightened times where churches had to be closed during the daytime to protect them'.[33] By 1986 the falling attendance numbers led the church authorities to lease the building to the local community. Two years later the pews were put up for auction and two years after that the building was sold and became the St John's Arts Centre. In the process a wall that surrounded the church was knocked down, leading one churchman to lament the insult 'to the Protestant heritage'.[34]

The arts centre attracted controversy in the 1990s when it put on a stage adaptation of *Lady Chatterley's Lover*. The Protestant Rector of Tralee, Reverend Warren, described it as 'insensitive to those who had worshipped there'[35] – though it was not exactly 'profane' as the church had been deconsecrated. There was criticism too from a member of the Listowel town council who called it 'insulting for the women of the town'.[36] Today St John's is thriving, a place of plural expression and cultural diversity. A new evangelical community has evolved and includes former Catholics among the congregation. Across rural Ireland small evangelical churches have attracted some who are disaffected with the scandal-ridden Church of Rome. And on the road to Ballydonoghue, not long after you pass the Famine graveyard at Teampallin Ban, there is the new evangelical church. In the old days there might have been a riot at such conversions. Today there is sublime indifference.

14

Inheritance

So I say only: bear in mind
Those men and lads killed in the streets;
But do not differentiate between
Those deliberately gunned down
And those caught by unaddressed bullets:
Such distinctions are not relevant ...
Bear in mind the skipping child hit
By the anonymous ricochet ...
And the garrulous neighbours at the bar
When the bomb exploded near them;
The gesticulating deaf-mute stilled
by the soldier's rifle in the town square
And the policeman dismembered by the booby trap
in the car ...
Patriotism has to do with keeping
the country in good heart, the community
ordered by justice and mercy;
these will enlist loyalty and courage often,
and sacrifice, sometimes even martyrdom.
Bear these eventualities in mind also;
they will concern you forever:
but, at this moment, bear in mind these dead.

John Hewitt, 'Neither an Elegy nor a Manifesto', 1972

I

At first I looked at the war they fought and asked if there could have been another way. Yes, of course, there *could*. At the outbreak of the Great War, Home Rule within the empire still defined the bound-aries of political ambition for most Irish nationalists.

But Ireland was not a peaceful realm in the first decade of the twentieth century. Other possibilities shuffled for prominence. The forces of loyalist irredentism that arose in response to the Home Rule campaigns fuelled an atmosphere in which revolutionary violence could again become imaginable. Not inevitable. This is a critical distinction. Before a war breaks out there are always other choices. It is the power of events, the influence of personality at critical junctures, the decisions made or avoided, the chance encounter, the starting shot fired that ignites a fusillade that can tilt the public mood from passivity to epoch-changing fury.

In Ireland the actions of the rebel leaders in 1916 did not propel Ireland into insurrectionary warfare. It took the blunders of the executions and martial law, followed by the conscription crisis to move a critical mass of Irish people towards support for guerrilla war when it eventually broke out.

Deeper emotions were waiting to be stirred. The punitive nature of the state response after 1916, and the campaign of counter-terror in the War of Independence, accommodated themselves well into the narratives of British perfidy that slept in the inherited memories of so many Irish families.

In the course of this war my grandmother and her brother became involved in inflicting terror on members of the Crown forces. This also meant terror and sorrow for the families of policemen and soldiers. The terror of the Crown forces brought grief to thousands of Irish people. My forebears made a choice that might have led them to prison or an early grave. They were idealists and they had immense courage. They could have remained uninvolved or taken a less dangerous role. Nobody compelled them to take up arms and the majority of people did not engage in violence. My paternal grandfather confined himself to working in the cultural sphere for the Gaelic League, though his greater age may have been a factor in this. The family of my maternal grandmother avoided any involvement in the revolutionary war. Here a family connection might explain the choice: my maternal great-grandmother had been orphaned as a young girl and her much-loved guardian was a Major McCarthy, retired from the Indian Army. The man she married, my great-grandfather John Sexton, worked for a Protestant firm in Cork. These connections, to empire and to the existing order, might have made her daughter, my mother's mother, less likely to follow the path of Hannah Purtill. Yet the man she married, Patrick Hassett, had grown up as the son of an RIC sergeant, a man every bit as dedicated to his job as Tobias O'Sullivan had been, and yet he ended up as an IRA man in the cauldron of Cork city. There was no absolute telling how the mood of the times and the circumstances of family, the generational shifts and, possibly, resentments could change the way in which young men and women saw the world.

I often thought about Hannah and Mick's war when I lived in the north. Its echoes were there when I heard the bomb that killed forty-seven-year-old Nathaniel Cush – a van driver and former army reservist – at the Tomb Street post office one June day in 1987. I reported on his funeral and remember a boy, possibly a close relative, passing the corner where the media was standing, his eyes catching mine and looking straight through me. I heard the echoes again one night in November 1989, on the shores of Lough Neagh, at one in the morning, when a woman washed blood from the floor of a bar after loyalists killed Liam Ryan and Michael Devlin. I saw the shadows of the old war in the eyes of mourners at the funeral of Gillian Johnston, who was shot forty-seven times by the IRA as she sat in a car with her fiancée. A mistake, the IRA said later. That earlier war, the one that changed the lives of my grandparents, that created the country in which I grew up, would follow me through all the wars of my own reporting life.

I lived in the North for five years. I listened to bigots and absolutists on both sides. I learned how the British state had colluded with loyalist death squads in its war against the IRA. I met Republican politicians who I knew had given orders for atrocities that killed hundreds of civilians. I also met those who, by acts of omission or silent support, had enabled the killings. At weekends I would sometimes go to Dublin and listen to people in bars or at dinners declaim loudly and often ignorantly about the north. 'I wish it would float away into the sea' ... 'They are a shower of fucking whiners' ... 'It's sick, the whole society is sick ...' If they did take time to reflect on the past, they would act as if the Troubles had nothing at all do with our revolution. They forgot our own wars, the assassinations and disappeared civilians of the Revolution, the executions of the Civil War, the shrieking families with their mangled dead after Ballyseedy.

When de Valera retired from public life in 1974, after spending fourteen years as president, Jack Lynch, the leader of Fianna Fáil, said that 'those who pursue their own misguided course of violence, can claim no identity with the man who fifty-seven years ago took up arms ... and who fought for Irish freedom'.[1] Well they could. And they did. The Provisionals' claims of legitimate violence were rooted in the violence ignited by Pearse and his comrades, who had no electoral mandate for revolution when they struck in 1916 against a government they declared to be illegitimate; Collins had directed a campaign of terror against the government and so had Liam Lynch in the Civil War. Both claimed a legitimacy rooted in 1916 as well as the election victory of 1918. To the armed keepers of the sacred flame of Irish Republicanism, the people's will was very much secondary to the will of the notional Republic declared on the steps of the General Post Office in 1916. The dissidents of today can find solace in the words Dev used after the Irish people elected a majority of pro-Treaty Dáil deputies: 'The people have no right to do wrong'.

If it was legitimate for the IRA of my grandmother's time to kill soldiers and policemen and to execute informers, the Provisionals asked, why should different rules apply today? The example of Collins's war was freely quoted by the new IRA. In November 1985 the Provisional's propaganda wing released a pamphlet that explicitly justified their campaign by referencing the IRA of the Revolution: 'How did Collins deal with them? He had his men shoot them down without mercy; a bullet in the back, in the dark, on their way to or from Mass, when they were unarmed, or with their families – it mattered not to Collins. Many more native RIC men were killed than Black and Tans and Brits.'[2]

The Provisionals listed killings from the Tan war, among them that of District Inspector Tobias O'Sullivan, repeating the claim that he was with his young son when killed. Sixty years after the killing, the policeman's death was being used to justify the killing of a new generation of policemen. It was a logically alluring argument, this justification through retrospective comparison, but only if you believed that Irish people were incapable of advancing the progress of their hopes through peaceful means, and that the violence and grief of past wars offered an example to be followed, not avoided. This last is the essential point.

The cost to civilians in lives lost, maiming and psychological trauma during nearly three decades of the Troubles was immense: over fifty per cent of the casualties were civilians.* As with the revolutionary war, British blunders and cruelties helped swell support for the IRA and keep the war going. Bloody Sunday in Derry in 1972, internment without trial, curfews and midnight raids, beating of suspects, the intimidation of Catholics at roadblocks by soldiers – some of them Protestant neighbours – helped bring young men into the paramilitaries' ranks. So did the threat from loyalist murder gangs, sometimes operating in collusion with the British state. The leadership of the IRA reaped the benefits. What began as a defensive campaign in support of Catholic communities

---

* Of the civilian casualties the full breakdown is: forty-eight per cent killed by loyalists; thirty-nine per cent by Republicans; ten per cent by the security forces. The Republican paramilitaries were responsible for sixty per cent of Troubles deaths.

under attack from loyalist mobs and paramilitaries was turned into an offensive war for a united Ireland. By the early 1970s the IRA had split into two factions with the Provisionals pursuing the military campaign for territorial redemption and the Official IRA beginning the political journey that led them away from violence. Peace invariably foundered on the opposition of hard men and bigots. The Sunningdale power-sharing Agreement between Catholic and Protestant in 1973 was wrecked by hard-line Unionist opposition and the continued violence of the IRA for whom militarism remained a sacred principle. Hannah and Mick Purtill's wars lasted three and a half years. They reached a pitch of intensity and involved reprisals and security measures that would have been impossible in a modern democratic state. The modern Troubles spanned over three decades and took the lives of more than 3,600 people. There were many times in that later nightmare when the people who ordered the killing could have made a different choice. Politics was always an option. Always. There was no absence of a democratic alternative if the gunmen had been willing to work with it. Thirty years. The IRA persisted with the bloody folly of believing that they merely had to defeat the British troops and police to drive the Protestants into a United Ireland. When I arrived in Belfast in 1985, armed Republicans were still proclaiming the dream of victory through the gun and the ballot box, wilfully ignoring the reality that killing Protestant police and soldiers only deepened the hatred and mistrust between the communities. That year the IRA declared 'confidently that it *will* successfully conclude the national struggle'.[3] But the war ended without a united Ireland. A war-weary population, growing electoral success and belated acceptance that Protestants were not going to be abandoned by London and bombed into a united Ireland, brought the IRA leaders into a government under the auspices of the British Crown, minus any troublesome oath of allegiance. When peace finally came in April 1998 it was based on the power-sharing formula, prompting the prominent constitutional politician Seamus Mallon to call the Good Friday Agreement 'Sunningdale for slow learners'.

We in the Republic voted to abandon the territorial claim over the six counties of Ulster. North and south accepted the principle of consent: a united Ireland would only happen if the majority of people in the north voted for it. By the standards of the IRA who fought the Civil War, this was every bit as great a betrayal as Collins's decision to sign the Anglo-Irish Treaty. In the north they voted by more than seventy per cent for their politicians to do the sane and moral thing: give up the gun for good. Work together. In the Republic on the same day we also had a referendum asking if we would give up the legal constitutional claim to the North and replace it with the language of aspiration and consent. The result was over ninety-four per cent in favour. Like the rest of the country, Listowel returned an overwhelming 'yes' vote and shunted IRA dissidents to the margins. From there they still snarl and occasionally kill, but the gun has been largely removed from the politics of our island.

The nationalist electorate did not look back on thirty years of violence and reject Sinn Féin. On the contrary. The men and women who chose peace from the start – people like John Hume, who was made a Nobel Peace laureate and whose voice pleaded reason on our airwaves for decades – were sidelined and their party eclipsed by Gerry Adams and his supporters. For Sinn Féin was the party that got things done. It was better organised; it spoke to needs of voters in deprived areas, north and south; its leaders were ruthless in ensuring that dissenters or those who threatened the party's image were ostracised and, when possible, silenced. If this took threats and violent intimidation so be it. The party was united and exuded a muscular confidence. On the Protestant side the party of Ian Paisley overpowered the more moderate Unionism of David Trimble. The great divider and bigot, the man who did so much to advance sectarianism, ended up sitting in government with the former IRA commander, Martin McGuinness.

The media started calling them 'the Chuckle Brothers', and with barely a glance backward the island 'moved on'. Except that history is rarely so accommodating. The peace walls in Belfast got longer and higher. The grieving and the traumatised were left to make their own way, just as they had been left after the Revolution ended, but in a society where sectarian alienation showed no signs of easing. Catholic and Protestant children still went to different schools. The power-sharing deal between Sinn Féin and the DUP broke down and remains broken at the time of writing. Direct rule from Westminster loomed. A slim majority of the British people decided to leave the European Union and in doing so raised the possibility of a physical or 'hard' border returning to the island of Ireland. Sinn Féin called for a border poll which they knew would not be granted. But Unionists were unsettled. Nobody thought the war would start again. But so much of our island history is about how unforeseen consequences play out over the long run that I cannot say violence will never return.

In north Kerry peace delivered a dividend for Sinn Féin with the election of former IRA commander Martin Ferris as a local TD.* By contrast Fine Gael, the party of the Purtills, lost the Dáil seat held by a close family friend, Jimmy Deenihan. There had always been a lingering Republican support in north Kerry but the election, and subsequent re-election, of Martin Ferris was not decided on the basis of Civil War antagonisms. Sinn Féin appealed to those who were excluded from the prosperity of the Celtic Tiger years and to many who were angered by the corruption and clientelism that brought the country to the brink of economic ruin in 2008. Money. Who made it. Who squandered it. Who paid the bill. Who promised to clean up the mess. Money, not memory, was the heart of the matter now.

---

* Martin Ferris served three prison terms relating to his IRA activity, including a ten-year sentence for attempting to import seven tonnes of arms, explosives and ammunition. When the killers of Garda Jerry McCabe, shot by the IRA in County Limerick in 1996, were released from prison, Ferris was present to greet them. Jerry McCabe was a fellow Kerryman and came from Ballylongford. He was guarding a post office van carrying cash when three IRA men arrived and opened fire.

II

For the first time I see you rising,
Hearsaid, remote, incredible War God,
How very quickly the terrible action has been sown
Among the peaceful fruits of the field, action
grown suddenly to maturity.

Rainer Maria Rilke, 'Hymn One', 1914

Towards the end of the 1980s my father came to visit me in Belfast. He was ill and nearing the end of his life. Alcoholism had ravaged his body and spirit. It was his first visit north since the beginning of the 1960s and on the road from Dublin he asked me if he would be safe. 'You're fine with me,' I told him. 'I'm living in a grand safe place.' I did not know what memories he held of this place when, as young actors with a touring company, he and my mother stayed here in the early days of their courtship. Belfast was a sleepy provincial city then. An IRA campaign along the border in the late 1950s had petered out and the Unionist monolith, with its tweeded elite and militant working class, seemed destined to endure forever. Eamonn was not ready for the army patrols on Great Victoria Street. I took him on a tour of the city's 'Troubles landmarks': up the Falls Road, across the peaceline to the Shankill via Lanark Way, down past the paramilitary murals, across the Lagan to the east and the gantries of the Harland and Wolff shipyard, and then back again to drive up the Antrim Road to Duncairn Gardens where he had stayed as a young man. He was silent. The street had become one of the worst flash-points of the conflict, divided between Protestant and Catholic districts at either end, with boarded-up houses and empty spaces where buildings had vanished; there were abundant weeds, broken glass and masonry, sectarian slogans and swear words scrawled by kids. The house where my parents had stayed was gone along with its owner Mrs Burns who had treated the young actors to hearty

With my father in Belfast in 1988 on his first visit back since the Troubles began

Ulster fries and late-night sandwiches when they returned from the theatre.

We drove up and down several times, my father shaking his head. It was later, after we had returned to the southern suburbs where middle-class Catholics and Protestants coexisted contentedly, that he started to talk. This man whose stories of the mythic Irish past had fired my child's imagination was shocked by what he had seen. He was thinking of his own beginnings, about the stories handed down and the silences around our own family's violent past. 'Look how long it's taken us to get over that,' he said. 'This will take longer. How will people ever get on again after what's happened?'

On this evening in Belfast my father realised that he would not live to see the united Ireland for which the revolutionary leaders had fought. But it was less this that troubled him, than suddenly facing the human mess made in the long decades of war in Ireland. Born in 1925, in the bitter aftermath of Civil War, he died in January 1990, eight years before the Good Friday Agreement that brought the long struggle to an end. I wish he had lived to see peace. Even this imperfect and troubled peace. He would have rejoiced in it.

15

Afterwards

When I was single I wore a black shawl
Now that I'm married, I've nothing at all
Still I love him, I'll forgive him
I'll go with him wherever he goes.

Still I Love Him, nineteenth-century ballad

I

In the year the Civil War would end Hannah Purtill became Hannah Keane. She was married in Ballydonoghue church near her father's farm and where her brother Mick and Con Dee had hidden from the Tans. The wedding took place on 5 September 1922, as the Civil War raged across Kerry. Less than a week later came the Republicans' attack on Tarbert barracks where Mick Purtill and Con Brosnan, and their comrade from Ballylongford, Brian O'Grady, were stationed. The IRA pumped petrol into the building and fired incendiary bullets to start a fire. This was the same tactic used against Tobias O'Sullivan in Kilmallock turned now against Irish soldiers. Eventually the remaining defenders, no more than seven men, were forced to surrender. In the following weeks, the first of my grandmother's married life, the National Army, humiliated by the Tarbert attack and another in south Kerry, swept the countryside. There were dozens of arrests. Hannah moved to the Keane house on Church Street, where her husband's parents, his sister and brother had determined to spend the rest of their days. It was not in Bill Keane's generous nature to ask them to move. Nor would Hannah have dreamed of encouraging him. Others in rural Ireland acted differently. The mental hospitals and county homes, successors to the workhouse of colonial times, were full of bachelors and spinsters pushed out by a married brother.

Within two years of their marriage the first child, a son, was born. As one child followed another – there would be nine altogether, one died as a baby – the pressure of space became acute. The only money was my grandfather's schoolmaster's salary and whatever his brother Dan could earn at cattle fairs. This was the time of the Great Depression and of de Valera's economic war with Britain.* Rural communities were hard pressed.

Yet Hannah did not rebel against the status quo. She had grown up in a family that had gained a crucial footing on the land late in the previous century. The Purtills had everything to lose if radical redistributive politics gained ground. Three years before, as the war against the British was starting to escalate, farm labourers around Listowel had gone on strike demanding to be given an acre of land each. The strike failed but it would have unsettled the Purtills and other landowners.

Paternalism was an abiding legacy. The colonial rulers had not trusted the Irish peasantry. Somebody further up always knew what was best. Power was pulled to the centre, into the maw of the great bureaucracies of Dublin Castle and Whitehall. The two big parties and the clerical establishment easily slotted into the vacant space

---

* The economic war followed de Valera's refusal to repay the loans made by the British government to Irish farmers to buy land before independence. De Valera reasoned that land which had been seized from the native Irish should never have to have been paid for in the first place. The British placed a tariff of twenty per cent on Irish exports to the United Kingdom. It is estimated that the conflict cost the Irish Free State around £48 million, with unemployment rising from 29,000 in 1931 to 138,000 in just a few years.

left by the British. Why give political or intellectual autonomy to the people when ministers in Dublin, and the bishops in their palaces, could do their thinking for them?

A handful of brave souls tilted against this hegemony and suffered exile, censorship or the penance of irrelevance in a society that seemed content with the status quo. My auntie Anne remembered the power of the Church in Listowel: 'The canon and priests in the town were put on pedestals to be revered. No one dared question its authority.' My bluff great-uncle Dan was a lonely exception. He was attending the mission one day when the priest began to summon up visions of the fires of hell.

'No such thing,' bellowed Dan from the congregation.

The priest focused on the insolent countryman.

'Be quiet,' he shouted, 'or I'll turn you into a goat. I'll put two horns on you!'

To which Dan replied: 'If you do I'll fuckin' puck you with them.'

Dan Keane might cause shock but he could be written off as an eccentric. In the land where Hannah Keane raised her children, girls and young women were constantly reminded of the need to maintain their purity. The priests railed from the pulpit against dancing and any co-mingling of the sexes. Sex was 'the deed of darkness', as one visiting mission priest told the Listowel congregation. Our Church Street neighbour and a celebrated writer, Bryan McMahon, wrote of the 1950s that 'in the Ireland of today the conception of sin is everywhere',[1] and he quoted from the catechism being taught to Catholic children:

> The chief dangers to chastity are: idleness, intemperance, bad companions, improper dances, immodest dress, company keeping and indecent conversation, books, plays and pictures.[2]

Young women were urged to emulate the example of the Virgin Mary. Piety. Suffering. Forbearance. The cult of domestic martyrdom. The old joke: how many Irish mothers does it take to change a lightbulb? None. *Sure I'll just sit here in the dark.*

A woman learned to put up with her lot. A woman who fell from grace in the eyes of the Church became an exile in her own community. One of the saddest stories I heard growing up concerned the short life of Peggy McCarthy. Peggy had become pregnant out of wedlock in the mid-1940s. In her own brother's account, she 'was refused admission to three hospitals in north Kerry and died giving birth on the side of the road . . . In death the gates of Listowel church were closed against her coffin.'³ Something of a rebellious spirit emerged in the aftermath when a large crowd of local men followed the coffin to the church gates in support of the McCarthy family. But the mood passed and the traditional order reasserted itself.

The Church controlled access to most education and health care, willingly subcontracted out by a state that had neither the immediate resources nor inclination to do the job on its own. There was no strict national ideology; instead the Irish people were corralled by a mishmash of clerical authoritarianism, instinctual conservatism and safe, gun free, nationalism. Books were censored, contraception and divorce denied, and abortion unthinkable. English building sites absorbed our unemployed and England's doctors carried out the abortions banned at home. But the people did not rebel against the impositions of the Church. My grandmother remained devout until her death. She could make disobliging remarks about certain priests in private, and was scathing about the crony politics of the time, but would never have dreamed of rebelling in public.

Why did this woman of the Revolution accept a society that shunted her back into the kitchen? The power of Church and state acting in malign congress does not explain it all. The answers come from Hannah's life and personality and from her immediate community, as well as from the larger forces that created the post-revolutionary nation. I come back again to the desire for stability. Hannah longed for it at home and in the country. Most of the families on Church Street, or on the farms around Ballydonoghue, would have shared that ambition. There had been enough chaos. A stable social order meant that your children could hope to inherit a thriving farm, or go to college or get a job in the civil service. It meant food on the table. For this, above and beyond the historic attachment to their faith, people were willing to tolerate a great deal. The empire of the Church could never have survived so long without the cooperation of its subjects.

Hannah and Bill's sons, my father and uncles, went to a local school presided over by a notorious brute. Father Davey O'Connor beat the boys in his care savagely and did so in the full knowledge that their parents would never confront him. He sat at the apex of power in Listowel, free to warp the lives of the boys and young men in his care. I know of him because my father spoke of his brutality repeatedly. Others in the family endorsed his accounts.

John B remembered being called on to recite a poem by O'Connor and decided to perform his own poem about Church Street.

'"Who wrote that?" he asked when I had finished.

'"I did father!" ... there followed the worst beating of all and ejection from the class ... What made the beating worse was that there was no explanation for it, but it was this beating which contributed more than anything to my being a writer.'[4]

'That was how it was. That was the way in those days,' Hannah would say. She had risked her life to fight the Tans but drew back from confronting a priest. 'That was how it was. That was the way in those days,' a relative told me. Everybody in the older generation I asked said the same thing. *That was how it was.* Violence was normalised. The child who complained was a liar. Or they must have done something to deserve what they got.

My grandfather made a symbolic protest. Some time afterwards he encountered O'Connor in the street and walked straight past without a salute. The priest ran after him and demanded: 'Why don't you salute a priest when you see one?'

To which Bill Keane responded: 'When I see one.'

Change came in the next generation. My father left for Dublin in his late teens without telling a soul, simply vanishing one morning. True to a childhood dream, he made his way as an actor, arriving at the Abbey Theatre in the late 1940s and going from there to work with the national radio station Radio Éireann. In the process he became involved in a public fracas about culture with a narrow-minded government minister and lost his job. The Fianna Fáil minister Neil Blaney had criticised the drama department of RTÉ, the national broadcaster, where my father worked. An official memo from 1957 said my father had 'hurled offensive epithets across the table at the Minister and had to be forcibly removed from the hall ... Keane came very deliberately to the place where he knew the Minister would be and ... he did not appear to have much, if any, drink taken'.[5] (Knowing him as I did, I would be inclined to dispute this last sentence.) My father was suspended and put on a boat to England and told to stay out of the way until the scandal died down. That was how things were handled in those days. More than a decade later, Blaney lost his own job, accused of plotting to send arms to the IRA in Belfast.

Eamonn was allowed to return and resume his acting career after a sojourn in England, during which he picked hops in Kent and worked for a furrier in Covent Garden. John B, meanwhile, wrote plays that captivated Ireland with their raw evocation of rural life: child marriage, murder over land, the struggle of women for control of their lives, were his great themes. Some of his finest characters

John B. The most independent-minded man I ever knew

– women made weary by the world men had made, but women who endured – were based, to a greater or lesser degree, on Hannah Keane.

My grandmother was ambitious for her children. Education and exam results were her abiding preoccupation. To the neighbours on Church Street she became known as 'Hannie Honours' for her habit of enquiring how many honours a child had received in their Leaving Certificate examinations. This was more than petty boasting. Education gave her children access to opportunities undreamed of in the age of the Revolution. What was her fight for if her children could not live lives of ambition and prosperity? Her youngest son Denis went to university in Dublin and became a maths teacher. Her daughter Peg joined the new national airline as a stewardess, marrying a refugee from communist Czechoslovakia who built his own successful business selling agricultural machinery to Irish farmers. Another daughter, Kathleen, became a nun and later a liberal-minded reverend mother, loved by the girls whose lives she shaped. In my auntie Kathleen's compassionate Catholicism I saw a rejection of the judgemental morality of the Church in which she had been raised. Hannah's children all went on to lives that offered infinitely greater prosperity than she had known in her youth. The trajectory of the family in the late 1950s reflects a country on the cusp of profound change: two of her children, William and Anne, emigrated – among nearly a sixth of the population (more than 400,000 people) who left the Republic between 1951 and 1961. They found better lives in England and America.* Auntie Anne remembers how many of her friends in Listowel were leaving and how 'the influence of American cinema painted a very rosy picture'.[6]

Hannah ran the household, hoarded the pennies and disciplined the children. Her husband often sought refuge from reality in

---

* The scholar Enda Delaney noted that the figure of 400,000 emigrants represented a sixth of the total recorded population. By 1971 one in three of those aged under thirty had left the country. See Delaney, *The Vanishing Irish*, in Dermot Keogh, Finbarr O'Shea and Carmel Quinlan (eds), *Ireland: The Lost Decade*, Cork, 2004.

Hannah

alcohol. Sometimes Hannah struggled to pay the bills when he spent much of his pay in the pub. There was shame in this for her. Hannah was a Purtill with the fierce pride of those country people who had never depended on charity. Her relatives in the countryside saw her distress and sent in meat and vegetables from the farm.

Hannah and Bill loved each other. It was the dreamer in him, the reciter of poems and teller of stories, that she was drawn to in the first place. So she left him to his books, his pipe and whiskey and struggled on. I have turned again and again to the writing of my uncle to glimpse the grandparents whose inner lives were hidden from me. John B wrote a poem about his father that lovingly captured the complex truth of life in Church Street.

He was inviolate.
Clung to old stoic principle,
And he dismissed his weaknesses
As folly.
His sinning was inchoate;
Drank ill-advisedly
… I am terribly proud of my father
For he was a loveable man.[7]

Bill Keane died in August 1963. Hannah would outlive him by twenty-six years. There was much to be proud of in her life. None of her children knew hunger or war. They had, as the saying goes, 'made well for themselves'. But my grandmother sheltered a sadness. She feared the shadow of drink. 'The curse of the Keanes,' she'd say. Hannah feared what it might do to her son Eamonn, my father. By the beginning of the 1970s he had already lost his marriage and been hospitalised repeatedly through alcoholism. In the end it would kill him, though Hannah did not live to see this. I saw her weep one New Year's Eve when he arrived home late and we stood to sing a poignant 'Auld Lang Syne'. When I was a teenager she would ask me occasionally: 'What's to become of him?' I had no answer. I was past the point of reassuring pieties.

Mother and son were unable to communicate except about horses. I watched her and Eamonn trade tips at the dining-room table and then carried their bets to the bookies. I would always enjoy that brief ease between them. Beyond this, there were only terse sentences, and silence, the great full silences of an Irish kitchen where none are at peace. I knew that my father was proud of her, especially of her stand against the Tans. But he could no more tell her this than he could abandon the bottle. As a child he had sought an attachment to her that she could not give, burdened as she was by the cares of the household. A shy, sensitive boy with a stutter – a dreamer – he was ill suited to the hard world of post-revolutionary Ireland. His aunt, Juleanne, my grandfather's sister, stepped into the vacuum and became the protector and spoiler of my father, sheltering him behind her countrywoman's shawl. Eamonn became the child of the spinster aunt and drifted away from his mother.

Hannah suffered bouts of depression. It came and went, an endlessly turning and returning tide. It could send her to bed for days. Where did it come from? The Purtills were not depressives. Was it from struggling to raise nine children with a husband who was loving but beset by a weakness for drink? Did some of it come from the war?

As a child I could only observe the silent sadness. Once I climbed the stairs to bring her a cup of tea in her bedroom. I remember her lying still, tears flowing down her cheeks. I came to the side of the bed and placed the tray on the small straw chair. She did not look at me but stared into the distance. It was explained to me as 'bad nerves', the failsafe description for all emotional disturbance in those days. Hannah was also plagued by imagined bouts of ill health, complaining of aches and pains which always, in her mind, hinted at the probability of terminal ailments.

It is tempting to project backwards, now that I know what war can do to a human being, what it can plant and how long the malady can take to grow. I do think the war was part of it: the fierce excitement of those years, and the dawning knowledge of the human cost, and then living in the world that grew out of the war, a landscape of marginal choices where power in public life was claimed by the men. This strong, intelligent and courageous woman joined the majority of her fellow women rebels in a life of child-rearing, cooking, budgeting, cleaning, and obeying the dictates of a church which strove to command their minds and bodies. This was the rural world in which Hannah Keane lived and whose rules she quietly accepted. But I believe it wore her down.

At the end of John B's play *Big Maggie*, about a matriarch fighting to dominate her family after the death of a feckless husband, the principal character delivers a monologue that is both a startling expression of sexual liberation and a denunciation of the state in which she grew to womanhood. Bear in mind it was written in

1969 while the Church still enjoyed considerable power, especially in rural Ireland:

> Oh I curse the stifling, smothering breath of the religion that withered my loving and my living and my womanhood. I should have been springing like a shoot of corn ... and all too soon I'll be dead but I can have anything I want for a while. By God I can have any man I fancy and who fancies me ... The weal of the chastity cord is still around my belly and the incense is in my nostrils. I'm too long a prisoner but I'll savour what I can, while I can and let the last hour be the sorest.[8]

Auntie Anne recalled that her mother was quietly proud of her role in Cumann na mBan. That was on the very rare occasions Hannah spoke about it. The state made little of the women's contribution until recent years, long after my grandmother's death. There is still no dedicated memorial to the volunteers of Cumann na mBan.

I am nearly finished with my writing when my grandmother's file comes into the light. War stories in a thick dossier in the Military Archives in Dublin. The letters, forms and testaments are from the late 1960s. Bill is dead by then and Hannah is applying for her war service medal and the military pension due to all who fought for Ireland. At first the state will not recognise the stand she took for her country. The bureaucracy is faced with vast numbers of claims. There is no proof, she is told. A government minister writes: 'I regret that under the circumstances, the medal cannot be awarded to her and that consequently, she is not a qualified person for the award of a special allowance under the Army pensions Acts.'[9]

Then something remarkable happens. The divisions of the Civil War are set to one side. Old friendships assert themselves. It turns out that the files proving her service were taken in Free State raids on the home of her commanding officer, Mae Brennan, who had taken the Republican side. They have vanished in the intervening decades. Now, nearly forty years after the end of the war her former CO speaks up for my grandmother. Yes, she had been with her in the fight for independence and yes, she deserved her medal and pension. As I read on there is another surprise. The shadow of Tobias O'Sullivan comes out of the pages. One of those who testifies for Hannah is Jack Ahern, who was among the four men who killed the District Inspector. He writes a short note from his home in Newtownsandes, dated 4 November 1968: 'I Jack Ahern of the North Kerry Flying Column do hereby certify that I knew Hannah Keane (nee Purtill) to be an active member of Listowel branch of C, na mBan during the years 1920 & 1921.'[10]

May Ahern, who also fought against the Free State, writes and tells of how she and Hannah were together 'on many occasions acting on instructions from the Flying Column'. And for the first time the handed-down story of Hannah and the Tan Darcy is made real by an eyewitness. It happened on an April evening in 1921 and the two young women were assigned to track Darcy's movements, almost certainly as a prelude to an assassination. They walked into the square in Listowel and were passing the Bank of Ireland when 'suddenly he leaped out at us with a gun in his hand and threatened us, and ordered us out of town'.[11] Darcy also went to Hannah's employer, the draper Moran, and told him to sack her within twenty-four hours. The draper refused. Now in this old file the fear with which my grandmother lived comes to life. Darcy must have loathed her. Yet she refused to flee. There were relatives of her soon-to-be in-laws the Keanes living in the Stack's Mountains. Other family scattered around north Kerry. She could have gone deep into the country but did not. As I learned in researching this book, it was Darcy who was shot and ended up leaving Listowel.

One of the most poignant files I encountered in researching this book was the military pension application from Amelia Wilmot, an old comrade of Hannah's and the woman who had smuggled guns and letters out of Listowel RIC barracks under the noses of the Black and Tans. She was renting a room on Charles Street – once famous as 'the haunt of pro-British types' – and in December 1946 she wrote to the government telling officials that 'I am 76 years of age and now unable to do anything. I find it impossible to live on my present income ... as I am crippled I cannot manage to exist any longer on my present income ... I have had to go into debt for necessities.'[12] A further letter pleads that she needs help quickly to avoid having to go to the county home, the modern-day equivalent of the poorhouse. The state granted her request but it was a scandal that she ever had to plead for it.

Of the Civil War Hannah said nothing, but I know that she remained friends with May Ahern. The childhood bonds forged in the fields and lanes of Ballydonoghue were strong enough to survive the fratricide. Towards the end of her life, a studio photograph was taken where my grandmother is facing sideways towards the camera. The background is dark, looking as if it might overtake her. But Hannah faces the lens with equanimity. Hers is the face of a survivor. When the image was sent to me by a cousin I felt sadness, but also a surge of pride. She left no diaries or letters so it is this photograph that stands for me as the final testament to her character. This is a woman who knows what she has lived through and who does not wish to hide it. Her need to see things exactly as they are, is pure Purtill.

II

After the Civil War Con Brosnan settled back in his home village. The name had changed, from Newtownsandes to Moyvane. He rebuilt the pub and the home burned down by the Tans after the killing of Tobias O'Sullivan. But his family was scattered by then. The three girls were gone to America. Two brothers left for England. One of them joined the Royal Navy and became a doctor. Con had a Free State army pension and some income from the pub and the small family farm. Like many veterans of war, Con Brosnan did not speak of what he had seen and done or what had happened to his friends and comrades. It was as if the war had never happened. Except that it was everywhere. You couldn't miss it in the bitterness of the politics. Con wanted the hatred to stop. This much we know for certain.

In Kerry only Gaelic football could unite people. It provided a collective identity that transcended politics. If beating Dublin or Mayo in an All-Ireland final meant putting politics to one side, then that is what you did. "T'was football helped to cure the bad blood,' remembered Gerry Brosnan.[13] Con was talented – among the best players of his generation. In Kerry this made him a legend. He is remembered for reaching out to his Civil War enemies on the football field, even arranging safe passage for wanted IRA men so that they could represent Kerry. In 1924, a year after the Civil War ended, Kerry won the All-Ireland final with a team almost roughly divided between pro- and anti-Treaty players. When Con Brosnan was coming to the end of his playing career, a Republican, Joe Barrett, ensured that he was given the captaincy. Another old Civil War enemy, John Joe Landers, said Con had faced down the bitterness of both sides: 'Regardless of pressure from within his own side of the divide, or from the other side, he did what he believed had to be done to bring about peace and healing. He was the ultimate peacemaker in Kerry football after the Civil War.'[14]

Con played for Kerry and then trained the county team. He encouraged youngsters so much that 'he couldn't keep a halfpenny from buying footballs for them'.[15] It was only on a tour to the United States that the bitterness surfaced. In New York the exiled Republicans nurtured a remorseless hatred of the Free Staters. Con was warned not to go on the Kerry tour there after the Civil War. He ignored the threat. Another comrade was told that he would be taken off the pitch in a coffin if he played in New York. He chose to face down the intimidation once more. As it happened the man who made the threat was stretchered off.

Con was a Gaelic Athletic Association hero in a county where there was no higher accolade. He had the aura of a leader, a man who made magic on the pitch so that men wanted to be in his company when the final whistle went and the talk of sporting battle went on and on in the pubs. During the election campaign of 1932, Con Brosnan stood for Cumann na nGaedheal, loyal to the memory of Collins. There was big talk of him being elected, a candidate who

The older Con Brosnan. He prayed
every day for those he shot

was popular on both sides of the house and a crowned king of
football.

He failed by just four hundred votes to win a seat. It was around
this time that depression began to manifest itself. After the election
he still played local football and trained the Kerry team that won the
All-Ireland on the eve of the Second World War. Two of his sons
played for Kerry. But at times he drank more than was good for a
man who was starting to suffer from an emotional imbalance.
Depression would follow him all his life.

Con lived in a time before the widespread availability of talking
therapy in Ireland or treatment of conditions like post-traumatic
stress disorder. We know that he prayed, every day, for the men he
killed.

Gerry Brosnan believes his father might have suffered from
depression even if there had been no war, and his understanding of
his father's psychological make-up is far greater than that of any
outsider.

But Con Brosnan was only twenty-one when he took part in the killings of Tobias O'Sullivan and James Kane. He had lost friends killed in the War of Independence. And he had fought against friends in the Civil War. An image comes back: Ballybunion, a few days into the Truce, six months after the assassination of Tobias O'Sullivan, and three young men are wading into the surf, free after years on the run. Con Brosnan is knocked over repeatedly by the Atlantic waves, until the others come to rescue him. It is a picture that seems like a foreshadowing of what is to come in the long future. Con Brosnan died when he was seventy-five, having seen two sons become doctors, their university fees paid by his brother in the Royal Navy. He could also trust that Gerry would make a good life as a farmer. But it is hard not to believe that the war followed him to the end.

Jack Ahern who led the group that killed the District Inspector went back to the life of farming in Newtownsandes. But he too was shadowed by the memory of Tobias O'Sullivan. 'He prayed for that man every night of his life,' his son, Father Dan Ahern, told me. Apart from this solitary revelation, Jack Ahern never spoke of the war.[16]

I have reported on many killings: fathers and mothers killed in front of their children, entire families butchered together by cheering, laughing mobs. The first shootings I covered were in Northern Ireland. The killers I met were often hardened men. Some of them were twenty years into the conflict, veterans of police interrogation cells and prisons; men who looked at a spot on the wall and refused to answer the questions no matter how long they were kept awake. They had killed people in front of their wives and children. And they had kept on killing. For years in some cases. For obvious reasons the killers were not going to admit anything to me. It would have meant a swift arrest for murder. I knew I could have interviewed them for the next ten years and would only have been told that the violence was justified, however 'regrettable' were the effects on civilians. If they ever did accept responsibility it would be that offered by a soldier acting under the conditions of war against an occupying army.

After the Troubles ended I did meet some who struggled with ghosts. They were left to face the silences they had delivered into the lives of others. An IRA man from mid-Ulster who shot a neighbour, a part-time soldier, told me he had been a different person back then. 'I look back and wonder how I did it. I knew his children. I live with him Fergal and I always will.' I met a loyalist gunman who had shot a Catholic man in a sectarian murder in the 1970s. Billy Hutchinson went to prison for his UVF activities and afterwards emerged as a political leader of working-class loyalism. The man he killed had nothing to do with the IRA or politics. He was a Catholic in the wrong place at the wrong time. I asked Billy how he dealt with the memory of killing. His response was one sentence, darkly suggestive of inner upheaval: 'I sometimes wake up at the night thinking of the things I have done.'[17] *The things I have done.*

It wasn't until later, years after Belfast, that I started to think about the revolutionary generation, wondering how they dealt with their memories. The more I covered wars the more I wondered. I had never been called on to kill or to be part of the process of killing. Yet the memories of the dead follow me constantly. My guilt has been the guilt of omission. It was for the people I had left behind in the hands of killers in Rwanda. It lay in every gesture of farewell in ruined cities and refugee camps. Like my forebears I knew what it was to live in fear of my life, but only for short periods, a few weeks at most, with the prospect of a flight to another, safer place always glittering at the end of the road. Nobody hunted me down. But the wars followed me home, nonetheless. In my late thirties I experienced a severe depressive breakdown and was diagnosed with post-traumatic stress disorder as a consequence of war experiences. I shared therapy groups with soldiers returned from Afghanistan and Iraq. There was much that separated us, but we all felt that the experience of war was something we could never communicate back here in the normal world.

I did not belong to the solid band that went to the wars and returned essentially undamaged. I believe that Mick Purtill did. He built his farm, at Kilcolgan, not far from Ballydonoghue, and raised his family. My uncle Mick is remembered as a man who worked from dawn until night in his fields. At ploughing time he would be alert to the slightest error in the geometry of the drills 'and would do the whole thing over again if it wasn't right'.[18] His relaxations were coursing with greyhounds and Gaelic football, a sport at which he excelled and represented Kerry at junior level. When he died the army sent a colour party and gave him a military burial with shots fired over the grave.

None of the children remembered him being beset by haunted moments. This was not because he was callous or hardened. My cousin Liam remembered a man 'who never raised his hand to strike a child'. I believe Mick compartmentalised his experiences. They belonged in a time and place that was gone, and he had the ability to keep them there. Mick Purtill lived to see his sons and daughters prosper. They bought farms of their own. The fields around Listowel became the birthplace of one of the world's largest food corporations, Kerry Group, bringing prosperity to the town and billions into the national exchequer. Mick Purtill was an ardent supporter of Ireland's entry into what was then the European Economic Community. When Ireland eventually voted to legalise contraception and then divorce, Mick Purtill, though still devoutly Catholic, did not rebel against the liberalising spirit of the times. Once he was sure that his family, and the land they lived on, was secure, Mick was content to let individual conscience have its day.

III

They are begging us, you see, in their wordless way,
To do something, to speak on their behalf
Or at least not to close the door again.

Derek Mahon, 'A Disused Shed in County Wexford', 1973

After he was killed there was a big fuss. May O'Sullivan was brought to Dublin to meet the Lord Lieutenant. There was the funeral and what seemed like all the policemen in Ireland marching behind his coffin. On the little mass card for the dead policeman, he is called Toby. May was twenty-six, widowed with three children, the youngest not yet two years old.

Tobias was twelve years older than his wife, a good husband, a devoted father. He was her strong man, his were the solid arms that carried the family through dangerous times. Now he was gone. He was unmourned by the majority of his fellow countrymen and women. To many of them Tobias O'Sullivan obeyed the wrong leaders. He wore the wrong uniform. A child said that once to his daughter Sara. She was only a child herself, and it was something said in a playground. 'A pity he died in the wrong colours.' It was a thing a child would say in the Ireland of that time. But Sara never forgot those words. The pain was there at the very end when her mind was wandering back to the land where her father had grown up, and she would recite the names of villages and townlands and all that she could remember of the O'Sullivans of Connemara.

After her husband was buried May went back to her own people in County Mayo. They were small farmers whose fields looked out on the heights of Croagh Patrick. But even in this remoteness the war followed. Her twenty-four-year-old brother was harassed by the Tans and ended up becoming involved with the IRA.

There was no new chapter for the widow of Tobias O'Sullivan. Five months after he was killed May died in a Dublin hospital of 'galloping' Tuberculosis, a virulent form of the disease which would have wreaked havoc on a body weakened by the trauma of that January day in Listowel. Tobias's brother took over guardianship of the children, returning from Jamaica where he was chief of police and placing them in boarding schools. The boys went to de Valera's alma mater, Blackrock College in Dublin; little Sara was sent to the nuns at Sion Hill. 'She was basically reared by the nuns,' remembered her daughter Desiree. The orphaned O'Sullivan children grew up in a country which had disowned the memory of men like their father. The two boys, Bernard and John, emigrated. John went to America and Bernard to Malaya and later London. When he retired, the boy who remembered seeing his father's body on Church Street came home to live in County Galway. John went to Texas, raised a family but died at the age of fifty. His niece Desiree believed he suffered from post-traumatic stress disorder, the lingering effect of the trauma that occurred in Listowel more than four decades before. Only Sara stayed in Ireland and lived to see the country embrace modernity. She married a man who was a big supporter of de Valera and Fianna Fáil; the couple loved each other all of their lives but Sara would never attend any of the party functions.

When the fiftieth anniversary of 1916 came around, Sara's son Morgan, the grandson of Tobias O'Sullivan, was part of the military guard of honour at the official commemoration. He was a member of the FCA, the army reserve. But he did not connect the Revolution with the death of his grandfather. By this stage the killing of Tobias O'Sullivan was a mere whisper from the past. There were no family masses, the custom for some, to commemorate the anniversary of his death. It was only years later that Morgan and Desiree began to excavate their family history. 'I didn't know where my grandfather was shot, that he was shot in Listowel,' Morgan said.[19] Why did the family not speak publicly about their grandfather before now? What Desiree said in reply haunts me. 'Because nobody ever asked.'

Desiree had grown up in a country where the questions were not even asked, let alone answered. Her mother, the daughter of the dead policeman, believed no good would come of looking into the past, so much so that she refused ever to visit Listowel or countenance one of her children going to the place that had broken her family. Maybe that was the cost of that child's remark in the playground. *The wrong uniform.* The pain she felt was kept inside, her life devoted to the happiness of those closest to her. But Desiree was followed by questions. Who was Tobias? How did he die? She could not leave the past to rest. It was something of the brave O'Sullivan spirit, I believe, that made her go secretly to Listowel, aged seventeen, hitching down the country with a friend to see where her grandfather was killed. Later she returned with her husband and her own children. When she tells me all this there are tears in her eyes. We are nearly one hundred years on from the killing but the loss of generations sits on the table before us, among the family pictures, in the eyes of Tobias and his wife May, in the years before the war.

Ireland no longer disdains to speak of those days. Memory is no longer a penance. On the day that the Republic celebrated the hundredth anniversary of the Easter Rising I stood in Dublin opposite the reviewing stand where the nation's president and leading politicians reviewed the ceremonial march. How far it all felt from the monochrome of Dev's celebrations I had attended as a child fifty years before. The preceding months had been full of debates about the true meaning of the Rising and its legacy in all of our lives. The island had come through thirty years of bloody violence in the north; the Republic was emerging from an economic crisis that had been unleashed by venal politicians, greedy banks and reckless property developers. This time around there would be no revolutionary romanticism. As the procession passed there was an announcement: 'Now approaching are representatives of the families of Gardaí killed in the line of duty.' The crowd applauded. The dignitaries on the reviewing stand rose to their feet. I looked across and noticed that among those standing and clapping his hands was the former IRA leader, Martin McGuinness. I dropped my reporter's distance and joined in the applause.

I could not ignore the shadows around this day of commemoration. There was much in the evolution of the modern state to make this an occasion for careful self-examination: the cronyism and corruption that fermented unchecked for decades; we were shamed by the revelations of systemic sexual abuse in institutions run by the clergy, and of the appalling treatment handed out to unmarried mothers in church-run homes. With all this, knowing the sordid details, accepting they were part of the country that made me, I still felt proud of the Republic on that Easter Sunday 2016. My country was a democracy with an unarmed police force governed by the rule of law. It had an independent judiciary and a free press. Its citizens felt free to speak their minds and challenge the political classes whenever they wished. I have lived and worked in places where these things are denied; I believe I know their value.

My people played a small part in the Revolution. Like many other Irish families. Because they were the kind of people they were, who lived in the times they did, I finish with unanswered questions. I have written their story as best I know it, feeling much is unreachable, concealed by forgetting or the necessary fictions of a violent age, what people told and re-told in order to live with the consequences of war. I am reminded of the old Irish proverb: *Bíonn dhá insint ar scéal agus dhá leagan déag ar amhrán* — there are two versions of any story, and twelve versions of every song. As for the dead, from the quiet corner of Glasnevin cemetery, close by the River Tolka, where Tobias O'Sullivan is buried with May, to Ballydonoghue and Church Street and Moyvane, where Hannah and Mick and Con were born and fought their war, I believe they each loved their country. It was Ireland's tragedy that people who loved the same land could become such bitter enemies.

Acknowledgements

To my late father Eamonn I owe an enduring debt of gratitude for sparking my interest in history, and to my mother Maura for encouraging my reading of history and urging the necessity of fair-mindedness. To Anne, and to Daniel and Holly, all of your support through so much of my life has been central to any capacity I have had to tell the stories I need to tell.

I am grateful to my ancestral tribes in Kerry – the Keanes, Purtills, Schusters and O'Connors – who shared their stories and have always been supremely hospitable families. Denis Keane and Anne Klaben, the last surviving children of Hannah Purtill, supported this project from the beginning and have always understood the importance of looking back with clear eyes.

My cousin Conor Keane was an invaluable support in researching the story of the killing of District Inspector Tobias O'Sullivan and the life of Con Brosnan. It was Conor who opened the door into the deeper story of Tobias O'Sullivan's life and whose judgements I have come to value immensely. Thanks also to Joanna, who walked the lanes of Ballydonoghue with me, and to John and Billy for their memories of life at 45 Church Street, and cousin John Schuster whose last-minute assistance was inestimably important. To the Hassetts in Cork, thank you for your warm support through all my travels and occasional travails.

In Listowel I am indebted to Vincent Carmody for his support and guidance and amazing store of historical knowledge. Eamonn

Dillon was hugely helpful in researching the story of the Protestants of the Listowel area. On the larger historical issues I am grateful to Marianne Elliott, biographer of Wolfe Tone and Robert Emmet, and Professor Emeritus at Liverpool University, who read the manuscript closely with an acute eye for the eruption of unsupported generalisations.

At University College Cork, Dr John Borgonovo, whose own work on the Revolution has been illuminating, read the manuscript and supplied careful insights. Any mistakes are my own.

Thanks are owed to the staff of the National Library of Ireland; the National Archives of Ireland; and the staff of the Military Archives in Dublin where Commandant Victor Laing, now retired, first gave me access to the files of my forebears; in London I am grateful to the Imperial War Museum, the National Archives at Kew and the British Library.

Thank you also to editors Kate Johnson and Iain Hunt and publisher Arabella Pike at HarperCollins, and to my agent David Godwin, for their dedication in seeing this work through to completion. At the BBC Andrew Roy and Daniel Fisher have always showed a benevolent understanding of the temperament of those who report war for a living. My comrade on the road, Tony Fallshaw, is a constant source of wisdom. To the families of Con Brosnan and Tobias O'Sullivan my respect and immense gratitude for agreeing to speak about the traumatic past. Thanks to Jimmy Deenihan who always fought the good fight on the field and in the Dáil.

To Alice Doyard, thank you for the enduring gifts of your friendship. To my siblings Eamon, Niamh and Niall, thank you all for being who you are. Finally to my late aunt and uncle, John B. and Mary: I'd never have written a line of a book without your loving support.

A Short Note on Sources

In the absence of any family memoirs, diaries or letters, and with only the sparse memories of relatives and what I could recall from childhood conversations myself, I faced a considerable challenge in attempting to recreate the two Irish wars my grandmother, Hannah Purtill, had known.

I turned first to the archives of the Bureau of Military History, which contain the statements of 1,722 witnesses to the revolutionary period. This priceless resource gives us the Revolution in the words of the men, and some of the women, who were there. The interviews with the north Kerry veterans allowed me to piece together some of the action in which my forebears were involved. Memory is always selective, changed by time and circumstance. That is true of veterans of all wars, but the sense of a people in turmoil is vividly expressed. The Military Pensions Collection provided invaluable material relating to the war service of my grandmother and her comrades in Cumann na mBan. The records of the National Archives in London and the Imperial War Museum helped provide a British perspective on the conflict. I have also drawn on the writings and primary research of the IRA commander and gifted chronicler of the Revolution, Ernie O'Malley, who spoke to many who fought against the Treaty.

Anybody writing about the history of north Kerry does so in the long shadow of Father Anthony Gaughan, whose history of Listowel remains the defining work on the long story of my father's town. I am also indebted to the work of T. Ryle Dwyer, Tom Doyle, Tim Horgan and Sinead Joy, all of whom shed important light on the trauma of north Kerry during the War of Independence and the Civil War. For a deeper understanding of the events at Ballyseedy, I turned to Pat Butler's exemplary documentary *Ballyseedy*, broadcast by RTE in 1997. David Leeson's study of the Black and Tans was also an invaluable resource.

The advent of online archives and a multiplicity of documents, from unpublished theses to digital versions of centuries-old books, has hugely enhanced the possibilities of research. I will always cherish the feeling of a paper book in my hands but am an enthusiast for the possibilities of the digital age.

In particular I would commend the website www.theirishstory. com run by historian John Dorney. It is a source of reasoned and often fascinating reading. It was here I was first acquainted with the work of the young Kerry historian Thomas Earls Fitzgerald who has investigated attacks on civilians during the revolutionary period.

The website www.irishlifeandlore.com run by Maurice and Jane O'Keefe in Tralee is a rich source for anybody looking into the lives of Irish forebears, particularly those who grew up in rural areas.

I am particularly grateful to the Mercier Press Cork for permission to quote from their extensive list of writers on the revolutionary period, particularly the works of Ernie O'Malley and Father Anthony Gaughan.

The poet Derek Mahon has long been an inspiration to my understanding of the island on which I grew up. Lines from his 'A Disused Shed in Co. Wexford' from *New Collected Poems* (2011) are reproduced by kind permission of the author and the Gallery Press.

I am grateful also to Blackstaff Press for allowing me to quote the poem 'Neither an Elegy Nor a Manifesto' by John Hewitt, and to Bloodaxe Books for their permission to feature Brendan Kennelly's work *My Dark Fathers*.

All efforts have been made to seek copyright clearance where it is required. Where it has not been possible any omissions that are pointed out will be corrected in future editions.

A Short Note on Sources

In addition to the material available in various archives and books, I am grateful to the following scholars whose doctoral theses helped provide invaluable information and context:

Timothy Breen, *The Government's Executions Policy during the Irish Civil War 1922–1923*, National University of Ireland

Gemma M. Clark, *Fire, Boycott, Threat and Harm: Social and Political Violence within the Local Community – A Study of Three Munster Counties during the Irish Civil War 1922–23*, Queen's College, Oxford

David Leeson, *The Black and Tans: British Police in the First Irish War 1920–21*, McMaster University

Donnacha Seán Lucey, *Land and Popular Politics in County Kerry 1872–86*, National University of Ireland

Mike Rast, *Tactics, Politics and Propaganda in the Irish War of Independence, 1917–1921*, Georgia State University

Martin White, *The Greenshirts: Fascism in the Irish Free State 1933–45*, University College London

Notes

Abbreviations used in Notes:
BMH – Bureau of Military History, Dublin.
IWM – Imperial War Museum archives, London
MSPC – Military Services Pension Collection, Dublin
NAI – National Archives of Ireland, Dublin
NLI – National Library of Ireland
TNA – The National Archives, Kew, London

Prologue: We Killed All Mankind
1. *Dublin Penny Journal*, Dublin, 1836, p. 292.
2. Fynes Moryson, *An History of Ireland*, Dublin, 1604.
3. Ibid.
4. Quoted in *The Catholic Encyclopaedia*, London, 1914.
5. James Joyce, *Ulysses*, London, 1922, section 15 – Circe.
6. Anon. ballad, *The Merry Ploughboy*, released by Dermot O'Brien, 1966.
7. Quoted in Joseph Lee, *Ireland 1912–1985*, Cambridge, 1989, p. 27.
8. Dion Boucicault, *The Shaughraun*, London, 1874, Act I, Scene I.
9. Interview with author.
10. Thomas Kinsella, *The Táin*, Oxford, 1969, pp. 150–3.
11. J. G. Kohl, *Travels in Ireland*, cited in Fr J. Anthony Gaughan, *Listowel and its Vicinity*, Dublin, 1974, pp. 123–4.
12. Cited in Martin Dillon, *The Shankill Butchers*, London, 1999, pp. 20–3.
13. 2014/32/2058, 1984, NAI.
14. *Guardian*, 3 Feb 1972.
15. Robert Kee, *Ireland – A Television History*, BBC Television in co-operation with Radio Telefis Eireann, 1980, Episode 10.

16. Colum McCann, *TransAtlantic*, London, 2014, p. 252.

1: The Night Sweats with Terror

1. Author interview with Breda Thunder, Dublin, 2014.
2. Rajkumari Shanker, *The Story of Gandhi*, Delhi, 1969, p. 84.
3. 'Defence of the North-West Frontier', Hansard, 21 May 1921.
4. Sir Henry Wilson to Malcolm Arnold Robertson, 30 Mar 1921, from Karine Bigand, *Ireland and the End of the Empire*, in *British Decolonisation: 1918–84*, edited by Richard Davis, Cambridge, 2013, p. 9.
5. Peter Hart, *Mick: The Real Michael Collins*, London, 2005, p. 175.
6. A. Norman Jeffares, *W. B. Yeats: A New Biography*, London, 2002, p. 206.
7. Elizabeth Bowen, *The Shelbourne*, London, 1951, p. 211.
8. The Canadian academic Professor David Leeson reported that between 24 February and 1 July 1920 forty-seven prisoners had been shot dead while trying to escape. See *The Black and Tans: British Police in the First Irish War*, Doctoral Thesis, McMaster University, 2003.
9. David Lloyd George, Guildhall speech, 9 November 1920.
10. W. B. Yeats, '1919', *Collected Poems*, London, 2008.
11. *Ballymena Weekly Telegraph*, 29 January 1921.
12. Ernie O'Malley, *The Men Will Talk to Me: Kerry Interviews*, edited by Tim Horgan, Cormac O'Malley, Dublin, 2012, pp. 72–3.
13. J. Anthony Gaughan, *The Memoirs of Constable Jeremiah Mee RIC*, Dublin, 2012, p. 15.
14. T. Colville Scott, *Connemara after the Famine: Journal of a Survey of the Martin Estate 1853*, edited with introduction by Tim Robinson, Dublin, 1995, p. xvii.
15. Account of James Hack Tuke in *The Tourists Gaze: Travellers to Ireland, 1800–2000*, edited by Glenn Hooper, Cork, 2001, pp. 129–30.
16. Peter Hart, *The IRA and Its Enemies: Violence and Community in Cork, 1916–1923*, Oxford, 1998, p. 3.
17. Cited in James H. Murphy, *Abject Loyalty*, Washington, 2001, p. 286.
18. In Donal P. Mcracken, *Forgotten Protest*, Belfast, 2003, p. 57.
19. Douglas Hyde, 'On the Necessity of De-Anglicising Ireland', speech delivered to the National Literary Society in Dublin, 25 Nov 1892.
20. *Cork Examiner*, 19 Mar 1895.
21. Ibid.
22. Ibid., 8 Oct 1902.
23. IRA statement, 30 Mar 1920, in Richard Bennett, *The Black and Tans*, Staplehurst, 2001, p. 37.
24. Interview with Desiree Flynn, 11 June 2017.

2: The Ground Beneath Their Feet

1. Cited in Rosa González, *The Unappeasable Hunger for Land in John B. Keane's The Field*, Barcelona, 1992, p. 87
2. In http://www.duchas.ie/en/cbes/4666578/4663527/4688866
3. Lydia Jane Fisher, *Letters from the Kingdom of Kerry*, Dublin, 1847, p. 20.
4. James Fraser, *Guide Through Ireland*, Dublin, 1838, p. 213.
5. In *Work on the Farm*, Newtownsandes Online, http://www.geocities.ws/dalyskennelly_2000/farmingnts.html
6. John B. Keane, *The Field*, Dublin, 1966, pp. 196–7.
7. W. R. Le Fanu, *Seventy Years of Irish Life*, London, 1893, p. 32.
8. *Irish Press*, 5 February 1934.
9. NA: CSO/RP/SC/1821.275.
10. Thomas Wesley, *The Works of Thomas Wesley – Volume IV*, London, 1810.
11. In Peter Beresford Ellis, *A History of the Irish Working Class*, Worthing, 1972, p. 62.
12. Cited Richard Gott, *Britain's Empire: Resistance, Repression and Revolt*, London, 2011, p. 50.
13. Arthur Young, *A Tour in Ireland*, Cambridge, 1925, originally published 1780, pp. 190–2.
14. *Saunders's News Letter*, 6 April 1786.
15. Sir Richard Musgrave, *Memoirs of the Different Rebellions in Ireland*, Dublin, 1801, pp. 4–5.
16. J. B. Connell, *Hanging at the Cross: Where the Streets Meet in Newtownsandes*, http://www.reocities.com/dalyskennelly_2000/hang_cross.html
17. *Chute's Western Herald*, 3 December 1921, cited in Gaughan, *Listowel and Its Vicinity*, p. 142.
18. NAI:CSO/RP/SC/1821/321.
19. Niall O'Ciosain, *Print and Popular Culture in Ireland, 1750–1850*, London, 1997, p. 195.
20. Cited in Samuel Clarke and James S. Donnelly, Jnr, *Irish Peasants:Violence and Political Unrest, 1780–1914*, Madison, 1983, p. 114.
21. For more on the violence of this period see James S. Donnelly Jnr, *Captain Rock:The Irish Agrarian Rebellion of 1821–24*, Madison, 2009.
22. J. A. Murphy, *The Church of Ireland in County Kerry*, http://www.Lulu.com, 2012, p. 16.

3: My Dark Fathers

1. Brendan Kennelly, *Selected Poems*, Boston, 1972, p. 15.
2. *Kerry Evening Post*, 7 October 1837.
3. Ibid.

4. Cited in Gaughan, *Listowel*, p. 142.
5. William Makepeace Thackeray, *The Irish Sketchbook*, London, 1845, p. 184.
6. Ibid.
7. John D. Pierse, *Teampall Bán: Aspects of the Famine in North Kerry 1845–1852*, Listowel, 2014, p. 10.
8. William Trench, quoted in http://archives.evergreen.edu/webpages/curricular/2006-2007/ireland0607/ireland/eyewitness-accounts-of-the-famine/index.html
9. Cited in Stuart John McLean, *The Event and Its Terrors: Ireland, Famine and Modernity*, Stanford, 2004, p. 94.
10. *Cork Examiner*, 31 August 1846.
11. *Kerry Evening Post*, 28 November 1846.
12. Immigration Report of 1851 British Parliamentary Papers, 1852 XXXIII (1474).
13. Cited in *Legion Magazine Canada*, Kanata, 1 March 2006.
14. Immigration Report of 1851 British Parliamentary Papers, 1852 XXXIII (1474).
15. Letter from Father Bernard McGauran to Archbishop Signay of Quebec, Grosse Isle, Quebec, 24 May 1847.
16. *Duchas Collection*, http://www.duchas.ie/en/cbes/4613715/4611581/4658767
17. Ibid.
18. John D. Pierse, *Teampall Bán*, p. 145.
19. Ibid.
20. *Report of the Listowel Board of Guardians*, 12 September 1849, in Kay Moloney Caball, *The Kerry Girls: Emigration and the Early Grey Scheme*, Dublin, 2014 ebook, Location 650.
21. Brendan Kennelly, *Selected Poems*, Boston, 1972, p. 15.
22. William O'Connor Morris, letter to the *Irish Times*, October 1869, cited http://www.theirishstory.com
23. Diary of Sir John Benn Walsh, 1848–55, cited John D. Pierse, *Teampall Bán*, p. 244.
24. Joseph O'Connor, *Hostage to Fortune*, Dublin, 1951, p. 17.
25. Lord Dufferin in R. F. Foster, *Modern Ireland, 1600–1972*, London, 1988, p. 377.
26. T. P. O'Connor, MP, cited in Joseph Valente, *The Myth of Manliness in Irish National Culture*, Chicago, 2011, p. 37.
27. Cited in Edward H. Judge, *Easter in Kishinev: Anatomy of a Pogrom*, New York, 1992, p. 87.

28. Cited in Stephen J. Zipperstein, 'Inside Kishinev's Pogrom: Hayyim Nahman Bialik, Michael Davitt, and the Burdens of Truth', from *The Individual in History: Essays in Honour of Jehuda Reinharz*, edited by ChaeRan Y. Freeze et al., Waltham, MA, 2015, pp. 365–83.

29. Cited in Carla King, 'The Mahdi for an Irish Constituency or at least a Seat in Dublin Town Council – Davitt and Africa', *History Ireland* magazine, Issue 4, Jul/Aug 2006.

30. P. Grousset, *Ireland's Disease, Notes and Impressions*, London, 1888, pp. 129–30.

31. Ibid.

32. S. M. Hussey, *Reminiscences of an Irish Land Agent*, London, 1902, p. 236.

33. Cited http://www.igp-web.com/IGPArchives/ire/kerry/newspapers/evictions-1887

34. Ballybunion Relief Committee to Mansion House Relief Committee, 17 Feb 1880, Mansion House Relief Fund Papers, CH 1/52/320 letter no. 5, Dublin City Archive, cited in doctoral thesis of Donnacha Seán Lucey, *Land and Popular Politics in County Kerry, 1872–86*, Maynooth, 2007, p. 58.

35. South Western Division monthly police report, 1 Dec 1885, NAI, cited in ibid.

36. Outrage Report: proceedings at Firies, 26 Jan 1886, NAI, p. 241, cited in ibid.

37. Cited in Marc Mulholland, *Land War Homicides, Uncertain Futures: Essays about the Irish Past for Roy Foster*, Oxford, 2016, p. 93.

38. Outrage Report: proceedings at Firies, 26 Jan 1886, NAI, p. 243, cited in Lucey, *Land and Popular Politics in County Kerry, 1872–86*.

39. *Freeman's Journal*, 11 Feb 1886.

40. *Freeman's Journal*, 1 Aug 1888.

41. *Kerry Sentinel*, 1 Aug 1888.

42. Michael Davitt, *Speech in Defence of the Land League*, London, 1890.

43. *Freeman's Journal*, 7 Mar 1902.

4: Revolution

1. Interview with Gerry Brosnan, 23 March 2016.

2. Gabriel Fitzmaurice, *My Own Place*, cited in *The Middle Plain*, http://www.moyvane.com/people/gabriel-fitzmaurice/

3. Message sent to Belfast and read to crowds by Sir Edward Carson on 12 July 1913.

4. *Kerryman and Kerry Evening Post*, 20 Dec 1913, cited in Gaughan, *Listowel and Its Vicinity*, p. 436.

5. Ibid.
6. *Kerry Sentinel*, 2 Jun 1909.
7. Ibid.
8. *The National Volunteer*, cited in 'An Abundance of First Class Recruits': The GAA and the Irish Volunteers 1913–15,' http://www. theirishstory.com/
9. *Belfast Telegraph*, 24 Apr 1914.
10. Speech by John Redmond MP at Woodenbridge, Co. Wicklow, 20 Sep 1914.
11. Cyril Kelly, 'The Bibles, the Brotherhood & the Booze: A Listowel Family's Divisive 1916 Experience', *Irish Independent*, 30 April 2016.
12. Thomas Carmody, Witness Statement 996, BMH.
13. Ibid.
14. House of Commons Debates 11 May 1916, Hansard, Vol. 82 cc935–70.
15. Judge Charles Wyse-Power, Witness Statement 420, BMH.
16. Statement of Thomas Collins, company commander, to Military Service Pensions Board, 19 May 1940.
17. Mary Colum, *Life and the Dream*, London, 1947.
18. Ernie O'Malley, *Raids and Rallies: Ireland's War of Independence*, Dublin, 2012, p. 11.
19. Cornelius Brosnan, Witness Statement 1,123, BMH.
20. WO 35 098/30, TNA.
21. Ibid.
22. Ibid.
23. Statement of the Catholic Hierarchy, 9 April 1918.
24. Thomas Carmody, Witness Statement 996, BMH.
25. 'The Condition of Ireland', Hansard, 6 May 1920.
26. Seamus O'Connor, *Tomorrow Was Another Day*, Dublin, 1970, p. 38.
27. Diarmaid Ferriter, *A Nation and Not a Rabble*, London, 2015, p. 344.
28. Edward J. Walsh, Witness Statement 1,170, BMH.
29. Brian O'Concubhair (ed.), *Kerry's Fighting Story*, Dublin, 2009, p. 208.
30. James Collins, Witness Statement 1,272, BMH.
31. Ibid.
32. L. Fogarty (ed.), *James Fintan Lalor, Patriot & Political Essayist (1807–49)*, Dublin, 1919, cited in *Tactics, Politics and Propaganda in the Irish War of Independence, 1917–1921*, Master's thesis by Mike Rast, Atlanta, 2011, p. 73.
33. T. Ryle Dwyer, *Kerry's Real Fighting Story*, Dublin, 2001, p. 130.
34. Denis Quille in O'Malley, *The Men Will Talk*, Location 500.

35. May Ahern interview with Military Service Pensions Board, 24 May 1940.
36. Statement of Thomas Collins to Military Service Pensions Board, 15 May 1935.
37. Rory O'Connor, *Tomorrow Was Another Day*, Dublin, 1970, p. 38.
38. John O'Riordan, Witness Statement 1,117, BMH.
39. Ibid.
40. Ibid.
41. Seamus O'Connor, *Tomorrow Was Another Day*, Dublin, 1970, p. 89.
42. Ibid., p. 84.
43. William McCabe, Witness Statement 1,212, BMH.
44. Cornelius Dee file, Military Service Pensions Board 34REF26352.
45. Jeremiah Mee, Witness Statement 379, BMH.
46. Patrick McElligott, Witness Statement 1,013, BMH.
47. May Ahern Witness Statement, Military Service Pensions Board, 24 May 1940.
48. Liam McCabe, Witness Statement 1,212, BMH.
49. Ibid.

5: Tans

1. Tape number 6720, interview with Private Arthur Robinson, IWM.
2. Tape number 8990, interview with Private Thomas Henry Flower, IWM.
3. Tape number 6048, interview with Private Horace Todman, IWM.
4. Ibid.
5. Tape number 10699, interview with Brigadier John Rymer-Jones, IWM.
6. Ibid.
7. Statement of John McNamara, 7 Mar 1921, American Commission on Conditions Ireland, 1921.
8. Jeremiah Mee, Witness Statement 379, BMH.
9. Ibid.
10. Ibid.
11. Ibid.
12. Richard Bennett, *The Black and Tans*, Staplehurst, 2001, p. 57.
13. Cited in Peter Cottrell, *The Anglo-Irish War: the Troubles of 1913–22*, Oxford, 2006, p. 48.
14. House of Commons Debates, 14 Jul 1920, Hansard, Vol. 131, cc2385–91.
15. Ibid.

16. John M. Regan, 'A Catholic Officer in the RIC and RUC, 1909–48', cited in *History Ireland* magazine, Jan/Feb 2008.
17. James Collins, Witness Statement 1,271, BMH.
18. Weekly Summary, 1 Oct 1920, cited in D. M. Leeson, *The Black and Tans*, Oxford, 2011, p. 213.

6: The Abode of Wolves

1. Aubrey de Vere, in *Poems of Places: An Anthology in 31 Volumes*, Bartleby. com, 2011.
2. Richard Berleth, *The Twilight Lords*, Lanham, MD, 2002, p. 77.
3. *Annals of the Four Masters*, M1571.4, CELT collection, University College Cork, p. 1655.
4. James Joyce, *Gas from a Burner*, in *Pomes Penyeach*, Paris, 1927.
5. Rev Samuel Hayman (ed.), Unpublished Geraldine Documents, Dublin, 1870, p. 55.
6. Cited in Mainichin Seoige, 'The Story of Kilmallock', Kilmallock Historical Society, 1987.
7. Patience Pollard Adams, cited in *History Ireland, 18th–19th-Century History*, Issue 1 (Spring 2003), News, Vol. 11.
8. Seoighe, *The Story of Kilmallock*.
9. Tomas O'Maoileoin, Witness Statement 845, BMH.
10. Ibid.
11. Cited by Lt Col J. M. MacCathy, *With the IRA in the Fight for Freedom: The Red Path to Glory*, Dublin, 2010, p. 52.
12. Tomas O'Maoileoin, Witness Statement 845, BMH.
13. Edmund Tobin, Witness Statement 1,451, BMH.
14. *Belfast Telegraph*, 29 May 1920.
15. Lieutenant M. Guirke, *Raid on Kilmallock RIC Barracks*, reprinted from *An t-Oglach*, in Terence Kelly (ed.), *Our Struggle for Independence: Eyewitness Accounts from the pages of An Cosantoir*, Cork, 2009, p. 83.
16. Ibid.
17. Ruan O'Donnell (ed.), *Limerick's Fighting Story*, Cork, 2009, p. 159.
18. Ibid., p. 90.
19. Seán Moylan, Witness Statement 838, BMH.
20. Seán 'Bertie' Scully, Witness Statement 788, BMH.
21. Ibid.
22. Ibid.
23. Seán Moylan, Witness Statement 838, BMH.
24. Nicholas O'Dwyer, Witness Statement 680, BMH.
25. Ibid.

7: Sunshine Elsewhere

1. Elizabeth Bowen, *Bowenscourt*, Dublin, 1998, p. 160.
2. Will and Probate of Sir Arthur Vicars, 1922, NAI.
3. Ibid.
4. Michael Murphy, Witness Statement 1,081, BMH.
5. Irene O'Keefe and Laura Doran, *Presentation Convent Yearbook*, 1988.
6. Ibid.
7. Charles Smith, *The Ancient and Present State of the County of Kerry*, London, 1756.
8. Ibid.
9. Arthur Young, *A Tour in Ireland*, Belfast, 1983, p. 120.
10. Ibid.
11. Bertha Beatty, *Kerry Memories*, Listowel, 2007, p. 27.
12. William Makepeace Thackeray, *The Irish Sketchbook*, 1842, p. 180.
13. Beatty, *Kerry Memories*, p. 30.
14. Arthur E. McGuinness, *George Fitzmaurice*, Lewisburg, 1975, p. 18.
15. Cyril Kelly, 'The Bibles, the Brotherhood & the Booze: A Listowel Family's Divisive 1916 Experience', *Irish Independent*, 30 April 2016.
16. Henry Grey Bennet, *Thoughts on the Protestant Ascendancy in Ireland*, London, 1805, pp. 82–4.
17. J. A. Murphy, *The Church of Ireland in County Kerry*, Dublin, 2016, p. 176.
18. Sir George Arthur, *Life of Lord Kitchener*, New York, 2007, orig. published 1920, p. 2.
19. PRO 30/57/108, TNA.
20. Elizabeth Bowen, *The Last September*, London, 1929, p. 146.

8: Assassins

1. Kuno Meyer, 'The Tryst After Death', in *Selections from Ancient Irish Poetry*, London, 1911, p. 20.
2. *Inspector O'Sullivan – The Philosophy of a Murdered Officer, Yorkshire Post*, 25 Jan 1921.
3. Ibid.
4. Hugh Martin, *Insurrection in Ireland*, London, 1921, p. 122.
5. Ibid., pp. 128–9.
6. Peter Hart (ed.), *British Intelligence in Ireland: The Final Reports*, Cork, 2002, p. 87.
7. Gaughan, *Memoirs*, p. 143.
8. Ibid., p. 144.
9. Ibid., p. 149.
10. Martin, *Insurrection in Ireland*, p. 145.

11. *Weekly Freeman's Journal*, 6 Nov 1920.
12. Martin, *Insurrection in Ireland*, p. 149.
13. James Houlihan, Witness Statement 1,118, BMH.
14. Statement of Michael Kelly, 7 Mar 1921, American Commission on Conditions in Ireland, 1921.
15. Houlihan, Witness Statement 1,118, BMH.
16. Brian O'Grady, Witness Statement 1,390, BMH.
17. Dr A. A. Hargrave, cited in T. Ryle Dwyer, *Tans, Terror and Troubles: Kerry's Real Fighting Story 1913–23*, Cork, 2001, p. 239.
18. Summarised findings of Military Court of Inquiry (William Muir), January 1921. NA: CO 904/189, cited in D. M. Leeson, doctoral thesis, *The Black and Tans: British Police in the First Irish War, 1920–21*, McMaster University, 2003, p. 203.
19. Ibid.
20. Thomas Carmody, Witness Statement 996, BMH.
21. Brian O'Grady, Witness Statement 1,390, BMH.
22. A majority of the dead were working in some intelligence capacity for the army. Most were shot at point-blank range in execution-style killings.
23. Tomas O'Maileoin, alias Seán Forde, Witness Statement 845, BMH.
24. Ibid.
25. House of Commons Debates, 21 Oct 1920, Vol. 133 c1111W.
26. House of Commons Debates, 20 Oct 1920, Vol. 133 cc925–1039.
27. Ibid.
28. Interview with the author.
29. Jack Ahern, Witness Statement 970, BMH.
30. Eoghan Corry, *The History of Gaelic Football: The Definitive History of Gaelic Football from 1873*, Dublin, 2011.
31. Edmund Walsh, Witness Statement 1,170, BMH.
32. WO 35/153A/25, TNA.
33. Ibid.
34. Ibid.
35. Ibid.
36. Ibid.
37. Ibid.
38. Ibid.
39. Con Brosnan, Witness Statement 1,123, BMH.
40. Patrick McElligott, Witness Statement 1,013, BMH.
41. Jack Ahern, Witness Statement 970, BMH.

9: Between Gutter and Cart

1. Lola Ridge, *Sun-Up and Other Poems*, New York, 1918, citing Project Gutenberg online edition, 2012.
2. John B. Keane, *The Street and Other Poems*, Dublin, 1961.
3. WO/35/157A/50, TNA (file on murder of District Inspector Tobias O'Sullivan).
4. Ibid.
5. Jack Ahern, Witness Statement 970, BMH.
6. WO 35/151/B, TNA.
7. WO/35/157A/50, TNA.
8. Con Brosnan, Witness Statement 1,123, BMH.
9. Interview with Conor Keane, 24 Mar 2016.
10. WO/35/157A/50, TNA.
11. John 'Jaco' Lenihan, Witness Statement 968, BMH.
12. Ibid.
13. Ibid.
14. Ibid.
15. Ibid.
16. Ibid.
17. 'Cork Courtmarshall – Kerry Murder Charge: Four Civilians Accused.' Account supplied to author by Vincent Carmody, 08/07,2017.
18. Correspondence with author, 21 July 2017.
19. *Nottingham Evening Post*, 26 Jan 1921.
20. Ibid.
21. Ibid.
22. Ibid.
23. Ibid.
24. O'Malley, *The Men Will Talk*, p. 74.
25. *Irish Bulletin*, 8 Feb 1921.
26. Patrick McElligott, Witness Statement 1,013, BMH.
27. Brian O'Grady, Witness Statement 1,390 BMH.
28. Tom Barry, *Guerrilla Days in Ireland*, Dublin, 1962, pp. 50–1.
29. Ibid.
30. Ibid.
31. Ibid.
32. Timothy 'Ted' Houlihan, Witness Statement 969, BMH.
33. Thomas Pelican, Witness Statement 1,109, BMH.
34. Ibid.

10: Executions

1. G. K. Chesterton, in A. P. Wavell, *Other Men's Flowers*, London, 1945 edn, p. 405.
2. *Kerryman*, 13 Apr 1935, cited in Gaughan, *Listowel*, p. 390.
3. 'The Condition of Ireland', Hansard, 6 May 1920.
4. O'Malley, *The Men Will Talk*, p. 73.
5. Patrick McElligott, Witness Statement 1,013, BMH.
6. Ibid.
7. James Costello, Witness Statement 1,091, BMH.
8. Thomas Carmody, Witness Statement 996, BMH.
9. Patrick McElligott, Witness Statement 1,013, BMH.
10. Ibid.
11. Michael Murphy, Witness Statement 1,081, BMH.
12. James Costello, Witness Statement 1,091, BMH.
13. Ibid.
14. Michael Murphy, Witness Statement 1,081, BMH.
15. Ibid.
16. Ibid.
17. O'Keefe and Doran, *Yearbook*.
18. Brian O'Grady, Witness Statement 1,390, BMH.
19. Gaughan, *Listowel*, p. 395.
20. Cited in Hore Herbert Francis, *An Inquiry into the Legislation, Control, and Improvement of the Salmon and Sea Fisheries of Ireland*, Dublin, 1850, p. 8.
21. Brian O'Grady, Witness Statement 1,390, BMH.
22. O'Malley, *The Men Will Talk*, p. 73.
23. Seán Moylan, Witness Statement 838, BMH.
24. Ibid.
25. O'Grady, BMH.
26. O'Grady, BMH.
27. O'Grady, BMH.
28. Cited in Gaughan, *Listowel*, Appendix 8, p. 457.
29. Brian O'Grady, Witness Statement 1,390, BMH.

11: The Republic Bold

1. Cited in Brendan McConvery, 'Hellfire and Poitin Redemptorist Missions in the Irish Free State (1922–1936)', *History Ireland*, Autumn 2008.
2. Affidavit of Cornelius Dee, given at Tarbert, Jun 1921.
3. Ibid.

4. Statement from Dublin Castle Publicity Department, 21 May 1921, cited in http://www.moyvane.com/people/gabriel-fitzmaurice/where-history-meets-poetry-the-valley-of-knockanure/

5. Timothy Houlihan, Witness Statement 969, BMH.

6. Michael Hopkinson, *The Irish War of Independence*, Dublin, 2002, p. 183.

7. Peter Hart, *Mick: The Real Michael Collins*, London, 2005, p. 270.

8. John Borgonovo, *Florence and Josephine O'Donoghue's War of Independence: 'A Destiny that Shapes Our Ends'*, Dublin, 2006, cited pp. 154–6.

9. Cited in Hart, *Mick*, p. 275.

10. Sir Alfred Cope, 'Lessons from the Irish Rebellion', talk given at Tabernacle Chapel, 7 Mar 1927, cited in http://www.cwmammanhistory.co.uk

11. Bishop Michael Fogarty, Witness Statement 0362, BMH.

12. Michael Hopkinson (ed.), *The Diaries of Mark Sturgis*, Dublin, 1999, p. 32.

13. Paul McMahon, *British Spies and Irish Rebels: British Intelligence and Ireland 1916–1945*, Woodbridge, 2008, p. 58.

14. See http://www.militaryarchives.ie/en/collections/reading-room-collections/truce-liaison-and-evacuation-papers-1921-1922

15. Ibid.

16. Tadhg Kennedy, Witness Statement 1,413, BMH.

17. Ibid.

18. Ibid.

19. Ibid.

20. Order of General Richard Mulcahy, IRA Chief of Staff, 9 Jul 1921.

21. Jack Ahern, Witness Statement 970, BMH.

22. Michael Finucane interview with Maurice O'Keefe, Irishlifeandlore.com

23. Seán Moylan, Witness Statement 838, BMH.

24. Colonel Éamon Broy, Witness Statement 1280, BMH.

25. Ibid.

26. Ibid.

27. James Leahy, Witness Statement 1,454, BMH.

28. *The Times*, 10 Dec 1921, cited in http://www.theauxiliaries.com

29. John Sharkey, Witness Statement 1,100, BMH.

30. Maurice Meade, Witness Statement 891, BMH.

31. Donal McMahon, 'The Story of a Thurles RIC Man', *Tipperary Star*, 28 Dec 2011.

32. Éamon de Valera to Michael Collins, 15 Jul 1921, No. 139, UCDA P150/151. Vol I, *Documents on Irish Foreign Policy*, http://www.difp.ie

33. Seán Moylan, Witness Statement 838, BMH, 1913–21.
34. Ibid.
35. Fearghal McGarry, *Eoin O'Duffy, A Self-Made Hero*, pp. 76–7.
36. Cal McCarthy, *Cumann na Mban*, Cork, 2007, p. 280.

12: The War of the Brothers
1. Denis Quille, quoted in O'Malley, *The Men Will Talk*, p. 385.
2. Treaty debate, 19 Dec 1921.
3. Treaty debate, 6 Jan 1922.
4. Treaty debate, 20 Dec 1921.
5. Treaty debate, 9 Jan 1922.
6. Speech at Killarney, 17 Mar 1922.
7. *Yorkshire Post*, 3 Jul 1922.
8. *Northern Whig*, 3 Jul 1922.
9. Tom Doyle, *The Civil War in Kerry*, Cork, 2008, p. 15.
10. Letter from Edward Sheehy, 31 Jan 1923, to Board of Investigators, Department of Defence, Dublin, MSPC.
11. Letter to Mr E. Sheehy, Officer I/C Personal Services, Office of Adjutant General, 14 Feb 1923, MSPC.
12. *New York Times*, 28 Jul 1922.
13. *New York Times*, 30 Jul 1922.
14. Ibid.
15. *Cork Examiner*, 26 Jul 1922, cited in Doyle, *The Civil War in Kerry*, p. 112.
16. Major General P. O'Daly, Witness Statement 387, BMH.
17. Cited in Calton Younger, *Ireland's Civil War*, London, 1979, p. 488.
18. Ibid.
19. National Army communiqué, in *Weekly Freeman*, 12 Aug 1922.
20. Cited in Doyle, *The Civil War in Kerry*, p. 127.
21. General Emmet Dalton interviewed in Robert Kee, *Ireland, A Television History*, Pt 10.
22. John O'Connell in ibid.
23. Moss Twomey Papers, p/69/93 (177), UCD Archives cited in *Denis O'Neill and the Road to Béal na Bla*, MSPC.
24. Department of Defence Intelligence Report, 9 Apr 1924, MSPC.
25. Peter Hart, *Mick: The Real Michael Collins*, London, 2005, p. 403.
26. 'Address to the Army on the Death of Michael Collins', 22 Aug 1922.
27. Michael Laffan, *Judging W.T. Cosgrave*, Dublin, p. 124.
28. National Library of Ireland, MS36, 251/26 18 Apr 1922.
29. National Library of Ireland, MS36, 251/29 16 Sep 1922.
30. 'The New Horror', *Freeman's Journal*, 11 Dec 1922.

31. Irish Military Archives, CW/OPS/3/C. cited in Gemma M. Clark, *Fire, Boycott, Threat and Harm: Social and Political Violence within the Local Community – A Study of Three Munster Counties during the Irish Civil War, 1922–23*, doctoral thesis, The Queen's College, Oxford, 2010. See also Gemma M. Clark, *Everyday Violence in the Irish Civil War*, Cambridge, 2014.

32. A letter from the Judge Advocate General to Mulcahy, 12 Dec 1922, U. C. D. Archives, Mulcahy papers, P7/B/101 (29. cited in Timothy Murphy Breen, *The Government's Executions Policy during the Irish Civil War 1922–1923*, doctoral thesis, National University of Ireland, 2010.

33. May Ahern, MSPC, 24 May 1940.

34. Wireless message from Paddy O'Daly to Richard Mulcahy, 19 Jan 1923 (M.A., Irish Civil War Operational/Intelligence Reports, Box 16/10), cited in Timothy Murphy Breen, *The Government's Executions Policy during the Irish Civil War, 1922–23*, doctoral thesis, National University of Ireland, 2010.

35. *Northern Whig*, 27 Jan 1923.

36. Ernie O'Malley, *The Men Will Talk to Me*, p. 1825.

37. Seamus O'Connor, *Tomorrow Was Another Day*, p. 89.

38. Dorothy McArdle, *Tragedies of Kerry*, Dublin, 1924, p. 22.

39. Niall Harrington, *Kerry Landing*, Cork, 1987, pp. 148–9.

40. IRA report, cited in Breen, *The Government's Execution Policy during the Irish Civil War*.

41. Ibid.

42. O'Malley, *The Men Will Talk to Me*, location 1784.

43. Ernie O'Malley, *The Singing Flame*, Dublin, 1978, p. 240.

44. O'Malley, *The Men Will Talk*, pp. 51–2.

45. Ibid., pp. 69–70.

13: A New Ireland

1. Niall Jordan, *The Past*, London, 1982, p. 22.

2. Michael Hopkinson, *Green Against Green: The Irish Civil War*, Dublin, 1998, p. 391.

3. De Valera to Joe Garrity, 5 Feb 1923, cited in Michael Hopkinson, *Ireland's War of Independence*, Dublin, 2014 edn, p. 388.

4. Hopkinson, *Green Against Green*, p. 389.

5. Cited in Kieran Glennon, *The Execution of the Drumbo Martyrs*, The Irish Story, http://www.theirishstory.com

6. Seamus O'Connor, *Tomorrow Was Another Day*, Dublin, 1970, p. 92.

7. National Library of Ireland, MS36, 251/30 6 Jul 1923.

8. Hopkinson, *Green Against Green*, p. 393.

9. Financial Compensation Claim, 2/8/847, NAI.
10. Financial Compensation Claim, 2/8/253, NAI.
11. Cited in Joseph Lee, *Ireland 1912–1985*, Cambridge, 1989, p. 98.
12. Richard English, *The Armed Struggle: The History of the IRA*, London, 2003, p. 44.
13. *Northern Whig*, 29 Nov 1923.
14. Gaughan, *Listowel*, p. 425.
15. Mary Keane, aunt, in conversation with the author.
16. *Northern Whig*, 15 May 1934.
17. Ibid.
18. Ibid.
19. Interview with author.
20. Ibid.
21. Ibid.
22. Máirtín Ó Direáin, 'Strong Beams', in *The Penguin Book of Irish Poetry*, edited by Patrick Crotty, London, 2010, p. 666.
23. Éamon de Valera, St Patrick's Day speech, broadcast on RTÉ, 17 Mar 1943.
24. Marcus Tanner, *Ireland's Holy Wars*, New Haven, p. 314.
25. Tom Barry, *Guerrilla Days in Ireland*, p. 174.
26. Jack White, *Minority Report: The Anatomy of the Southern Irish Protestant*, Dublin, 1975, Chapter 8: 'Part and Parcel'.
27. Cited in Marcus Tanner, *Ireland's Holy Wars*, p. 315.
28. The words mean 'Lest rashly' and are taken from the opening sentence of the 1907 papal decree which insisted that any marriage between a Catholic and non-Catholic had to be solemnised by a Catholic priest.
29. Theobald Wolfe Tone, *Speech from the Dock*, 10 November 1798.
30. Senate debate on divorce legislation, 11 Jun 1925.
31. Brian Inglis, 'No Petty People', *Spectator*, 25 October 1957.
32. Eamonn Dillon, correspondence with the author, 7 Jul 2017
33. J. A. Murphy, *The Church of Ireland in County Kerry*, p. 178.
34. Ibid.
35. Ibid.
36. Ibid, p. 179.

14: Inheritance

1. *RTÉ News*, 24 Jun 1973.
2. *The Good Old IRA: Tan War Operations*, Sinn Féin Publicity Department, Dublin, Nov 1985, p. 7.
3. *The Good Old IRA*, p. 1.

15: Afterwards

1. Cited in *The Lost Decade: Ireland in the 1950s*, ed. Dermot Keogh, Finbarr O'Shea, Carmel Quinlan, Cork, 2004, p. 16.
2. Ibid.
3. M. Lennon, from the play *And All His Songs Were Sad*, London, 2006.
4. John B. Keane, *Self Portrait*, Cork, 1964, p. 17.
5. Fergal Keane, *All of These People*, London, 2005, pp. 10–11.
6. Correspondence with author, 20 Oct 2016.
7. John B. Keane, 'My Father', from *The Street and Other Poems*, Monument Press, Dublin, 1961.
8. John B. Keane, *Big Maggie*, Cork, 1969.
9. Files no. MD44630 and MD41314, MSPC.
10. Ibid.
11. Ibid.
12. MSP34REF32473, MSPC.
13. Conor Keane interview with Gerry Brosnan, 24 Mar 2016.
14. *Kerryman*, 26 Jun 2013.
15. Keane/Brosnan, 24 Mar 2016.
16. Father Dan Ahern, conversation with author, 26 July 2017.
17. In conversation with author, October 2013.
18. Liam Purtill, 23 Mar 2016.
19. Morgan Flynn, 31 Mar 2016.

Chronology of Major Events

1916
24 April: Easter Rising to establish an independent Republic.
25 April: Martial law declared.
3 May: Executions of the leaders of the Rising begin.

1917
20 June: Kerry prisoners return home from internment after the
Rising. Welcome parades in Listowel and Ballybunion.
11 July: Volunteer killed by police during march in Ballybunion.
Dates unknown: Con Brosnan and Mick Purtill join the Irish
Volunteers. Volunteer drilling takes place in their home districts
of Newtownsandes and Ballydonoghue.

1918
13 April: First raid in Ireland on police barracks takes place in
County Kerry. Two Irish Volunteers are killed.
18 April: British government introduces Military Service Bill
which seeks to extend conscription to Ireland. The move is
widely condemned in Ireland and by Irish MPs at Westminster.
14 December: General election victory for Sinn Féin which
increases its number of Westminster seats from 6 to 67.

1919

21 January: Establishment of Dáil Eireann which will provide an underground government for the Revolution. On the same day the IRA ambushes and kills two policemen at Soloheadbeg in County Tipperary in what is regarded as the first attack of the War of Independence.

1920

Date unknown: Hannah Purtill goes on active service with Cumann na mBan.

12 March: IRA attacks Ballybunion RIC barracks. Since late 1919, attacks on remote RIC posts have escalated.

25 March: First Black and Tans arrive to augment regular police force.

3 May: RIC sergeant shot dead near Listowel – the first policeman killed in the district in the growing violence.

28 May: North Kerry Volunteer organiser Liam Scully is killed in an attack on Kilmallock RIC barracks in County Limerick. The defence of the barracks is led by Sergeant Tobias O'Sullivan, who is shortly afterwards promoted to District Inspector.

19 June: RIC constables mutiny in Listowel against shoot-to-kill instructions from senior British officer.

27 July: First Auxiliaries start to arrive in Ireland.

September–October: District Inspector Tobias O'Sullivan takes up his command in Listowel.

October–November: Violence escalates in north Kerry between the IRA and the RIC and Black and Tans.

22 November: Raid on Ballylongford by regular police and Black and Tans led by District Inspector Tobias O'Sullivan. Volunteer Eddie Carmody killed.

1921

1 January: Clerical student John Lawlor dies after being beaten in public by the Black and Tans in Listowel.

20 January: District Inspector Tobias O'Sullivan is shot dead in Listowel. The town is placed under curfew for three days. Eight men are arrested and two sentenced to death for the killing.

February–July: Violence continues with ambushes, assassinations and the killing of suspected informers. The most notorious acts include the killings of Sir Arthur Vicars at Kilmorna in April – by the IRA – and of three IRA men at Knockanure by the Black and Tans in May.

11 July: Truce comes into force that ends the War of Independence.

6 December: Anglo-Irish Treaty signed.

1922

7 January: Treaty ratified by Dáil by 64 votes to 57, forcing open split in Sinn Féin.

28 June: Civil War begins with the shelling of Republican positions by the new National Army at the Four Courts in Dublin.

29 June: In Listowel National Army forces surrender after day-long exchange of fire with Republicans.

2 August: National Army lands in force at Fenit near Tralee.

3 August: Listowel falls to National Army.

22 August: Michael Collins killed by Republicans in County Cork.

15 October: Emergency Powers Act allows for execution of all caught in possession of arms.

30 November: In retaliation for Emergency Powers Act the IRA leadership issues order to kill members of Dáil who voted for the legislation as well as hostile judges and newspaper editors opposed to Republicans.

7 December: Pro-Treaty member of the Dáil is killed and colleague wounded by IRA.

8 December: The Free State government executes four senior Republicans in retaliation.

1923

6 March: Five Free State soldiers killed by IRA mine in Knocknagoshel, north Kerry.

7 March: Nine Republican prisoners taken to Ballyseedy Cross and tied to landmine. Eight are killed.

14 March: Two Listowel men executed by Free State in County Donegal.

10 April: IRA leader Liam Lynch killed in the Galtee Mountains.

18 April: IRA Column surrounded at Clashmealcon Caves in last significant fight of the Civil War in north Kerry. The leader of the Column is killed and several survivors are subsequently executed.

30 April: The IRA calls a ceasefire.

24 May: IRA leadership tells Volunteers to dump arms and go home.

Glossary

Auxies: Their formal name was the Auxiliary Division of the Royal Irish Constabulary. They were recruited from the ranks of former military officers who had served in the Great War. The majority of these men had obtained their commissions from the ranks. Around 2,000 served in Ireland where, like the Black and Tans, they earned a reputation for brutality and ill-discipline.

Black and Tans: These paramilitary police reinforcements were overwhelmingly recruited in Britain to support the regular Royal Irish Constabulary. They were so called because of their uniform of dark green tunic and khaki pants. Many had served in the ranks of the British military in the Great War. Up to 10,000 men were recruited into the Black and Tans.

Cumann na mBan: The organisation was set up in 1914 as a women's volunteer movement to campaign for an independent Irish Republic. The women acted alongside the militant faction of the Irish Volunteers during 1916 and in the War of Independence. Cumann na mBan split after the signing of the Anglo-Irish Treaty, with the majority of its members opposing the Free State.

Free State: The 26-county state which came into being after the withdrawal of the British from the south in 1922. Under the terms of the Anglo-Irish Treaty, the Free State remained within the British empire but was self-governing with its own army, control over taxation and foreign affairs. The British monarchy was represented by a Governor General, in much the same fashion as countries like Canada and Australia. The other six counties of Ireland remained under British rule and became the Unionist-dominated state of Northern Ireland.

IRA: The Irish Republican Army grew out of the militant faction of the Irish Volunteers that had staged the Easter Rising of 1916. The IRA waged war against Irish police, British paramilitary police and the British military during the period 1919–23. In the aftermath of the War of Independence, the IRA split into pro- and anti-Treaty factions. One of these became the National Army of the Irish Free State. The anti-Treaty side continued to call itself the IRA and was defeated after a civil war. To the present day armed Republicans claim the mantle of the original IRA and regard both British and Irish governments on the island of Ireland as illegitimate.

IRB: The Irish Republican Brotherhood was an oathbound secret society founded with the avowed aim of overthrowing British rule in Ireland. Known popularly as the 'Fenians', the IRB staged an abortive rebellion in 1858. However, its leaders would influence the generation of Republican activists who carried out the Easter Rising in 1916, as well as forming a core group who dominated the IRA in the years afterwards.

Irish Volunteers: The organisation was established in 1913 in response to the mobilisation and arming of northern Protestants who had formed the Ulster Volunteer Force to fight against Home Rule. The Volunteers were a mix of constitutional nationalists who joined in order to defend Home Rule and other more militant activists who believed in armed rebellion to end British rule in Ireland.

RIC: The Irish police force under British rule. The Royal Irish Constabulary was founded in 1836 and operated as both a civil and political police force. There were an estimated 10,000 members when the guerrilla war broke out. The RIC was disbanded after the signing of the Treaty between Ireland and Britain which led to the foundation of the Irish Free State.

Select Bibliography

Barrett, J. J., *In the Name of the Game*, Wicklow, 1997

Barry, Tom, *Guerrilla Days in Ireland*, Lanham, MD, 1995 edn

Beatty, Bertha, *Kerry Memories*, Listowel, 2007 edn

Bennett, Richard, *The Black and Tans*, Staplehurst, 2001 edn

Berleth, Richard, *The Twilight Lords*, Lanham, 2002 edn

Bielenberg, Andy and John Borgonovo, with James S. Donnelly Jr, '"Something in the Nature of a Massacre": The Bandon Valley Killings Revisited', Éire-Ireland, Cork, 2014

Borgonovo, John, *Florence and Josephine O'Donoghue's War of Independence: 'A Destiny that Shapes Our Ends'*, Dublin, 2006

Bowen, Elizabeth, *Bowenscourt*, Dublin, 1998

Bowen, Elizabeth, *The Last September*, London, 2011

Boyd, Andrew, *Holy War in Belfast*, Belfast, 1969

Brendon, Piers, *The Decline and Fall of the British Empire*, London, 2008

Brouder, Simon, *Rebel Kerry*, Cork, 2017

Caball, Kay Moloney, *The Kerry Girls: Emigration and the Earl Grey Scheme*, Stroud, 2014

Coogan, Tim Pat, *Michael Collins*, London, 1990

Coogan, Tim Pat, *De Valera*, London, 1995 edn

Dillon, Martin, *The Shankill Butchers*, London, 1999

Doyle, Tom, *The Civil War in Kerry*, Cork, 2008

Doyle, Tom, *The Summer Campaign in Kerry*, Cork, 2010

Dwyer, T. Ryle, *Tans, Terror and Troubles: Kerry's Real Fighting Story*, Cork, 2001

Dwyer, T. Ryle, *The Squad: And the Intelligence Operations of Michael Collins*, Cork, 2005

Elliott, Marianne, *When God Took Sides: Religion and Identity in Ireland – Unifinished History*, Oxford, 2009

English, Richard, *The Armed Struggle: The History of the IRA*, London, 2003

Fanning, Ronan, *Éamon de Valera: A Will to Power*, Faber and Faber, 2013

Fanning, Ronan, *Fatal Path: British Government and Irish Revolution 1910–1922*, Faber and Faber, 2013

Ferriter, Diarmaid, *The Transformation of Ireland 1900–2000*, London, 2004

Ferriter, Diarmaid, *Judging Dev*, Dublin, 2007

Ferriter, Diarmaid, *A Nation and Not a Rabble: The Irish Revolution 1913–1923*, London, 2015

Foster, R. F., *Modern Ireland*, London, 1988

Foster, R. F., *Vivid Faces: The Revolutionary Generation in Ireland*, London, 2015

Gaughan, J. Anthony, *Listowel and Its Vicinity*, Cork, 1974

Gaughan, J. Anthony, *The Memoirs of Constable Jeremiah Mee RIC*, Cork, 2012 edn

Harrington, Niall C., *Kerry Landing*, Cork, 1987 edn

Hart, Peter, *The IRA and Its Enemies: Violence and Community in Cork 1916–1923*, Oxford, 1998

Hart, Peter, *Mick: The Real Michael Collins*, London, 2005

Hart, Peter (ed.), *British Intelligence in Ireland: The Final Reports*, Cork, 2002

Hopkinson, Michael, *Green Against Green: The Irish Civil War*, Dublin, 2014 edn

Hopkinson, Michael, *The Irish War of Independence*, Dublin, 2014 edn

Horgan, Tim, *Dying for the Cause*, Cork, 2015

Joy, Sinead, *The IRA in Kerry 1916–1921*, Cork, 2005

Keane, Fergal, *All of These People*, London, 2005

Keane, John B., *Self Portrait*, Cork, 1964

Keogh, Dermot, Finbarr O'Shea and Carmel Quinlan, *The Lost Decade: Ireland in the 1950s*, Cork, 2004

Kiberd, Declan and P. J. Matthews, *Handbook of the Irish Revival: An Anthology of Irish Cultural and Political Writings 1891–1922*, Dublin, 2015

Kinsella, Thomas, *The Táin*, Oxford, 1969

Laffan, Michael, *Judging W. T. Cosgrave*, Dublin, 2016

Lee, Joseph, *Ireland 1912–1985*, Cambridge, 1989

Leeson, D. M., *The Black and Tans: British Police and Auxiliaries in the Irish War of Independence*, Oxford, 2011

Lucey, Donnacha Seán, *Land, Popular Politics and Agrarian Violence in Ireland*, Dublin, 2011

Lyons, F. S. L., *Ireland since the Famine*, London, 1985 edn

McArdle, Dorothy, *Tragedies of Kerry*, Dublin, 1924

McCarthy, Cal, *Cumann na mBan*, Cork, 2014 edn

McCarthy, John P., *Kevin O'Higgins: Builder of the Irish State*, Dublin, 2006

McKittrick, David, Seamus Kelters, Brian Feeney, Chris Thornton and David McVea, *Lost Lives: The Stories of the Men, Women and Children Who Died As a Result of the Northern Ireland Troubles*, Edinburgh, 1999

McMahon, Paul, *British Spies and Irish Rebels: British Intelligence and Ireland 1916–1945*, Woodbridge, 2008

Marley, Laurence, *Michael Davitt: Freelance Radical and Frondeur*, Dublin, 2007

Mishra, Panjak, *From the Ruins of Empire: The Revolt Against the West and the Remaking of Asia*, London, 2012

Moryson, Fynes, *An History of Ireland*, Dublin, 1604

Murphy, J. A., *The Church of Ireland in County Kerry*, Dublin, 2016

Murphy, Jeremiah, *When Youth Was Mine*, Dublin, 1998

O'Concubhair, Brian (ed.), *Kerry's Fighting Story*, Cork, 2009 edn

O'Connor, Frank, *The Big Fellow*, Dublin, 1991 edn

O'Connor, Seamus, *Tomorrow Was Another Day*, Dublin, 1970

O'Donnell, Ruan (ed.), *Limerick's Fighting Story*, Cork, 2009

O'hEithir, Breandan, *The Begrudger's Guide to Irish Politics*, Dublin, 1986

O'Malley, Ernie, *The Singing Flame*, Dublin, 1978

O'Malley, Ernie, *On Another Man's Wound*, Cork, 2002 edn

O'Malley, Ernie, *Raids and Rallies*, Cork, 2011 edn

O'Malley, Ernie, edited by Cormac K. H. O'Malley and Tim Horgan, *The Men Will Talk to Me*, Cork, 2012 edn

Pierse, John D., *Teampall Bán: Aspects of the Famine in North Kerry 1845–1852*, Listowel, 2014

Rieff, David, *In Praise of Forgetting: Historical Memories and Its Ironies*, Yale, 2016

Ryan, Annie, *Comrades: Inside the War of Independence*, Dublin, 2007

Ryan, Meda, *The Real Chief: Liam Lynch*, Cork, 2005 edn

Sheehan, William, *British Voices: From the Irish War of Independence 1918–1921*, Cork, 2005

Smith, Gus and Des Hickey, *John B.*, Dublin, 2002 edn

Tanner, Marcus, *Ireland's Holy Wars: The Struggle for a Nation's Soul, 1500–2000*, Yale, 2001

Thackeray, William Makepeace, *The Irish Sketchbook*, London, 1845

Thomson, David, *Woodbrook*, London, 1974

Townsend, Charles, *The Republic: The Fight for Irish Independence 1918–1923*, London, 2013

Walsh, Maurice, *Bitter Freedom: Ireland in a Revolutionary World*, London, 2016

With the IRA in the Fight for Freedom, 1919 to the Truce: The Red Path of Glory, with introduction by Gabriel Doherty, Cork, 2010

Young, Arthur, *A Tour in Ireland*, Cambridge, 1925, Blackstaff Press 1983 edn

Younger, Calton, *Ireland's Civil War*, London, 1979 edn

Illustration Credits

My father the actor *(Author's Private Collection)*
Tobias O'Sullivan and his wife May *(Desiree Flynn)*
Hannah and Bill, my grandparents *(Family Collection)*
Rural labourer in Famine era *(Sean Sexton Collection)*
Con Brosnan, revolutionary and footballing legend *(Brosnan Family)*
My great-uncle Mick Purtill in his Free State army uniform *(Purtill Family)*
Tans in Dublin *(Bettmann / Getty Images)*
After the siege of Kilmallock, Tobias O'Sullivan centre *(Photo by FPG / Hulton Archive / Getty Images)*
Sir Arthur Vicars *(George Grantham Bain Collection, Library of Congress)*
Captain Rose McNamara, Cumann na mBan officer *(English Photographer, 20th Century / Private Collection / The Stapleton Collection / Bridgeman Images)*
Church Street in the early nineteenth century *(Laurence Collection)*
IRA graves, Listowel *(Author Photo)*
St John's Protestant Church, Listowel *(History collection 2016 / Alamy Stock Photo)*
A Flying Column in County Tipperary *(Wikimedia Commons)*
My grandmother's idol Michael Collins *(Pictorial Press Ltd / Alamy Stock Photo)*

Armoured car outside the Listowel barracks during the Civil War
  (Vincent Carmody)
Mick Purtill on his wedding day with Madge, after the war *(Purtill
  Family)*
My grandmother's comrades in the Blueblouses, the women's wing
  of the Blueshirts *(Vincent Carmody)*
The Blueshirt leader, General O'Duffy speaking in Listowel
  (Vincent Carmody)
Éamon de Valera *(Library of Congress, Prints & Photographs Division)*
With my father in Belfast in 1988 on his first visit back since the
  Troubles began *(Author's Private Collection)*
John B *(Domnick Walsh)*
Hannah Purtill *(Keane Family, Listowel)*
The older Con Brosnan *(Kerryman newspaper)*

Index

Index

Index